PRAKṚTI
The Integral Vision

VOLUME 1

Primal Elements — The Oral Tradition

PRAKṚTI

The Integral Vision

General Editor

KAPILA VATSYAYAN

VOLUME 1

Primal Elements—The Oral Tradition

Edited by

Baidyanath Saraswati

Indira Gandhi National Centre for the Arts
New Delhi

D. K. Printworld (P) Ltd.
New Delhi

Cataloging in Publication Data — DK

Prakṛti : the integral vision / general editor,
Kapila Vatsyayan.
Includes bibliographical references.
Includes index.

1. Nature. 2. Cosmology. I. Vatsyayan, Kapila, 1928-

ISBN 81-246-0036-8 (set)
ISBN 81-246-0037-6 (vol. 1)

First Published in India in 1995

Publishers
Indira Gandhi National Centre for the Arts
Central Vista Mess, Janpath, New Delhi - 110001

D.K. Printworld (P) Ltd.
Regd. office : H-12, Bali Nagar, New Delhi-110015

Printed at : D. K. Fine Art Press (P) Ltd., New Delhi

In Memory

of

Prof. D. S. Kothari

Foreword

In 1986 when the first of the Multidisciplinary and Cross-cultural Seminars was held under the aegis of the Indira Gandhi National Centre for the Arts, there was a trepidation. In my Introduction to the Volume on ***Concepts of Space : Ancient & Modern*** I have shared with the readers the sense of challenge as also of gratification. Then, it was not easy, nor has it been easy in the subsequent years to bring together people from different parts of the world of diverse disciplines and levels of society to speak through a multiplicity of languages to reflect and converse, and have a meaningful dialogue on the fundamental concerns of humanity in the past or present, in science or religion, philosophy and the arts, in civilizations as far apart as Egyptian, Chinese, Greek and Indian, permeating expressions through the written or the oral word, generating a language of myth and symbol which communicates across cultures.

The gathering, the dialogue and the discussion on a single concept of **Space** (*Akasa*) made it evident that the more fundamental and universal the concept, the greater the probability and possibility of diverse interpretations at multiple levels. The single concept of **Space** had taken us through the journey of the concepts of cavity, cave, aperture, fountainhead, body, air, sky, vacuity, cipher, point and much else. The scientist and the technologist explored the concept through their method of empirical investigation, the philosopher and the metaphysician, artists and the sociologist through perennial questioning and speculation. The two approaches and methods we learnt were complementary and not in conflict. The arts, architecture, sculpture, painting, music and dance enclose, embody and evoke space. Poetry creates vast edifices of space as spatial situations, and evoke the experience of outer and inner space.

The concern with **Space (*Akasa*)** could not be dissociated from the concern – the concept of **Time (*Kala*)**. Two years later, a similar gathering with many familiar faces (who communicated with one another with greater ease) gathered to deliberate upon the many dimensions of **Time (*Kala*)**. Once again, the discussions at that Seminar revolved round the micro and the macro levels of the single concept, from molecular time to the cosmic time, from the time of biologists to the time of astronomer, from the time of the seer and meditator to the time of the architect, sculptor, musician, dancer and the poet. Besides the familiar faces, there were others who had joined the family of the IGNCA. The enlarged family gave this Seminar a depth and richness, unique and unparalleled. The experiences His Holiness The Dalai Lama articulated in words lucid and resonant, were juxtaposed with the precision and meditation of a scientist – the late Professor D.S. Kothari. The depth of the experience of **Time** in religious traditions, Islamic, Christian, Hindu, Buddhist, Jain and Hebrew, and the embodiment of inner and outer **Time** in poetic language was shared through rapt silence through the voice of the Poet Kathleen Raine.

Logically and naturally, from these two fundamental and universal concepts the next step in our quest for exploration of a single universal theme through diverse paths recalling the Rgvedic Verse, **Truth is one; man knows it by different names**, was to explore the concept of the primal elements (five or four) in different civilizations which have governed and determined the evolution of civilization and culture. Perhaps, the first conscious awareness of Man was the fact that his life depended on water, Earth, air, fire and, above all, space. Understandably, in all civilizations, at the most sophisticated level as also at the simplest level, the recognition that the primal elements were primary and indispensable for Man, is universal. Myths of the origin of the universe, creation, cosmology and cosmogony, have been developed on the concept of the elements which are four or five. There is a vast body of primary sources and equally extensive and complex a history of critical discourse on the nature of primal elements and their indispensability, not only for Man but for all life on Earth.

The subject was too vast and too monumental to be taken up in a single Seminar. Organizationally, therefore, this time it was decided to hold five successive but interlocked Seminars, one leading to the others, so that they could all culminate in a final international cross-cultural multidisciplinary Seminar. Since cultures, disciplines, and levels of society are not completely autonomous and insulated, there was a planned and understandable overlapping between one Seminar or Workshop and another.

The five Seminars were divided more for facility than the autonomous nature of each area or field. The discussions, therefore, at one Seminar were taken up and did interpenetrate into the next.

Logically, the first of these Seminars focused attention on the articulations of cohesive communities in the world who have lived in harmony with nature and who have communicated with the five elements in a continuous unceasing dialogue. To them the nature of the five elements – water, earth, air, fire and space – is not a matter of intellection or breaking down into separation and divisions of totality or a whole; instead, it is a question of life here and now. This is manifested in ritual practices which sacrilize nature so that man can live as an integral part of the universe, the rhythmic movement of the changing seasons, and the symmetrical punctuation and cycle of seed sprouting, growing, flowering, fruiting, decaying and renewing. In modern discourse this is understood as the need for man to live in harmony with the environment for an evolution of socio-cultural systems and methodologies for ensuring the maintenance of ecological balances. The lives and lifestyles of these cohesive groups have begun to acquire renewed validity on account of what man has done to pollute, contaminate, desacrilize and desecrate the very fundamentals that sustain him and make it possible for him to live on earth. The first Volume is based on the papers submitted at this Seminar.

The second Seminar moved the emphasis to the textual traditions. There is a vast body of literature in Greek, Chinese and Indian sources where philosophic discourses have been held on the nature of the universe, the nature of matter, the elements and the possibility of transmutation of the gross to the subtle. In India all branches of the philosophic streams have discussed the nature of the *Bhutas* and the *Mahabhutas*. The discussion ranges from the earliest articulation on the subject in the *Rgveda* to the philosophic schools of Vaisesikas, Vedantins, Saiva and the *Agamas*. The old system of *Ayurveda* in India, as much of medicine in Greece in a very different way, is based on the concept of the *Mahabhutas* in the constitution of the body itself. The very conception of the five elements constitutes the body. Texts for Indian astronomy, chemistry, metallurgy are replete with discussions on the elements. This discussion cannot be dissociated from a speculation, and discourse of, the nature of the universe, cosmology, cosmogony. The second Seminar delved deep into each of these aspects specially in the Indian tradition – Vedic, Brahmanical, Upanisadic and Tantric. In addition, there was a consideration of the concept of the *Mahabhutas* in Buddhism and Jainism. This Seminar unfolded the very complex and subtle aspects of the discourse on the nature of the matter, the fivefold organic matter and the five external objects. It also brought forth the many convergences as also divergences of viewpoint between and amongst these different streams of Indian thought as exemplified in the textual tradition. The Seminar was hosted by the Department of Sanskrit, University of Poona, Pune. The second Volume of this series is based on the papers and the discussions held at this Seminar.

Logically, the third Seminar had to and did explore the discussions as also the manifestations of the five elements in the Indian arts, along with their Agamic background. As is wellrecognized, while the *Upanisads* provide the basis for speculative thinking, the *Brahmanas* give the methodology of ritual practice (*Yajna* and *Prayoga*). Parallel is the development in early and later medieval India where the texts on *Vastu* and *Silpa* provide the frame-work of the abstract principles of creating concrete structures through different media and in different forms. The *Agama* is the twin which provide the methodology of enlivening, giving life and breath to the concrete structures and forms of art. If monumental architecture, sculpture, painting, music or dance, poetry or theatre, is created on the comprehension of space and time, they are even more built on the system of correspondences first for embodying and then evoking the five elements. The fascinating and unceasing cycle of the movement from the inner experience to the creation of form, which would incorporate the five elements and the employment of a methodology of ritual, is outlined in the Agamic texts only to achieve the end experience of the transformation of the gross to the subtle. This was the subject of this Seminar. From different vantage points of the architect, sculptor, painter, musician and dancer, the field was re-opened to examine the structure of the Indian arts at its primal level.

Naturally, theories of aesthetics which have emerged from such a viewpoint had to be discussed and many questions asked. The third Volume incorporates the span of the papers presented and the discussions held at this Seminar.

If the arts deal with the process of transmutation and mutation of the subtle to the gross, and the evocation of the subtle from the gross, in other words, the process of the abstract and the concrete suggesting, stimulating and evoking the abstract, then the astrophysicist deals with the nature of primal matter itself. No discourse on the elements could have been completed by excluding the discussion on modern physics of elementary particles and the most recent developments in microbiology. The fourth Seminar took up the question of the nature and function of matter itself and discussed the theories of the creation of the universe and emergent cosmologies in the modern physics. This was juxtaposed with the consideration on the nature of matter and consciousness. It was obvious that the new developments in science were, perhaps, not all that far remote from the earlier insights in the context of consciousness. The debate between the nineteenth Century mechanistic science and the modern physics was re-opened. This was juxtaposed with speculations and the philosophic discourses in the Indian philosophic schools. If the second Seminar dealt with the textual traditions and the philosophic schools of *Samkhya*, *Mimamsa* and the *Vaisesikas*, this Seminar looked at these traditions as structuralistic traditions from a scientific point of view. The dialogue created between the method of science and the method of speculation was invigorating. The fourth Volume comprises papers and discussions at this Seminar.

The fifth and the last Seminar was a coming together of cultures as also disciplines. Coordinators of the earlier Seminars presented brief Reports on each of the Seminars which provided the background and the landscape. The international community, comprising scientists, biologists, philosophers, anthropologists, ecologists and artists shared not only the myth and cosmology of their particular societies but also there was a most meaningful dialogue between those who lived in the awareness of the primordial myths of the elements and those who had employed the tools of science to explore the nature of the phenomenon of matter.

The putting together of the deliberations of the five major Seminars, as a single or a multiple-volume, is a daunting task. Through the combined efforts of the Coordinators of each of these Seminars and, particularly, the Chief Coordinator – Professor B.N. Saraswati and his associates – it has been possible to prepare the five Volumes based on the deliberations of these Seminars as also a companion exhibition which was called "**PRAKṚTI: The Integral Vision**".

It is my hope that these Volumes will provide material for further discussion and dialogue. The perennial nature of the theme and its urgent and contemporary validity will, I hope, make these Volumes significant. As I have said earlier in my Introduction, Man stands today at a moment where he is threatened by the pollution, inner and outer, of his own making. The primal elements and the urgent need for purification through austerity and discipline are not the matters of intellectual discourse alone. Their maintenance and sustenance, and the purity of these that are primary and primal, are the objectives of our life, lest death overtakes us.

9th June, 1994 **Kapila Vatsyayan**

Preface

It is my pleasure to introduce the first of the five Volumes, entitled ***Prakṛti : The Integral Vision***. This Volume focuses attention on the cosmogonical myths prevalent in cohesive societies which are articulated not as theory but are manifested in lifestyle, ritual practice, medical systems, art forms, music, dance and in the craft tradition.

The Seminar brought together a number of scholars who had been working at the field level for the programmes of the Indira Gandhi National Centre for the Arts. Besides, there were others, who have, for years, been pursuing the role of understanding of the five elements in body systems – medicine – preventive and curative medicine and in healing. This was a rich fair. The Volume comprises the Papers and gives an inkling or insight into some of the discussions held at the Seminar.

Professor B.N. Saraswati's introduction presents the essence as also the dynamics of the discussions which took place at this Seminar. However, no record of this Seminar would be complete without sharing with the readers, the wisdom, the insight, the scientific as also the meditative, outer and inner, vision of a scientist, thinker and philosopher, a modern *rishi* – who is no more amongst us – Professor D.S. Kothari – who inaugurated the Seminar, or, one should really say, the series of Seminars. He began with the simplicity of a child's question – a simplicity which can only be given to one who had gone beyond the narrow boundaries of mere intellectual argumentation.

"Why do we feel warm in the sunlight?" "Why does the sun feel warm?", he asked. This is the first and the last question. An attempt to give an answer to this question has been the history of civilizations, he said . Is it a physical phenomenon? Is it the body that feels warm? Is it nature that provides the warmth? Is it only the sun that provides the warmth? Or are there other elements in interaction with the body which produce the warmth? If it is the body that feels warm then what is body? Is it matter? Is it an aggregation of the five elements?

These are simple, child-like questions and within them is embodied the history of philosophy, science and the arts. Turning his attention from this, a very simple question, he elaborated lucidly on the eighth, thirteenth and the eighteenth chapters of the *Bhagavad Gita*, especially on *sarira* (body) as defined by the *Gita*. The question asked was: what is *sarira*? What are the epithets chosen even in seeking an answer to this fundamental question?

Krishna calls Arjuna 'Kaunteya', i.e., the son of Kunti – that is the biological link. But is *sarira* only a physical organism? *Sarira* is the *ksetra* (field). Krishna enjoins upon Arjuna to be the 'knower of the field'. He who has the capacity of 'knowing' (comprehending) the field is the *ksetrajna*.

Body, therefore, is equal to the *ksetra*. And what is this field? The field is the fivefold body – the sheath of nature, comprising the five elements. Almost as a scientific equation, Professor Kothari extracted the essence of the *Gita* by stating, body = *ksetra*, *ksetra* = five elements. And where from do these five elements come? They come from nature, nature here understood by its Sanskrit name *prakrti*. Is nature dead without attributes? No, there is no absolute dead matter, because nature itself is psycho-physical, psycho-somatic because it is *gunatmaka* (i.e., with attributes and qualities). Thus the system by which man comprehends nature and its elements is not just physical or material, it is a psycho-physical system. It begins with the wholeness. Professor Kothari continued to remind us that the material component of the universe is always changing from moment to moment, body to body, the macrocosm to the microcosm, and yet there is something which remains constant. What is that something? He continued, is it not logical that "I am more than the assembly of the parts and the moment I am more than the assembly of the parts, the implications are clear?" I am part of *ananta* and infinity, and infinity and a continuity despite every moment of flux and change. Consciousness is the eternity and the immutable, he said.

From an enumeration of the thirteenth chapter of the *Gita* he took us to the eighteenth, where nature of the consciousness of total surrender and of meditation and reflection is articulated. It is thus consciousness and not dead matter, but the combination of consciousness and matter which makes us feel warm in the Sun.

Modern science, he reminded us, has realized for the first time that the atom has a wholeness of its own. It is also *ananta*, its growth is a dynamic process and it is not merely an aggregation of electrons and protons. Time has now come, said he, when science has to be spiritualized, just as the ritual of the indigenous people had been spiritualized so as to sacralize nature. Science and the perceptions at the level of textual traditions, the metaphysics and the arts and those lived by cohesive communities must converge. Science, he said, has arrived at the dictum that the velocity of light is absolute. It is only modern science which is linking physical matter with consciousness, and if the IGNCA has begun this exploration then it must be complimented and congratulated for its courage. Such questions can only be asked in a spirit of humility, modesty and with an openness of mind where the barriers of disciplines and cultures, ideologies and positions are transcended. The symbiosis of knowledge, vision and values alone can bring about a consciousness of the wholeness.

How can this happen? It can happen with a sense of feeling, *bhavana*, of reflection and of meditation. All this is possible only if man lives by the perennial consciousness that he is one amongst all particles of nature, and is also conscious of the probability and possibility that he can be *Brahman*.

The audience was blessed and stood in silence and in grace because a scientist and mystic had spoken. The journey of the Seminar had begun.

Kapila Vatsyayan

Contents

Introduction

Ancient vision of the cosmic order has certain fundamental features that separate it from the modern science perspective. The exchange of views between the two systems of knowledge seems to be problematic. Yet, as humans, we cannot dispense with searching for our foundations.

Human science presents a picture of the cosmos as *seen* by man, the master of the universe. It describes the role evolution plays within the biological and cultural spheres; constructs a theory of culture as the tribal microcosm conditioned by human instincts; and creates a super-ideology of power that places man at the centre of the universe. The result of this anthropocentric attitude is that the cosmos sharing the human adventure is overwhelmed by the tension between nature and culture.

The traditional vision of man, on the contrary, is cosmocentric. Man is made up of four or five cosmic elements. The cosmic order that governs the dynamism of all reality, envelops human life, creates awareness, and signifies patterns of culture. As a result, the cosmic equilibrium is maintained both in nature and in culture. This primal vision is incontestable and fully integrated in two different but related traditions – the textual and the oral. The textual tradition offers a complete and systematic analysis of the universe. Reflections of the oral tradition are more concentrated in practice than systematic in analysis.

The essays compiled here are based on papers presented in the seminar on 'Perceptions of *Bhutas* (Elements) in the Oral Tradition' held at the Indira Gandhi National Centre for the Arts (IGNCA) in February 1992. They trace the areas where reflections on man and the universe emerge. Of these presentations, eleven are the fruits of the IGNCA pilot projects on cross-cultural lifestyle studies.

Primal Elements of the Universe

Tribal cosmogony refers to a variety of elements, some of which are self-existing and others created. For instance, the tribes of Arunachal Pradesh speak of water, cloud, mist, egg and wood as the basic elements from which all other elements are known to have originated (Saraswati). For them, as also for other archaic groups, creation is a male-female principle, allegorically termed 'marriage' or 'sexual union' (Adhikary,

Prasad, Purohit, Saraswati). It has also been held that the world was created in phases by a number of heavenly bodies and not by one Creator-God, a single supreme being (Saraswati). The hunter-gatherer Birhors divide the world into two halves: the sky and the earth. There is a world beyond the sky and another below the earth. The earth is a round-shaped flat surface; the sky a hollow concave over-arching the earth. The structure of the universe is thus somewhat like a cone, similar to the structure of the Birhor leaf-hut (Adhikary).

It is curious that many of the tribes who have never seen the sea, or even large sheets of water, should visualize a primeval ocean from which the universe is said to have emerged. Another remarkable feature of the tribal vision is the notion of the pluriverse. There is, however, no clear distinction between this world and the other worlds.

Structured Sequence of Elements

The idea that the world was created in phases made the elements structured in a sequence. In the beginning was a state of nothingness. But this nothingness is described not as an absolute void. Before the earth was created, everything was water, or cloud, or nothing, nothing at all but two eggs which shone like gold. From that state of nothingness came the earth and the sky; and when the sky made love to the earth, every kind of tree and grass and all living creatures came into being (Saraswati). The Santhals claim that water and earth came first, air fourth, man fifth and fire was sixth and the last (Prasad). In the Garhwal Himalayas, the sequence is visualized as follows: from the mysterious syllable *onkar* to the primeval whizzing; from whizzing air; from air clouds; from clouds water; from water to lotus; and from lotus the creator Brahma was born. In yet another sequence of creation, the earth was first and afterwards the sky; first female then male; first night then day; first *guru* then disciple; first daughter then son (Dhasmana).

The archaic cultures developed their own jargon, just as the modern specialists have complex theories. The tribal notion of the beginning of the universe as 'not absolutely void' seems to be in line with the scientific cosmology. The archaic realization of the origin of the universe from a primeval sound is another interesting resemblance with the theories in modern physics.

Gross and Subtle Elements

The primal elements are said to have personal (material) as well as spiritual attributes. The Angami Nagas assign positive quality to water, and both positive and negative qualities to fire. Water is perceived to have cleansing properties; fire, though not capable of cleansing, is regarded as an agent of good and bad fortunes (Joshi). The

Bhuiyans ascribe sacredness to all five elements. The earth is associated with their entire lifestyle, rituals and festivals. Fire is an object of worship; it is kindled in a special manner. It epitomizes the fundamental principle of the cosmic order. The power of water is utilized against evil. It is also a medium for transferring sin or impurity to the enemies. For the Bhuiyans the sky and the sun are synonymous. The sun and the earth are always viewed as benevolent deities. The ritual act of blowing (air) heals the sick (Mohanty). The Birhor hunters believe that fire also has life and death; the sun is the supreme creator of all things on earth; a female presides over the earth; and there are deities of rain and storm, thunder and meteor, wind and so on (Adhikary). The marine fishers of Kerala think that every element has a spirit or demon (Mathur). The farmers of Karnataka worship the earth, consider water divine and fire auspicious, associate air or wind with life, and regard the sky as a home for the countless celestial bodies (Chandran).

These examples make a great impression on the gross and the subtle aspects of an element; but the cognitive distinction between them remains unexplained. According to Adhikary, the Birhors think that the deities who control the elements are the natural phenomena superior to man. Purohit, reporting on the folk myths of Garhwal, observes that a recognizable pattern of the gross and the subtle is found in the form of the concrete matter and the all-powerful souls of gods, goddesses, men, animals and birds. All souls are believed to be the subtle form of the five basic elements. Khubchandani cites an example of the incarnation of the Sindhi's lord of the river in a family of boatman. Thus three types of cognitive distinctions are identifiable:

(i) in the tribal perception the gross and the subtle are inter locked;

(ii) in the folk beliefs the two levels overlap;

(iii) at a higher abstraction, the reality of the subtler plane is responsible for the reality of the grosser plane.

Integral View of Man and Nature

The Arunachal tribes consider man as an integral part of nature. In their perception man is not unique insofar as his origin is concerned. There is no ontological difference between man and non-man. Every element has a form, a location, a function and a dependent relation with other elements. Man is not unique even in the possession of knowledge; for primordial knowledge came to him from birds and animals (Saraswati). The Santhals also think of man and nature as an inseparable whole. According to them the human body is made up of three elements – air, earth and water (Prasad). Different parts of the body are associated with different elements – head and ears with sky, neck and chest with air, stomach with fire, and body with earth (Mital). Thus man as a microcosm fits harmoniously with the macrocosm, both being subject to the rule of the sphere (Patnaik). There are examples of human groups claiming their origin from one specific element. The Bhuiyans (derived from *bhumi*, land) associate themselves with earth (Mohanty), and the Birhors (*bir* = forest, *hor* = man) with forest (Adhikary). In Karnataka each caste of craftsmen is associated with one of the five elements (Brouwer). The fact of an intrinsic relationship between the human body and elements of nature is ritually demonstrated by the Paiks of Orissa. Their *danda* ritual involves group pantomimes on the ground (rolling in dust), acrobating in water, walking on burning coal, and swinging upside down on burning ashes (Citaristi).

In traditional lifestyles nature is an arena for the play of man. Man's understanding of the natural phenomena depends on his attitude towards nature, and the kind of relationship he establishes with the natural environment. The analysis of the myths of Arunachal tribes shows that in the tribal perception the forces of nature are set into a creative harmony to the extent that there is no intrinsic disorder in nature (Saraswati). In the Santhal worldview all opposites are united by the male-female principle: air-water, seed-earth, earth-sky, dry-wet, and so on. Fire symbolizes destruction and water restores the world order (Prasad).

This ancient vision of spiritualized nature has been destroyed by the modern 'technocentric' civilization. Reporting on the pastoral transhumants in the Garhwal Himalayas, Negi observes that although man and animal are still symbiotically related, man's relationship with nature (ecology) has turned parasitic. Miri's analysis of the Lingami Naga stories shows how man-animal-nature continuum has been disrupted in today's tribal consciousness.

Oral and Textual Modes of Perception

The discussion on the five-element theory in oral tradition has shown that different categories of people – the hunter-gatherer, the fisher, the farmer, and the pastoral transhumant – visualize, more or less, the same basic pattern of the universe. Minor variations occur only in the specificity of the ecological conditions and social systems. Since the basic elements of nature are the same everywhere, one can understand perceptual similarity among many of the preliterate groups.

The oral mode presents an experiential view of the environment that co-ordinates human life in concrete terms with things and beings around. The textual mode, on the contrary, provides instruments for logical analysis that takes one to a higher level of abstraction. The question, then, is: does the difference in the mode of perception constrain the projection of reality ? Several contributors to this volume (Brouwer, Dhasmana, Mathur, Patnaik, Verma) have demonstrated that as far as India's traditional cosmology is concerned, there is little difference between the oral and the textual views. This again stands to reason, because India's wider system of beliefs and practices has been operating through crossed-link populations from time immemorial.

How does traditional cosmology work across civilizations ? As appears from Tan Chung's investigation of the ancient Chinese cosmology, the belief that the world is made up of material elements is deeply rooted in human thinking. Of the five elements of the Chinese tradition – water, fire, wood, metal and earth – only metal does not figure in the Indian system of basic elements. There are areas of conspicuous similarities in the two traditions. Both the civilizations share in common views on the gross and the subtle aspects of elements, on the fivefold constitution of man and the universe, on the association of elements with colour, sensory organs, emotions, etc., inter-relatedness of the five elements through a chain of reactions, understanding the world in terms of the male-female principle, and the idea that opposites form a harmonious whole.

The IGNCA has planned a number of conferences devoted to the study of the basic elements in the ancient philosophies and modern sciences. This venture, being the first in the series, may seem to be largely descriptive; but, whatever the form, it does show that the search for the human foundation has been a common concern of both spiritual and scientific enquiries.

Baidyanath Saraswati

1

Cosmogonic Myths in Northeast India

Forces of Nature

Baidyanath Saraswati

One of the most inscrutable mysteries confronting man is that of his own existence. Reflections of man's place and purpose in the universe are found in all cultures at all times, but the ways of understanding are different. Profound answers have been sought through religion, science and popular wisdom.

Science and Scriptures

Two opposite paradigms have been constructed in the post-Renaissance European science and Christian scriptures: evolutionism and creationism.[1] Evolutionism considers man to be a product of nature, moving progressively from simplicity to complexity, from unorganized to organized, from lesser to greater. Creationism holds god as an active agent in the creation of man and the universe. The opposition between the formulation of science and the Christian ideas of creation is more apparent than real, for both are structured around the homocentric view of the universe. From the viewpoint of science, man makes his own history and civilization. Protagoras, the Greek sophist, has said, "Man is the measure of all things." The Biblical account places man at the centre of the purpose of creation. Man alone is entitled for progress and salvation.

The eastern view counters the western homocentrism. This could be best illustrated by the Indian theory of elements. The basic assumption of this theory is that, like the rest of the material world, man is made up of elements, which after death disintegrate and dissolve into nature. The elements have been spiritually identified and metaphysically debated for thousands of years. The texts of the religio-philosophical traditions differ in respect of both identification and classification of elements. At the most general level, there are nine *tattvas*: *prthvi* (earth), *jala* (water), *tejas* (fire), *vayu* (air), *akasa* (sky), *kala* (time), *dika* (directions), *atma* (soul) and *manas* (mind). Of these, the first five are called *bhutas* and the last four *dravyas*. The gross and the subtle aspects of elements are differentiated. Traditional thinking leaps over the dichotomy: the reality of the subtler planes is responsible for the grosser planes, and at a higher level of understanding the distinction between the gross and the subtle gets obliterated.

Oral Culture

In oral cultures, man's fascination with the world is embodied in his language, myth and ritual, in fact, in everyday life of the whole community. Regrettably, there have been no systematic studies of this specific aspect of oral culture so far. However, a beginning has been made at the IGNCA in a consistent way.

Tribal Cosmogony

In the textual philosophical tradition, man has a fivefold constitution called *bhutas* – earth, water, fire, air and sky. It is not yet known whether such a conceptual category exists in the oral mythic tradition. In order to grasp its implicit philosophy, it is important to investigate and analyze the cosmogonic myths of a particular culture.

Tribal cosmogony refers to a variety of elements, some of which are self-existing and others created. The tribes of Arunachal Pradesh,[2] for instance, refer to water, egg, cloud, rock, wood and the great personage as the self-existing elements of the first order. According to the tradition, from these were created elements of the second order: earth, sky, sun, moon, wind, fire and all living creatures. The third order of elements were then formed: colour, direction, form, smell, etc. The fourth order was attributed to knowledge.

A general description of the creation myths summed up in close identification of the elements now follows.

WATER

Before the earth was made, everything was water. There were two brothers who were supreme in the Sky. One day they said to each other, "When men are created, how will they live if there is nothing but water in the world?" There was a lotus flower growing in the sky. The brothers threw this down and immediately the water was covered with flowers. Then they called the winds from the four quarters. The east wind brought white dust and scattered it on the flowers. The west wind blew yellow dust, the south wind red dust and the north wind black dust. The wind blew the dust round and round and mixed it up together until the earth was formed. This is why the earth is made up of different colours.[3]

EGG

At first there was nothing but two eggs. They were soft and shone like gold. They did not stay in one place, but went round and round. At last, as they went round, they collided and both eggs broke open. From one came the earth, from the other the sky, her husband. When the sky made love to the earth, every kind of tree and grass and all living creatures came into being.[4]

CLOUD

At first there was no earth nor sky, but only cloud and mist. From it a woman was born; and since she came from the mist she was a sort of cloud. In time she gave birth to a girl and a boy. They had the appearance of snow. When they grew up they married each other and from them were born a girl called Inga (earth) and a son called Mu (sky). Inga was mud and Mu a cloud. These two also married and had a boy called Imbung (wind). When he was born he blew so strongly that he raised the cloud, his father, into the sky and dried up his mother, the mud. In this way heaven and earth were made.[5]

ROCK

At first there was nothing, nothing at all, but rocks and water. The first living beings were the rocks, but they were not as rocks are now: they were soft and could move about. From the rocks, a female rock was born. She married another rock and her first child was the fish. Then she gave birth to the big frog, and then the little frog, and then to the land frog. After that she gave birth to the insect which lives in water and then to another fish. Then she left her husband and went to the sky-village among the stars, where she married and had many children, and when she had borne them all, she died. The children prepared rice-beer for her funeral. When the millet was ready and they poured water over it, a great cloud arose, and from the cloud was born the *mithun* (*bos frontalis*). The *mithun* dug a great pit with his horns, and when water poured into the pit, dry land appeared. After this the rocks became hard as they are today.[6]

WOOD

Everything was water — water as far as the eye could see. But above the water rose the tree Teri-Ramula. As time passed a worm was born in the tree and it began to eat the Wood. The dust fell into the water, year after year, until slowly, the world was formed. Then, at last, the tree fell to the ground. The bark on the lower side of the trunk became the skin of the world; the bark of the upper side became the skin of the sky. The trunk itself turned into rock. The branches became the hills.[7]

Great Personage

At first Kujum-Chantu, the earth, was like a human being. She had a head, arms and legs, and an enormous fat belly. The original human beings lived on the surface of her belly. One day it occurred to her that if she ever got up and walked about, everyone would fall off and be killed; so she died of her own accord. Every part of her body became a part of the world, and her eyes turned into the sun and the moon.[8]

Some of these oral myths have parallels in textual myths. For instance, the tribal notion of creation from water, or from the cosmic egg, or from the transformation of some great personage, has a remarkable similarity with the vision of the classical texts. In the Hindu scriptures, one finds mention of the primeval ocean, Hiranyagarbha, the Golden Germ, and the sacrifice of Prajapati.[9] The other motifs which the tribal cosmogonic myths share in common with the classical texts are lotus, snake, boar, fish, tortoise, mountain, and so on. Yet, apparently, there is no complete agreement between the tribal perception and the textual enumeration of the basic elements. Wood, for instance, is not an element in the classical texts, but finds a place in tribal oral myths. Interestingly, wood is one of the five elements in Chinese tradition.[10]

Another curious feature of tribal cosmogony is that in its vision of the phenomenal reality there is no single creator of the universe. There are creators for each specific element: Nili and Nipu, who were without form, made the earth and the sky respectively.[11] Creation is a male-female principle, often brought about by marriage or sexual union.

Tribal Epistemology

Most tribes do not seem to have a clear notion of the fivefold constitution of the human body. Different tribes speak differently of the various elements responsible for man's origin. Man has descended from the union of the earth and sky, who are regarded as wife and husband.[12] Humankind is traced to the marriage between the daughter of the Sky-God and a spirit on Earth.[13] The sun makes images of a man and woman from clay and puts a breath of life into them.[14] The daughter of the lord of sky gave birth to a lump of flesh which was neither living nor dead. She dried it by the fire, and it soon burst open and bits of it scattered about the world and turned into human beings.[15] In the beginning there was a great tree, from the berry of which grew a flower; out of this flower came a pair of human beings, the first man and woman.[16] The first human beings came out of a gourd.[17] Many of the first men and women came out of the tusk of an elephant.[18]

There are also stories of how the first human race was destroyed and a new race created. Seven suns destroyed humankind for its iniquity; then, after the world has been washed clean by rain, it was re-peopled with a new race.[19] The first men were destroyed by fire and flood, and only one man and woman were saved; from them modern humanity has descended.[20] The world was destroyed by flood and the tribe descended from a girl who was impregnated by the wind.[21]

Tribal myths deny the uniqueness of man insofar as his origin is concerned.[22] There are no real distinctions between man, animal and spirit. A woman gives birth to twins, of whom one is human and the other a tiger; animals talk and often behave like men; of two brothers, one is the father of mankind and the other the father of spirits. There are many stories of marriage of human beings with gods, spirits, animals, as well as leaves, trees and, sometimes, even fire. Man is not unique even in the possession of knowledge.[23] Primordial knowledge came to him from birds and animals. The knowledge of ritual is revelatory. The priests of all creatures were born at the beginning of creation. The implication of these myths is that the universal knowability lies with what could be called the Cosmic Intelligence, symbolized in the myth of the Cosmic Egg.

In contrast to the classical scriptural myths, tribal cosmogony asserts that the world was created in phases by a number of heavenly bodies and not by the one Creator-God, a single Supreme Being. It also makes no distinction between the creature and the creator. The early phases of creation were characterized by total integration of all that came into being. Everything that has been created has its own life, and hence there was no ontological difference between man and non-man. The truth of the unity of all experience and the harmony of all existence is expressed through the mythic confirmation of the relation between various elements of nature: the earth and sky are a divine couple and universal parents. Fire and whirlwind are brothers just as water and mist are brothers. But water and fire have always been enemies. Wind is the friend of fire against water and he fights the rain and drives it before him.

Man's kinship with the earth and sky is reaffirmed by the eschatological belief that patterns of life on earth are the same as in heaven.[24] Man lives on earth in the company of good and evil spirits, above whom rises the majestic figure of the sun-moon, Doini-Polo.[25] The sun-moon was created after the *wiyus* (spirits) and, according to some traditions, later even than mankind.[26] Water[27] is believed to be under the control of the spirit; some dwell in streams and rivers; others are in the sky, making the world hot or cold, sending or restraining rain, snow and hail; they can be influenced by the *shamans*. Rituals are performed to avert drought and excessive rain. There is a general belief that early in history, fire took refuge in a stone or a tree. Men got fire from various animals: owl, monkey, crow, bat and others. Although it was known that fire[28] could be disastrous, either deliberately or by accident, many tribes believed in the fire-spirit – a spirit whose body is full of fire. He lives in the sky and wherever he sees evil he comes down and destroys it. There are protection rituals of various kinds. If a house catches fire the people leave a charm in a bowl of rice-beer and throw it at the house along with earth hurriedly collected from the grave and some black dye which is used to colour their cloth. It is believed that these objects drive away the spirits who cause the fire.

Order and Disorder

Three operant ideas have emerged: (i) Man is not unique in his origin, not even in the possession of knowledge; (ii) there is no ontological difference between man, animal and spirit; and (iii) there is no distinction between the creature and the creator. From these, it may be deduced that all elements, things and beings, are an organic part of the cosmos. Every element performs the same paradigmatic act of creation, preservation and destruction. The order of the cosmos is dependent on the harmonious functioning of all elements. Tribal cultures have not only a vision of this reality — they also live up to it. The Ongees are a good example.[29]

Ongees and spirits live on the same island. There are good spirits and bad spirits. When bad spirits are attracted to the living Ongees, they come and take away the Ongees. This act is known as death caused by *enegetebe* (to be embraced and taken away). Since good spirits do not have lower jawbones, they depend on the Ongees to provide them food. During negotiation, the good spirits convince the bad ones to let the Ongees live so that they may provide a continuous supply of food which all spirits may share. Bad spirits agree to the negotiation since the good spirits provide them with *maonale*, which good spirits alone are capable of making or directing the Ongees in making them. This relationship between spirits and Ongees is also the basis for seasonal translocation among the Ongees. Since the spirits and the Ongees depend on the island for food, the potential encounter with spirits who can cause death makes it necessary for Ongees and spirits to be on the same island but in different parts. Ongees explain:

> In each season spirits along with winds come from a particular direction. When they leave other spirits come in from a different side and it is a different season. When spirits come to the sea, then we move to the forest for hunting pigs. When spirits come to the forest we all go to the sea for hunting turtle. Spirits and Ongees both have to be on this island, sky and sea around. But the place where the spirits are feeding is the place in which Ongees should not hunt and gather. If the two are in the same place then all the Ongees will be taken away by the spirits to the sky and sea . . . by letting the spirits in a place in a season we get more plants, more animals and more children . . . . Ongees and spirits hunt and gather in the same *injube* (space), but in different *nanchugey* (place). Many *nanchugey* in the land, sea and sky make one big *injube* in which we along with animals, plants and spirits live.

The medium of interaction between the Ongees and the spirit world is the smell (kept in the ancestral bone, which the Ongees wear as an ornament). It is the smell[30] that keeps the Ongees on the island and the spirits in the sky and the sea.

The Ongees' awareness of the cosmic order is consistent with the cosmogonic myths of the Arunachal tribes.

To conclude, every element has a form, a location, a function, and a dependent relation with other elements. Water is the first element, from which all elements originate and to which all return. The earth and sky form a universal principle of creation, both concrete and abstract, expressed by such kinship terms as husband and wife, or by such conceptual terms as used in Hindu and Chinese traditions – *mithun* and *yin-yang*, respectively. Wind and fire are brothers; and fire and water are enemies. Together they perform the function of creation and dissolution. In such a configuration of elements, the dissolution of the earth, sky, wind and fire into water is not to be considered as disorder. For, water is the first principle of cosmic order. The forces of nature are set into a mutually creative harmony. There is no intrinsic disorder in nature. Hence the oral cultures in their wisdom have made a final reconciliation with nature.

Notes

1. Cf. Saraswati (1987).
2. The tribal cosmogonic myths discussed in this paper are based on Elwin (1968).
3. Sherdukpen, cf. Elwin, *op.cit.*
4. Hrusso-Aka, cf. Elwin.
5. Singpho, cf. Elwin.
6. Minyong, cf. Elwin.
7. Hill Miri, cf. Elwin.
8. Apa Tani, cf. Elwin.
9. See, the famous *Purusa Sukta* in the *Rigveda*.
10. Personal communication from Ms Meng Si-hui of Palace Museum, Beijing.
11. Bugun-Khowa, cf. Elwin.
12. Dhammai, cf. Elwin.
13. Nocte, cf. Elwin.
14. Hill Miri, cf. Elwin.
15. Moklems, cf. Elwin.
16. Khampti, cf. Elwin.

17. Singpho, cf. Elwin.
18. Mishmi, cf. Elwin.
19. Singpho, cf. Elwin.
20. Idu Mishmi, cf. Elwin.
21. Wancho, cf. Elwin.
22. Cf. Saraswati (1991a).
23. *Ibid.*
24. Cf. Saraswati (1991b).
25. Adi, cf. Elwin.
26. Cf. Elwin.
27. *Ibid.*
28. *Ibid.*
29. Cf. Pandya (1991).
30. Ongees describe how smell affects the form of life: "Smell is like the water of the sea and the tides. Nobody knows or affects the water coming to land and rising and then going back. It happens always. Smell also like the tide water comes and goes from all that is living, but just like the tides change the land at the coast, the loss of smell changes the form that is living. If the smell is not kept, there is no life, if the tides' water does not go back to the sea then there is no land and no sea." (Pandya 1991: 92).

References

Elwin, Verrier, 1968. *Myths of the North-East Frontier of India.* Shillong, North-East Frontier Agency.

Pandya, Vishvajit, 1991. "Tribal Cosmology: Displacing and Replacing Process in Andamanese Places", In *Tribal Thought and Culture: Essays in Honour of Shri Surajit Chandra Sinha*, Baidyanath Saraswati (ed.). New Delhi, Concept Publishing Company.

Saraswati, Baidyanath, 1987. "Man and Culture: the Exegesis of Science and Scripture", In *Sramana Vidya: Studies in Buddhism – Jagannath Upadhyaya Commemoration Volume*, N.H. Samtani (ed.), Sarnath-Varanasi, Central Institute of Higher Tibetan Studies.

———, 1991a. "Tribal Cosmogony: Primal Vision of Man and Cosmos", In *Tribal Thought and Culture: Essays in Honour of Shri Surajit Chandra Sinha*, Baidyanath Saraswati (ed.). New Delhi, Concept Publishing Company.

———, 1991b. "Rtual space : Tribal Non-Tribal Context", In *Concept of Space: Ancient and Modern*, Kapila Vatsyayan (ed.). New Delhi, Indira Gandhi National Centre for the Arts and Abhinav Publications.

2

Chinese Cosmogony

Man-Nature Synthesis

Tan Chung

This is not an in-depth study of ancient Chinese cosmogony as it requires a specialization of ancient philosophical writings and a close acquaintance with the rich folklore of China.

However, it can be said for certain that the theories of *yin* and *yang* and the five elements are a part of the ancient Chinese cosmogony. *Shangshu* (Book of Documents) contains the earliest textual reference of *wuxing* (five elements).

> First we have the five elements water, fire, wood, metal and earth. Water moistens downwards. Fire heats upwards. Wood is both crooked and straight. Metal can be changed into various shapes. Earth is for planting crops. Moistening downwards makes the salty taste. Heating upwards makes the bitter taste. Crookedness and straightness make the sour taste. Changing into shapes makes the pungent taste. Crops make the sweet taste.[1]

Chinese civilization was born with agriculture. Here *Shangshu* speaks of the five elements in the words of an ancient Chinese farmer who also had handicraft skills in making wood and metal into implements.

Kong Yinda (AD 574-648) was an important Tang court-scholar who was one of the ancient authorities in expounding the Confucian cultural tradition. While annotating *Liji* (Book of Rites), Kong wrote that water was created in the eleventh month, fire in the sixth, wood in the first, metal in the eighth and earth in the third month.[2] In agriculture, life was incorporated into the seasonal changes of the year which came to mankind repeatedly as a routine. Kong Yinda's comments are appended to one of the three chapters on *yueling* (lunar order) which deal with the twelve lunar months of the year.

Kong Yinda, in his commentary on the *Shangshu* passage cited above, elaborates the ancient Chinese creation of the five elements in the *xici* (preface) of *Yijing* (Book of Change).

> Heaven starts with one, Earth two, Heaven three, Earth four, Heaven five, Earth six, Heaven seven, Earth eight, Heaven nine, Earth ten.

This, said Kong, was the numbering in which the five elements were created. He continues:

> Heaven, being one, created water. Earth, being two, created fire. Heaven, being three, created wood. Earth, being four, created metal. Heaven, being five, created earth.

At this point, Heaven and Earth were without spouse.

> Earth, being six, created water. Heaven, being seven, created fire. Earth, being eight, created wood. Heaven being nine, created metal. Earth, being ten, created earth.

In this way *yin* and *yang* found their matches, and the beings of the universe took their forms.[3]

Jin Chunfeng, a modern Chinese scholar, has tried to find a diagram which can categorize traditional Chinese thought. He constructed the *yueling tushi* (diagram of lunar order) with the *yin* and *yang* and the five elements as its nucleus. He thinks that earth was the centre of the agricultural economic activities in ancient times, hence being placed in the centre (while wood, metal, fire, water are placed in the east, west, south, north respectively). The ancient Chinese linked space with time. East was linked with spring, south with summer, west with autumn, and north with winter. Earth controlled the four seasons and was the identification of men.

Jin thinks that the above-mentioned identifications have outlined the ecological environment of the cradle of Chinese civilization in the valley of the middle stream of the Yellow River (during the Xia, Shang and Zhou dynasties). Men in this country noticed that when the east wind blew there came spring, therefore the east created spring and wood. In summer, hot wind came from the south which was the creator of fire and summer. Autumn was the harvest season. When the west wind blew, the crops turned golden, hence west with autumn and metal was taken in one category. Winter brought cold wind from the north, and marked the time of hiding and storing which characterized water.[4]

Lushi chungiu (Lu Buwei's edition of *Spring and Autumn*) associates the five elements with five colours, and also with the development of ancient Chinese history. According to the textual tradition, Chinese civilization began with the Yellow Emperor (Huangdi). During the time of Huangdi the spirit of earth prevailed and its colour was yellow – hence the yellow earth and Yellow Emperor. During the time of Yu (the first king of the Xia dynasty), there was an exuberant vegetation in all the seasons which presented the colour of wood, i.e., green. During the time of Tang (the first king of Shang dynasty), the spirit of metal prevailed, presenting white colour. During the time of King Wen of Zhou, the spirit of fire prevailed, presenting red colour. Fire would be replaced by water which would present black colour. Water would, then, be absorbed by earth, and the rotation of the five elements would continue endlessly till eternity.[5]

The representative colours of the various seasons are the visual representations of the ecological environment. It makes sense to associate spring with green and wood as it is the season of growth of vegetation. Summer is associated with red and fire, as it is the hottest season with maximum sunshine. Associating autumn with white and metal needs a little more imagination. This probably had something to do with the withering of vegetation and transformation of a rich colourful world into whitish grey. Similarly the association of winter with water and black may be explained by the cold which forced people into hiding, thus bringing darkness. Besides this, black or other dark colours are used more often in winters.

The historical reference in *Lushi chungiu* is also interesting. The Chinese civilization began with the beginning of agricultural pursuit which was to get some yield from the yellow earth, with the Yellow Emperor being a typical symbol. Then, plantation brought about the increasing importance of wood and prevalence of green colour during the time of Yu which showed a stage of economic advancement. Further advancement was made by the utilization of metal during the time of Tang (which, according to Chinese tradition, was nearly a thousand years after Yu). The Shang dynasty founded by Tang was a period of magnificent bronze wares which are found in almost all the major museums of the world. King Wen of Zhou ushered in a new era of more brisk human activities with larger territories and greater population brought under the pale of Chinese civilization. The prevalence of fire signified cooking, lighting, handicraft industry and war.

Dong Zhongshu (176-104 BC), the famous Han prime minister who was responsible for creating a state ideology in the name of Confucius, used human temperament to analyze seasonal changes. Spring was the expression of happiness, there was warmth. The sun was the embodiment of joy and ecstasy which created summer. Autumn was created by anger. Sorrow made winter which was dominated by the concentration of *yin*, just like the sun marked the concentration of *yang*. Thus, spring was the spirit of love, summer was of joy, autumn of anger, and winter of sorrow. The spirit of love meant creation; that of joy meant growth; that of anger, success; that of sorrow, death and end. He concluded that:

> The dynamics of the four seasons are the ways guiding father and son. The will of Heaven and Earth is the relationship between the ruler and subject. The logic of *yin* and *yang* is the law of the sages.[6]

The Eight Trigrams (*bagus*) is a special growth of the Chinese cultural tradition in which both the *yin* and *yang* and the five elements play a vital role. There is no phenomenon in the universe which cannot be explained by the experts of the Eight Trigrams. Special theories of the working of the Eight Trigrams are found in the Chinese lunar calendar, and in the life of the users of the calendar even to this day of modern science and technology. Each day of the calendar is allotted one of the five elements, which dominates for two consecutive days and give way to the next in a rotation which works in the following manner :

> wood wood water water earth earth fire fire wood wood
> water water metal metal fire fire

Chinese fortune-tellers essentially use the five elements for their calculations. The five elements form a circle of one constraining the other: water constrains fire, fire constrains metal, metal constrains wood, wood constrains earth, earth constrains water. As each birth sign is associated with one of the five elements, matchmakers would normally ensure that the wife's element does not constrain that of the husband as it would result in endless family trouble. But the element of the husband constraining that of the wife will be regarded natural and logical.

The five elements along with other concepts form the Chinese non-alphabetic script. A large number of the Chinese written characters have one of them forming a part of the stroke combinations. According to folklore a person born in a particular year should prefer some ideographic parts in his written name. For instance, a person born in the year of Tiger can be blessed with a gentle and sagacious nature, and can achieve fame and richness if his/her name has both metal (*jin*) and wood (*mu*) in it. A person born in the year of Monkey will be romantic and optimistic if he/she has water as a part of his/her name.

The holy book of Taoists, *Daodejing*, traces Tao as the creator of the universe. Tao has created the five elements by its movements, revolutions, dynamics and motion-lessness. It has created the *yin* and *yang* and everything. Taoism as a religion has absorbed many of the domestic Chinese cults which have connections with ancient Chinese cosmogony. Taoists are ardent worshippers of the Earth-God. A variation of the Earth-God is the Wall-God (*chenghuang*) which guards the walled towns. Taoists also worship the Kitchen-God. According to legend, one of the culture heroes of China was Yandi who was the god of fire. After he died he became the kitchen. The five elements are also five star-gods in the Taoist tradition. The Wood-star is called

Suixing, the Earth-star Zhenxing, the Metal-star Taibaixing, the Water-star Chenxing, and Fire-star Yinghuoxing. The four famous Taoist supernatural animals, also called *zhenmushou* (guardian-angels of the graves), are Blue-dragon, Red-bird, White-tiger, and Xuanwu. The Blue-dragon guards the east, hence blue or green. The Red-bird guards the south, hence red. The White-tiger guards the west, hence white. Xuanwu guards the north, hence black. The four different colours are those of wood and spring, fire and summer, metal and autumn, water and winter, respectively.

The Yi nationality which populates the four southwestern provinces of Sichuan, Yunnan, Guizhou and Guangxi, worships sun, moon, Water-God, Fire-God, Mountain-God, Stone-God and Heaven-God. People believe in Water-God as the controller of rains, Fire-God as the force to dispel evil spirits, Mountain-God as a protector of men from the attack of wild animals, and Stone-God as a guardian-angel against theft and children's diseases.

Another very small nationality called Bulang in the Bulang Hill area in Yunnan (with a population of less than one lakh) worships Fire-God and Earth-God. People worship Fire-God for protection from fire. They worship Earth-God for safety to human life and for a bumper harvest. They conceive a Water-spirit which has a human-head with a snake-body. The Water-spirit comes out for mischief during heavy rains and flood. They also worship the Mountain-God to protect them and give them prosperity, as they are mountain-dwellers leading difficult lives. Many of them are Buddhists; but Buddhism does not conflict with their traditional beliefs.

The Bai nationality which resides in Yunnan, Guizhou and Hu'nan have an earth-breaking ceremony in the spring festival every year in order to have good weather and good harvest. People also worship the Mountain-God for good crops and protection of the domestic animals. The Miao race which was a major native population of south China and is now spread in Yunnan, Guizhou, Guangxi, Hu'nan, Sichuan, Hubei, has a strong Earth-God worship. Every village has a temple for the Earth-God. The temple for the Earth-God is equally popular among the Han residents of south China.

A teleological approach has been used here to study the five elements, and to ponder upon the purpose of the ancients in such an analysis. The major approach of ancient Chinese thinking was to synthesize human activities with their natural environment, which contrasts with the European approach of isolating various objects to gain a deeper insight into their nature and dynamics. Many Chinese feel that these two approaches have led the Europeans to develop modern science and technology, while such a development escaped China. The Chinese approach has been holistic. Although people did observe natural phenomena, they established too early an organic linkage between man and nature. One aspect of this man-nature synthesis was to humanize nature, attributing a human character to natural changes. Conversely, the other aspect of synthesis subjected men under the domination of nature, to bind human activities to movements of the sun, moon and stars.

Some modern Chinese scholars, like Jin Chunfeng, do not disparage the Chinese holistic tradition. Jin thinks it provides a very ideal scientific approach. First, the approach does not concentrate on isolated individual entities, but on the entirety or the system as a whole. Second it is not static, but dynamic, grasping the movements of the objective entities within the evolutions of time and *qi* (ether). Third, it does not take into consideration the inner structure and composition of an object, but on its function and nature. Since every object is a process of flowing and revolving, it only maintains a temporary stability which should not be mistaken as a fixed structure. Fourth, the approach does not eye on the functions and natures of the parts, but on the functions and responses of the whole. Fifth, it does not pay attention to the geometric models and trajectories, but tries to size up the entire developmental trend of the objects.[7] Jin illustrates these characteristics of the Chinese tradition by the example of Chinese medicine. Chinese pathology treats every organ of the body as a moving process, as the entire body is in a process of decaying, like the river flowing downwards. Stability is viewed as in a state of ephemeral whirlpool.[8] Chinese medicine treats ailment as a disturbance of the natural equilibrium in the body, and tries to send input to the body to sustain its vitality to slow down the process of decay. After all, the human body, like all other beings in the universe, is the combination of *yin* and *yang* and the five elements.

I would like to make clear that I am neither a believer of the five elements and *yin* and *yang*, nor sceptical about the expertize in them which I have no share in me. There could be some similarities between the Chinese ancient and tribal cosmogonies and those of India. Indian scholars are welcome to explore the field.

Notes

1. Kong Yinda, *et al.*, *Shisanjing zhengyi* (Annotated edition of the Thirteen Classics), reprint, Beijing, Zhonghua Bookshop, 1980, vol. I, p. 188.
2. *Ibid.*, p. 1354.
3. *Ibid.*, p. 188.
4. Jin Chunfeng, " 'Yueling' tushi yu Zhongguo gudai siwei fangshide tedian jiqi dui kexue zhexuede yingxiang" ("The Lunar Order Diagram and Characteristics of the Ancient Chinese way of Thinking as well as its Impact on Science and Philosophy"), In *Zhongguo wenhua yu Zhongguo zhexue* (Chinese Culture and Chinese Philosophy), comp. Shenzhen

University, Beijing, Eastern Publishing House, 1986, pp. 128-30.

5. Liu Yuanyan, "*Lushi chungiu* shi xianqin gejia sixiang zuidade zonghezhe" ("*Lushi chungiu* is the Greatest Summary of the Ideas of Various Schools in the Pre-Qin Period"), *ibid.*, p. 174.
6. Ye Xiaoqing, "Zhongguo chuantong ziran'guan Yu jindai kexue" ("The Traditional Chinese View of Nature and Modern Science"), In *Kexue chuantong yu wenhua: Zhongguo jindai kexue luohoude yuanyin* (Science, Tradition and Culture: Causes of China's Lagging Behind in Science in Modern Times), Xi'an, Shaanxi Science and Technology Publishing House, 1983, pp. 159-60.
7. Jin Chunfeng, *op cit.*, p. 132.
8. *Ibid.*, p. 133.

3

The Supernatural in Nature
Sindhi Tradition

Lachman K. Khubchandani

People of the Hindu faith demonstrate a great deal of variety in their everyday ritualistic expression. Most of these practices are rooted in the oral tradition.

Many different explanations of the cosmic reality, as perceived by a Hindu mind, are found in classical compositions – the *Vedas*, the *Brahmanas*, the *Puranas*, the epics, the *Bhagavad Gita* and so on. At the same time, many age-old folk beliefs have been orally transmitted through the intervention of *avataras*, *gurus*, or through miracles and *akasavanis*. These beliefs usually prevail among specific groups and their impact is confined to a smaller region. In this context, anthropologists distinguish two streams of tradition: 'high' tradition enjoying the legitimacy of scriptures or of philosophical interpretation, and 'low' tradition backed by syncretic beliefs and myths.[1]

Among the Sindhi Hindus is a popular sect known as the *Daryapanthis*, 'followers of the river', who worship a folk deity named Uderolal; the word is said to be derived from Sanskrit *odaka*, meaning water. Many temples named after the deity were built in different parts of the erstwhile Sindh in undivided India. The same deity is revered as *Zindah Pir* or *Khwaja Khizr* among Muslims as well, and has main places of worship: one on an island near Rohri (in northern Sindh) and another, at the Lal Shahbaz Dargah, associated with the Sufi mystic Mast Qalandar, in Sehwan (in central Sindh).

The believers of *Daryapanth* worship *joti* and *jalu*. They have elaborate rituals on religious and festive occasions throughout the year, particularly on *Chetichandu*, marking the beginning of new year. *Chetichandu* coincides with *Gandi Parva* the new year festival in Maharashtra. Various *pujas* are performed, initiated by the priestly class called Thakkurs (believed to be Khatris, the descendants of the first disciple of Uderolal). These practices have been transmitted orally. No claims are made about the existence of any written text in the name of the holy deity of his descendants (though, surprisingly, the legendary figure of Uderolal on river fish *palo* is shown holding a scripture in his hand). In recent decades in spite of the inception of the print media, few booklets have been compiled, formulated on the basis of oral transmission.

This chapter discusses the socio-historical background of the sect and various rituals associated with the folk beliefs of the *Daryapanthis*, exalting the miraculous powers of the cosmic order, particularly those of the flame and the water.

There are many legends concerning the river deity, called by various names, Uderolal, Jhulelal, Amarlal, associated with certain historical events in Sindh during the early Medieval period. It is commonly believed that, in response to persistent prayers to Lord Varuna from the oppressed folk, the river deity Darya Shah, River Lord, incarnated himself in a family of a boatman at Nasarpur (on the banks of river Sindhu in central Sindh), in the tenth century, as their saviour from the atrocities of a chief of Thatta named Mirkh Shah in lower Sindh. Having won the fierce battle, Uderolal through his miracles brought about a change of heart in the atrocious king, who also became his devotee. Devotional hymns, called *janam sakhia* and *panjiras*, are sung by the devotees of *Daryapanth*, exalting the river deity as a young warrior on a valiant horse emerging from river Sindhu, as a sage riding on *palo* 'sweet-water fish' against the tide, and as a *jogi* who received *guru mantra* from Gorakhnath and made a pilgrimage to the Hinglaj Devi (a holy place of *Nathpanthis*, situated on the Sindh-Baluchistan border).

Rhythmic compositions form a significant aspect of the folklore among the *Daryapanthis*. *Panjiras*, five-line devotional verses (sometimes stretched to seven lines), are composed by devotees for specific occasions and presented as an offering to the exalted deity. One such popular version is:

Munhinji beri athai vicha sira te
palau panyan thi man jinda pira te
jotiyuni vara lala udera
kei kani tha to dari pera
tunhinji mahira amira faqira te palau . . . .

My boat is in the mid-stream
I submit myself to the Jinda Pir
Oh ! Lala Udera ! decorated with eternal lights
Several devotees call upon at your doorsteps
Your blessings are alike for the rich and for the poor.
I submit . . . .

Jhulelal's mission is identified by

(i) performing many miracles as a messenger of Lord Varuna, pacifying conflicting sects with the doctrine of One Almighty.

(ii) mitigating miseries of the oppressed (Hindus as well as Muslims); and

(iii) promoting the worship of superior powers through *joti* 'holy flame' and *jalu* 'holy water' as the source of life.

A *samadhi* and a *qubo* (mausoleum), attributed to Jhulelal and Zindah Pir, are located at the same place near village Jhijhan (in Nasarpur), where Hindus and Muslims go for pilgrimage. The Sufi *dargah* of Lal Shahbaz in Sehwan is also associated with the worship of Zindah Pir. Till today a place in the interior of the *dargah* is maintained by the Sufis for the worship of Hindu devotees.

A forty-day vigil *chaliho saheb* is performed by devotees of the river deity, culminating with the thanksgiving festivities, awaiting the arrival of their saviour. *Chetichandu* (new moon of *chaitra*) is celebrated marking the event of Uderolal's birth.

One remarkable feature of *Daryapanthis* is that many of the elaborate rituals worshipping the flame and water have been transmitted orally in the past one thousand years or so. Followers of *Daryapanth*, called *shewaks*, perform various rituals at the initiation of Thakkurs, in temples or in individual homes; they take *bahrano*, an exquisite decorated offering in a *thali* (a big tray) for Uderolal to the river, and participate in a procession dancing their way with *chheja* 'crescendo, inundation', a dance of joy resembling the Gujarati *Dandia Raas*.

An elaborate ritual connected with *bahrano* 'offering to the flowing stream' has many parallels with *Vedic* rituals of *havan*, except that it substitutes water for fire, and after the *puja* the decorated *thali* is ceremoniously taken to the river (stream or ocean) for immersion, accompanied with chorus music and folk dancing. A large portion of wheat flour, kneaded with fresh water, is equally divided for preparing one or more (preferably five) *modakas* (round balls) and lamps; five wicks soaked in cooking oil or ghee are placed in each lamp. Flour balls are placed by the side of lamps, which are sprinkled with *kumkum* and adorned with cloves, cardamoms, sugar candy, flowers and fresh milk; *kumkum* is applied to the flour lamps as well. The tray is scented with burning *dhoop* and *agarbattis*; camphor and sandalwood are burnt for lighting the first wick, from which other wicks for the rest of the lamps are lit. Five assorted fruits, along with a coconut, are placed next to the flour balls; paddy and sugar are also set aside in the tray to be available for individual offerings to the river lord, called *akho (aksaya)*. Auspicious markings of *aum* and Ganesh are drawn with *kumkum* and a betel is placed over the markings.

A small *kalash* (earthen urn), filled with fresh water and covered with a coconut on the top, is placed next to the decorated tray. Another tray is filled with *prasada*, called *sesa*, made of sweetened rice and black grams; one-third of the *sesa* is immersed in river and the rest is distributed among the devotees after the ceremony. In the midst of singing *panjiras*, clinging of cymbals, and the frenzy of *chheja* dance on the riverbank, both trays are taken to the midstream for immersion. At the culmination of the ceremony, water taken from the midstream is sprinkled over the devotees as a mark of blessing from the river deity. There is an air of fanfare and festivity on the river bank.

Oblations to the flowing waters (river, stream, ocean) is quite widespread among the Sindhis, irrespective of sectarian affiliations, as the subsistence of the desert people has been largely on the river Sindhu. Devout believers regularly make an offering of *akho* (on occasions, along with an oil lamp preferably made of wheat dough), when crossing the river.

According to the legend, Uderolal, after having accomplished the worldly mission (as saviour of the down-trodden), took his chosen disciple Pagad (Pongad) to the bottom of *bhavasagar* to reveal the divine experience of creation to him. Taking him to the *joti mandaru* at the bottom of the fathomless waters, Uderolal identified *agni* as the almighty power of creation, and explained the significance of worshipping the omnipotent *joti* and *jalu* to his disciple.

On returning to the surface, Uderolal installed Pagad as the custodian of *joti mandaru* for his devotees on earth and handed over seven sacred articles to be part of every *joti mandaru*.

joti	a lighted earthen lamp, manifesting the omnipotent
jhari	a *kalash*
kantha	a silken cloth-cover, also called *pakhara*, as a shield against evil
veedha	a ring, fulfilling one's mission, like *kalpa* (*verho*) *vrksa*
dhokla	a *damru*, signifying the original *nada*
tegh	a sword, signifying control over external and internal lures; it protects from demonic forces
degi	a metallic vessel for cooking sweetened rice *tahiri* as *aksya patra* (for providing *sesa parsadu* to devotees)

Joti and *jhari* are to be installed in the centre-stage of the temple, *dhokla* is used for singing hymns, and *degi* for preparing *sesa parsadu*, and *kantha* and *veedha* invoke the blessings of the priest. The significance of *joti* and *jalu* rituals among *Daryapanthis* has a close parallel with the Zoroastrian rituals among Parsees in India connected with *atish* (eternal flame) and *ava* (holy water) as primary forces of nature. These rituals are supported by Avestan texts (Boyce 1989, Randeria 1992).

With the migration of a large number of Sindhi Hindus to India, scattered in distant places, professional Thakkurs continue making periodic visits to the homes of their *shewaks* to perform *pujas* or the *shewaks* making individual contributions to their priest to perform *pujas* on their behalf in newly installed Jhulelal temples in many Sindhi settlements in the country. Lately the celebration of *Chetichandu* has acquired an added significance of creating a cultural bond of unity among the Sindhis scattered in the heterogeneous milieu of the Indian subcontinent.

There are different ways of organizing and looking at the universe. Primal groups such as tribals in central and northeastern regions show an abiding faith in nature; they live in harmony with nature. In the tribal worldview, nature is conceived as an order that includes man.

The oral tradition of Uderolal worship highlights the bountiful powers of nature. In a way it illustrates the human faculties of perceiving and recreating the world as conditioned by the socio-ecological environment. The *Daryapanthis* of Sindh present a unique blend of folk rituals emerging from the desert conditions, integrated with the influences of the *Nathpanth*, *Bhakti* cult, and Sufi mysticism as prevailing in northern India in the early Medieval period.

Note

1. Taking another example of the Orient, "Buddhist tradition is ascribed to the oral formulation of the Pali canon to the first century after the Buddha's death, and it was supposedly not written down until the first century BC" (Bright, 1988). Pali literature strongly suggests the absence of anything that could be called 'scriptures'. In the monastic rules, there is no reference to owning books or manuscripts. The *Anguttara Nikaya* refers to 'a definition of scholarship which does not mention reading' but rather 'repeating over to oneself' (Davids, 1903; Bright, 1988).

References

Abbott, J., 1910. *Sind, an Interpretation of the Unhappy Valley*, Karachi.

Boyce, Mary, 1989. *A History of Zoroastrianism*, 2 vols. Leiden, E.J. Brill.

Bright, W., 1988. "Written and Spoken Language in South Asia", In *On Language: Rhetorica, Phonologica, Syntactica*, C. Puncan-Rose and T. Vennamann (eds). London, Routledge.

Davids, T.W. Rhys., 1903. *Buddhist India*. New York, Putnam (reprinted by Motilal Banarsidass,

Delhi, 1971).

Jiwatramani, Topandas, 1980. *Jal Awatar*. Pune.

Khubchandani, Lachman M., 1992. *Tribal Identity: A Language and Communication Perspective*. Shimla, Indian Institute of Advanced Study.

Malhi, Gobind, 1991. "Jhulelal: The Sindhi God", In *Sindhi International II*, 1-2. Bombay.

Randeria, Jer D., *The Parsi Mind: A Zoroastrian Asset to Culture*, (forthcoming). New Delhi, Munshiram Manoharlal.

4

The Order of Nature in Liangmais Myth

Sujata Miri

This chapter consists of a few remarks about the man-animal-nature continuum in the collective awareness of the Liangmais, a small Naga tribe living in Manipur. The remarks are based exclusively on consideration of two folk stories of the tribe. The first of these stories is entitled, "The Deal Between Man and the Rat", and goes as follows:

> There was a time when the Liangmais were in desperate need of food. The men, in their greed, had eaten up all the fruit of the fruit-bearing trees, thus depriving them of their basic function of serving the earth. As is usual for him, at times of crisis, man, then, thought of God. The strong men of the tribe went to the house of God and begged Him to find a way of feeding man for all time to come. God told the men to pick a grain of paddy each and eat it, from his fields rich in vegetables and rice-paddy. The men did as they were told, and lo and behold, all the extra hair which used to be part of man's body fell away from them. As they were leaving God's house, He gave them two bags of paddy, but warned them to go home directly with the paddy without stopping anywhere on the way. The men however felt tired along the way and decided to rest for a while on the banks of a river. They went down to the river to quench their thirst leaving the bags of paddy on the bank. On their return, they found, to their horror, that the bags had disappeared. They looked everywhere, but in vain. Suddenly they saw their bags walking into the river, and, then, being carried by its currents to the deep blue sea.
>
> Trying desperately to find a way of recovering the bags, they sighted pretty birds of many colours, Mazaima-na, Kinmana and Ake, and

> pleaded them for help. The birds wanted to help, but their beaks were not strong enough. The men could not turn to the birds with strong beaks for fear that they might eat up all the grains themselves.
>
> At last a small creature named Tazamakhepui (queen of the rats), feeling sorry for the helpless men, offered to bring back the floating bags of paddy, on the condition that the men gave half of the paddy to her. The men rejected this condition outright. Then the rat became more reasonable and demanded that man and his descendants share their life with her descendants for all time to come. They should give any spare paddy they had to her and her descendants. This condition was accepted. Accordingly, a boat of sixteen leaves of the Phemananyu tree was made; the rat rowed down to the bags of paddy, and brought them back safely to the men. It is because of the rat's help in recovering the bags and the agreement between her and man that they are allowed to live with man today.

The first thing to be noted about this story is that man, in his foolishness and greed, can precipitate a crisis for himself and the world. By eating up all the fruit of the fruit-bearing trees, man deprived the earth of its source of renewal, and thus ran out of food. But god ensures that man survives such a crisis, though he brings it on himself by his thoughtlessness. In this case, god saves man once again, but punishes him by making him hairless thus marking him as the violator of the natural order – the only animal without hair.

Man is not only thoughtless, but is also forgetful. On his way back home from god's house, he forgets god's warning which brings another crisis. The saviour this time is a tiny female animal, a rat. The bargaining between the rat and man illustrates the relationship between man and other creatures for survival. The story also shows how all the creatures on earth, including man, are responsible not only for themselves and their present, but for the world around and the future generations to come. The concern for future is a recurring theme in many Liangmai legends and stories. Life, in all its forms, is the supreme gift of god. It is therefore every creature's sacred duty to preserve it and flourish in it and make the future safe for it. This duty can be fulfilled only by harmony and goodwill between all creatures, big and small, animate and inanimate.

The other story, "How an Elephant Made a Poor Boy King", goes as follows:

> Once upon a time there lived a family of eight sons and their parents in a village. The family was so poor that the parents frequently had to eat all the food themselves, leaving nothing for the children. Consequently, the children starved and became very weak. The

parents would cook food at night when the children were asleep. One day while the parents were handling the pots, one of the children woke up. He was asked by the parents to stay quiet. They promised to give him a share of whatever they were going to eat. However, the commotion disturbed the other children and all of them woke up. The parents tried to distract them by asking questions. They asked them what they would do for their parents when they grew up. All the sons, except the youngest who had only just learnt to speak, replied that they would help their parents in all possible ways. The parents wanted the youngest son also to respond. The child replied that he would live off the left overs of his elder brothers all his life. The parents were so annoyed by this reply that they ordered the elder brothers to kill him. The eldest brother felt sorry for the child and took him to the forest where he sealed his eyes with some adhesive and left him there. From where the boy stood he could go in any one of eight different directions. The elder brother also left him a knife.

The child sat there the whole night and became extremely tired. As dawn came an elephant appeared and asked him about his problem. The boy told the elephant all that had transpired during the night. The elephant felt sorry for the child. "You are the most honest among all your father's children", said he. He unsealed the child's eyes so that he could see again. Then the elephant gave the child a reed and told him to chop it into small pieces of meat. These pieces of meat were to be hung on the reeds and the boy was to take shelter under the remains of the elephant. The boy did as he was told, and slept under the skeleton that night.

The next morning the boy found himself inside a big palace. The skeleton of the elephant had been transformed into the palace during the night. Where the boy had kept the pieces of meat, there was an annexe to the palace. Thus the little boy found himself the king of a beautiful rich city.

News spread far and wide of the sudden emergence of the new city. The cruel parents meanwhile had become poorer than ever and lived by begging. One day they, along with their other sons, came upon their youngest son, now a king. He recognized his parents and without any illwill towards them ordered a feast in their honour. However, during the feast his mother and father were to receive severe punishment from God for their misdeeds. They were made to confess their crimes against their own children. The moment they finished

> with their confession they were struck down by *chuk-kiubo* (a strange disease causing the tongue to fall out of the mouth). the mother's eyes too fell out of their sockets, and they both died. The brothers however stayed happily with the king for many years.

Man's inability to control his selfishness in difficult circumstances leads to his moral degeneration and destruction. The parents not only forget their natural duty to their progeny, but arrogantly expect their children to serve them in return in spite of the most unnatural and unpardonable neglect of duty. The natural moral order is thus reversed by them. It requires a tremendous sacrifice on the part of the elephant, the wisest and largest and most powerful of all animals, to restore the moral order. The elephant lays down his life to save the child of man, and, consequently, innocence and honesty triumphs over selfishness, deceit and arrogance. The elephant willingly lays down his life so the reversal of the natural order at the hands of the parents is effectively opposed. The parents must die because there comes a point when moral degeneration becomes irredeemable and death alone can restore the natural order. Renewal of life requires sacrificial nurturing and ruthless elimination of nature-negating forces.

These stories may have several more layers of meanings, with all kinds of unsuspected structural depths. Here, I have gone by what is the most obvious. However, it is very important to note that the animal characters in these stories are not just dramatic devices used for the plot and to illustrate the relationship of man with other men, as, for instance, in the *Pancatantra* stories or Kafka's *Metamorphosis* and the *Autobiography of a Dog*, but they stand for themselves and are not dramatic substitutes for human characters. Man, animal and nature form, in the Liangmai imagination, a continuum — they are the variegated embodiments of life on earth and it is in their mutually enhancing togetherness that life flourishes. This togetherness is most delicately balanced — disturb this balance and life is bound to degenerate and may even be destroyed.

5

The Nomads
Man, Animal, Nature

R.S. Negi

Human evolution is a success story of adaptation of the genus *homo* over a span of nearly two million years. Of these human ancestors subsisted as hunter-gatherers for all but the last 10,000 years, till they learnt domestication of animals and plants, leading to sedentrization. So, almost 99.5 per cent of the history of genus *homo* was spent as hunter-gatherer nomads. As such nomadism is the primal adaptation of the hominids and is deeply rooted in human ancestory.

Domestication of plants was the beginning of agriculture, but it did not put a complete stop to nomadism, since domestication of animals, simultaneously, made possible a new adaptation, which was mobile pastoralism. Historically, pastoralism is considered an offshoot of mixed agricultural and herding subsistence complexes in adaptation to the grasslands not so suitable for cereal plants. There are still some human populations in different and remote areas of the world who have maintained a nomadic way of life which to some extent may be similar to that of the earlier hominids. The present-day nomadic way of life is mainly of two kinds: one being hunting-gathering, the first adaptation of the hominids, and the other pastoral nomadism having a history since the Neolithic times. Both these life ways are adaptation to different ecological situations. This chapter studies pastoral nomadism as a special adaptation pattern in the Himalayan region of north-western India, particularly the Garhwal Himalayas.

Pastoralism as an adaptive strategy is based upon the three main resources of animal herds, pasture lands and water. Animals are usually available, and it is access to pastures and water, which requires seasonal migration of the herd and the herder, known as transhumance. The seasonal migration is often between two sites, which are predetermined and well-marked for the availability of pasture land and water sources.

Transhumance, thus, is a special form of nomadism requiring special adaptive measures on the part of the transhumant population, and it is somewhat different from the nomadic hunter-gatherer who are constantly on the move and do not return to the earlier sites in a cyclic manner. The transhumants, though nomadic, move in a cyclic manner, returning to earlier sites which more or less become permanent, seasonal bases. The pastoral transhumants in their cyclic movement allow time for regeneration and preservation of resources. They also have the option of drawing upon 'unearned resources' as in the case of the hunter-gatherer nomads, to some extent. The seasonal cyclic movements and utilization of resources in a rotational manner has placed the transhumant populations in a situation where they are nomadic on the one hand and transitionally or marginally sedentary on the other.

The Garhwal Himalayas support a number of transhumant populations, chief among them being the Bhotias, Gujars and highland shepherds. The Bhotias raise sheep and goats and combine trading with cultivation, the highland shepherds raise sheep and goats and are agro-pastoral. The Gujars mainly raise buffaloes and are pastoral. An attempt has been made here to study the Gujar lifestyle so as to have an insight into the pastoral nomad's perception of the relationship between the herder and the herd and the resources, that is, man, animal and nature.

The Gujars, who have got their name from the Sanskrit *gurjara*, were once a dominant population in western India. The territory is now called Gujarat. It is believed that earlier ancestral stock may have migrated from the central Asian region and they have been identified with the Kushans or the Yuchis by General Cunningham.[1] Later, for some unknown reasons, the Gujars migrated from Gujarat, spreading all over north-western part of the Indian sub-continent and to some pockets in central India. The present-day distribution of the Gujars is in the States of Jammu and Kashmir, Himachal Pradesh, Punjab, Haryana and western Uttar Pradesh. The Gujars were mostly Hindus, but from time-to-time sizeable sections of them got converted to Islam. At present there are both Hindu and Muslim Gujars in north-western India, but, curiously, while the Hindu Gujars inhabit the plains and are settled agriculturists, the Muslim Gujars inhabit the Himalayan region and are pastorals. In some areas, such as Garhwal Himalayas, they have been completely nomadic till very recently.

In western Uttar Pradesh, the Gujars have set up winter camps in the Shiwalik region. With the onset of spring they prepare to migrate with their herds to high altitude pasture lands, known as *bugyals*, in the Garhwal Himalayas. The journey is through the middle altitude region along the river valleys; and the migration, also termed as vertical transhumance, is seasonal between fixed sites, through fixed routes and according to more or less fixed time table. Generally, they spend May to October in summer camps, in high altitude pastures, and November to April in winter camps, in the Shiwalik region. The outward and inward journeys take fifteen to twenty days. Thus the actual camping in the winter and summer camps is nearly for five-and-a-half months each. The mode of migration has undergone some change over a period of time. Till about fifty years ago, the journey each way took longer as there were no modern means of communication through middle range valleys, and also the local population was less hostile towards the migrants. In earlier days the migratory Gujars and their herds were able to travel in the day time also, camping near villages where fodder and water were easily available for the herd. Besides, transactions would take place between the local populations and the Gujars. Buffalo herds of the Gujar were considered a good source of manure for the fields of the local population. In recent years the Gujars have begun to utilize modern means to transport. They travel with the herds mostly during night. This change in the mode of migration is an adaption response to the changing human and ecological conditions. The migratory routes and journeys have now been reconditioned by the availability of grass and other fodder, and water for the herd, and the necessity of secluded camping places away from the roads and villages.

The Gujars live in groups of families called *deras*, which are generally organized on the basis of kinship. The neighbourhood relationship is also maintained both during migra-tory journeys and the encampments. Each family or *dera* maintain on an average 30-40 head of buffalo, a few cattle and horses and ponies, for transportation of household effects.

It is reported that over the years the number of buffaloes per *dera* is on the decrease. This trend is considered to be a dangerous signal by the pastoral nomads. Since the subsistence of the pastoral nomads is totally dependent on the herd, decrease in the number of animals adversely affects the survival strategy of the population. However, in case of Gujars, the reported decrease may or may not be real, depending on extraneous factors as well as change in the survival strategy itself.

The Gujars have been in the Garhwal Himalayas for the past 100-150 years. It is said that they migrated to this part of the Himalayas from Jammu region through Himachal Pradesh, where there are Gujars in sizeable numbers. The main reason for their migration was depletion of resources to maintain the herd. In the Garhwal Himalayas, Gujars were allowed to take their herds to high altitude pastures, on the basis of a specific amount of fee per head of buffalo, paid to the forest department. The grazing fee is for the winter camps and has been periodically increased. The increase of fee per buffalo-head is one of the reasons for the reported unreal decrease in the number of buffaloes, as the Gujars would like to keep the amount of fee payable low by reporting lesser number of buffaloes.

Earlier, the Gujar *dera* migrated with all the animals from the winter camp in the Shiwalik to the high altitude *bugyal*. But recently the trend has changed and fewer *deras* migrate to the high altitude pastures. At the same time the *deras* do not migrate as a whole, but leave behind some members and buffaloes in the winter camps. This has resulted in more horizontal transhumance as well as partial sedentarization. In the Shiwaliks, in the vicinity of camp sites there is a gradual reduction in the grazing area and the drying of water sources with the rise in temperature, and therefore alternate grazing grounds and water holes are to be looked for, where the herd can be taken. All these factors also affect the milk yield of the buffalo and the economy of the Gujar.

In the case of transhumants, when they go to the high altitude *bugyals*, the Gujars find conditions changing year after year. Earlier, the herd could find grazing ground and water in the vicinity of high altitude villages, which is no longer the case now. The Gujars have to take their herds higher to where grass is available but there are not enough water holes for watering the buffaloes. Besides, the higher pastures have been the grazing grounds for the goats and sheep of highland shepherds. The presence of buffaloes in the higher pastures has created a situation of conflict. The sheep and buffaloes cannot share the same grazing ground as sheep do not touch the grass grazed by other animals. Therefore, the highland shepherds do not want the Gujars to take their herds to these pastures.

The Gujars would like to continue their transhumant adaptive strategy. They are very dependent on their buffalo herds and would like to take them to good pastures. They also recognize that their herds are conditioned to move to higher altitude pastures and cooler climate in summer months as the animals start becoming restive when the temperature goes up. There is thus an interdependence between the Gujars and their herds and a dependence of the herder and the herd on the pasture lands and water resources, both in the Shiwaliks and the high altitude regions. Up to a certain level this relationship can be symbiotic. But there is obviously an optimum level beyond which an imbalance is bound to occur due to some recognizable factors such as increase in the human and animal popu-lations and depletion of resources. The depletion of resources in itself can be due to over-utilization – a direct consequence of rise in human and animal population and some natural causes. The Gujar is aware that the optimum level has been reached and an imbalance has set in, because though man and animal are still in symbiotic relationship, their relationship with nature has turned parasitic instead, which is indicated by over-grazing and, drying up of water holes. Change in human relationship due to competition between sheep and buffaloes for the pasture land is also contributing to the imbalance that has set in.

The pastoral Gujar has perceived the change in the relationship and has begun to readjust the adaptive strategy. One is by reducing the number of migrant *deras*, and, consequently, lowering number of buffaloes. The other is by the process of sedentarization. Though the Gujar is reluctant to give up the pastoral nomadic mode of subsistence, he is aware that it is no longer a successful adaptive strategy as it used to be and needs to be either modified or given up altogether.

Note

1. Crook, W., *The Tribes and Castes of North Western India*, vol. II, pp. 439-54.

6

Perception of Bhutas in Kedarkhand

M.M. Dhasmana

Kedarkhand is an old name of Garhwal[1] region. The Shaiva scriptures describe nine regions[2] out of which four are in Himalayas. The *Kedarkhand* which is a part of the *Skanda Purana,* divides Himalayas into five[3] broad regions and glorifies the tract (Garhwal), rivers, mountains and places as Kedarkhand. The geographical outline described by the scripture as the area bound by white snow peaks[4] and the Gangadwar,[5] the river Tamasa[6] and the Nandadevi,[7] is exactly the boundary of the present-day Garhwal Commissionary.

The Regional version of the perception of *pancabhutas* and their mythological origin is given in *Kedarkhand* (A local edition of the Kedarkhand portion of the *Skanda Purana* glorifying the Garhwal region). The origin of *Pancabhutas* finds a mention in another regional text *Dhol Sagar,*[8] as also in lores and in folk songs sung by the musicians,[9] celebrating the occasion of child birth.

Genesis of *Pancabhutas*

In the first chapter of the *Kedarkhand,* Mahadev tells Parvati that in the beginning there was an inaccessible aqueous mass (*amburasi*) containing various universes (*brahmand*) in it. In the second chapter, Mahadev explains the flowing of *Tripathga* (Ganga) in heaven, hell and the earth from the watery mass. Narrating the origin of the animate and inanimate, He tells Parvati in the fourth chapter, that when Lord Vishnu desired to produce the world he created water and positioned himself in the aqueous mass in the form of a golden egg. The egg was divided into two portions making earth (*prthvi*) and heaven (*urdhwalok*) and the sky (*akasa*) was formed between the two. The earth surrounded by water (*jala*) was divided into ten directions (*disa*); of first of all time (*kala*) was formed, followed by mind (*manas*) and speech (*vani*). They were followed by desire (*kama*), anger (*krodha*) and love (*rati*); and in analogy to them the universe was created. Brahma, after producing his seven sons (*manasputras*),[10] created Rudra from wrath (*rosh*). The *manasputras* (*saptarsis*) and Rudra created progeny (*praja*) and invented lightening (*vidyut*), clouds (*megha*) and the rainbow (*indradhanus*). Then the Vedic hymns (*ricas*) were created to perform *yajna* and by dividing mind and body (*deha*) the man and woman were formed. To Manifest his glory Lord Vishnu made earth and sky stable and created Swayambhu Manu.

The sixth chapter narrates the birth of fire (*agni*) and air (*vayu*). The Pracetas, descendants of Dhruva and grandsons of King Prthu, originate fire, air and moon (*soma*) from their mouth. Fire and air start engulfing the trees and the forests perish. Then *soma* (moon) tells fire and air to accept very beautiful daughters of trees and become peaceful after receiving the gift of girls. A beautiful girl (*kanya*) named Marisha, adopting preventive measures with fire and air conceives the foetus of Pracetas and gives birth to Daksa Prajapati who is glittering, fiery-like *agni* and the progenitor of the universe. This was the genesis of *maithuni srsti* (origin of progeny by the union of male and female, i.e., procreation by copulation).

Dhol Sagar is a manual containing the methodology of rhythms, tunes and melodies of the drum musical instruments in Garhwal. It gives detailed notes on drum instruments and musical connotations and also dialogues on various related subjects. The musician who plays the drum instrument is called *auji* (literally a tailor). The *auji* who stitches the cloths is also a professional drum-player, hereditary singer and musician, folklorist and, in some cases, a talented extempore poet composing folklores suitable to the occasion. The *auji* plays the drum in front of village households on all social, religious and auspicious occasions. In *Dhol Sagar* dialogue the origin of the *srsti*[11] is given as follows:-

> Goddess Parvati tells the *auji* (drum-player) that first of all there was a large expanse of water and ocean of emptiness (*jal shunakaram*) everywhere. Neither there was earth, nor mountains, nor heaven but mist and darkness everywhere. *Iswar* (Mahadeva, Siva) then explains that in the beginning there was a formless (*nirankar*) state. From shapeless came the formal (*sakar*) and then appeared the water (*jal*) and earth (*thal*). On earth came the egg which split into nine regions (*khand*). Nirankar Gosain[12] by rubbing his eyebrows and feet produced Shiva and Parvati respectively. Adi Gosain[13] created the earth (*prthvi*). Then first ground (*dharti*) and afterwards sky (*akasa*), first female then male, first daughter then son, first guru then disciple, first night then day, was produced.

This narration appears to have been influenced by the Gosain (ascetic) sect which flourished in Garhwal after the Nath Sect of Guru Gorakhnath. The priority of female over male also appears to have been influenced by the Sakta[14] cult.

Origin of *Bhutas* in Legendary Ballads

The god almighty (*Nirankar*) is invoked in Garhwal in the form of singing of *jagar*[15] and a ritual dance. Legendary ballads sung on this worship of *Nirankar* describe the origin of universe and *bhutas* in two different versions:

> *Onkar* (mysterious syllable) to *fonkar* (whizzling sound)
> Whizzling sound produced air (*vayu*)
> which in turn created clouds (*megh*).
> The clouds originated water (*jal*).
> Which produced lotus (*kamal*).
> and from lotus the Brahma (the creator) was born.
> The Gosain (ascetic) sat in meditation,
> of the God in the Ocean of water
> and created the Universe.
>
> Goddess Parvati fed up with her loneliness requests Lord Shiva to create *srsti*. Shiva rubs his thighs and from the dross produces two eagles named Soni and Bramha. When they become young, Brahma proposes to Soni to marry and become his wife. Soni reminds him of their brother and sister relationship. On hearing this Brahma sheds tears which are swallowed by Soni and she conceives. After some time she delivers an egg on the wings of the Brahma eagle. The egg splits and forms earth and sky and the liquid portion becomes the sea.

In another oral tradition the hereditary folk singers and musical instrument players (*auji vadak*) sing this folk song on the occasion of child birth.

> First originated the earth (*prthvi*)
> Then sprang up the sky (*akasa*)
> Then were produced air (*vayu*) and water (*pani*)
> In Mahadev's house a son is born;
> Raja Karna[16] is born in the house of sun,
> Narayan[17] is born in Nandu's house.
> Whether the Narayan is born or the child?
> The child is born as offspring of the gods.

As residents of the valley of gods the local people of Kedarkhand worship many local gods and deities in open air temples or in oromorphic forms and where liturgical performances are conducted by *sastric* sacred specialists or local ritual masters. Interacting with snow, avalanches, hailstorms, excessive rainfalls, floods, landslides, forests, wild animals and other natural phenomena the highlanders have a complete inventory of gods, protecting spirits, harmful supernatural forces, benevolent and malevolent spirits controlling the entire natural phenomena which may be described as Kedarkhand cosmogony. The belief in regional cosmogony, i.e., faith in local gods, invocation, propitiation, exorcism of supernatural powers, is of indigenous origin as the worship pattern and the sermons and rites of folk rituals have an oral tradition.

In the oral tradition expressed in the folk ritual, folk religion, customs and the *ksetriya parampara*, there is no systematic conception of the *bhutas* except as indigenous invocations and rituals performed to appease local gods and deities controlling natural elements for the benefit of local masses. The role of *agni* (fire), *vayu* (air) *akasa* (sky) in various rituals clearly indicates that these elements (*tattvas*) have certain cognition, special status, recognition and expression in the indigenous cosmogony.

Symbolism of Earth and Fire

In a widely prevalent folk song there is a dialogue between the invoker and *agni*. Since the appellent is requesting *agni* to come to her *matlok* (mother earth), the supplicant appears to be a young girl. *Agni* expresses her concern and apprehensions about the *matlok* as earth is full of impurity and sin. The song hints at the divine origin of fire and its sacrosanct and purificatory virtues on earth.

> Agni come! O Agni! Come to my *matlok*
> Agni without you Brahma remained hungry.
>
> Agni replies:
> How shall I come to your *matlok*!
> There is misdemeanor, dissipation and
> turpitude in your *matlok*.
>
> Invocation to Agni
> Agni come! O Agni! Come to my *matlok*!
>
> Agni replies:
> How shall I come to your *matlok*!
> There is blemish and impious conduct there.
> People there will trample me under their feet,
> People there may spittle on me.
> How shall I come to your *matlok*!

Man has always tried to harness and utilize natural forces to his advantage. In another instance fire is invited to come to the *matlok* to bestow food to the hungry masses. The statement that without *agni* Brahma (creator of the universe) remained hungry implicates that without fire mankind is deprived. The importance of *agni* as benefactor, as satisfier of appetite, desire and bestower of victuals is expressed.

Fire descends on earth as a purifier and *paphanta* (destroyer of sins). The ignition of fire in the indigenous rites and rituals is because fire is considered as a saviour, a protective force against all wicked spirits, evil forces and malignant and obnoxious forces. In the purifying process it absolves the guilty and salvages the sinner and in addition to *paphanta*, performs the role of pardoner of sins (*papkshama*).

Expecting a self-resolution of faith and fidelity and maintaining a state of self-purification, piety and devotion in the invoker, fire latently initiates a character of ethics and good behaviour and bears testimony to purity of conduct, noble deeds and virtuous life. In this role *agni* is aptly described as *paprakshak* (saviour from sinful acts/ behaviour).

The apprehensions of fire about the profane earth can be attributed to the fact that *agni* is an embodiment of purity and by descending to the *matlok* (earth) she may become impure by interaction with the masses. *Agni* wishes to caution the involver and through her, the people, about her inclination to refrain from evil, sinful and profanatory deeds. This appears to be a latent hint to treat fire with sanctity, reverence and holiness and deter men to desist from the path of sin as fire will not tolerate this. Thus holding fire in supreme reverence and as a symbol of purification is a pointer to the faith and awareness of the local people in purity of *agni* as one of the *bhutas* and its usage in their socio-cultural life.

Invocation of fire in the form of a ritual dance performed during the annual worship of an indigenous god Jakh[18] presents glimpses of the evocation pattern of the people of Mandakini[19] valley who live in the lap of mountains and snow peaks and are ensconced in the geomorphic wonders of nature. The local population is subjected to natural phenomena like snowfall, avalanche, sleet, cloud-burst, landslide, earth-quake, etc., of natural furies. The local cosmogony and the autochthonous ritual invocations are manifestation of the awareness of the people of the supremacy of the *bhutas* (elements), of cosmic forces, and their constant endeavour to harness them gainfully for their agro-pastoral pursuits. This is expressed in the appeasement of gods and ritual symbolism.

The people of Mandakini valley are generally staunch devotees of Siva[20] and Shakti[21] sects, but in upper reaches of the valley the local god is Jakh. The name Jakh appears to have originated from the word *yaksa*, who, along with Kinnar[22] and

Gandharvas, frequented the Gangetic Himalayas, which is their most favourite resort. Jakh is a very powerful god and is controller, distributor, regulator and dispenser of water in the shape of favourable and excessive rainfall, hailstorm, sleet, storms and clouds-bursts. Besides bestowing good crops in the agro-pastoral economy of this hill region, he also brings prosperity and removes obstacles of the devotees.

The worship of Jakh mainly consists of invocation of *agni* by the *nar*[23] (spirit medium) of the god and the glorification of fire as a sanctifying and purifying element. The ritual dance is a composite worship schedule covering invocation of air, sky and fire, and indicating an awareness of their creative and generative powers.

The main Jakh is called Harmuny[24] Jakh, whose temple is located at Jakhdhar[25] under the grove of *banj*[26] (*Quercus incana*) trees. The *dhar* (ridge) is situated on an open slope overlooking the snow peaks of Kedarnath[27] and Chowkhamba.[28] The temple structure has a four feet high wall on three sides and is open in the front. There is no cover or ceiling on the top. Inside only one icon of the deity, made of granite without decorations, is placed near the back wall of the temple. The temple is very old and thronged by numerous devotees, but the deity continues to remain under the open sky. Numerous attempts have been made by the beneficiary devotees to construct a structure above it, but the *nara* has repeatedly resisted to come under any shelter.

Harmuny Jakh is the tutelary god of eleven villages[29] and is also worshipped by another twenty-seven villages. He has several Jakhs associated with him. Influenced by the powers of the Harmuny Jakh, the villages situated in the sub-valleys of the tributary rivulets have made token temples of the Jakh in their areas and invoked the deity there. Howerver, they consider Harmuny Jakh as the main god and treat their temples as affiliatory to him. In case of a major crisis the villagers owing allegiance to affiliated Jakhs come to pray at the main temple at Jakhdhar. Some of the affiliated temples of Jakh are at Jal, Jougi, Ransi, Nyalsu and Trijugi villages.

The devotees of Harmuny Jakh offer masks of Jakh to the lithic icon at the Jakhdhar. The masks are in the form of moulds of faces of silver and copper made by the local smith craftsmen. The villagers also offer banners, flags, standards and canopical covers made of cloth for displaying on the ritual days. All masks and decorative material are stored in Deoshal[30] and taken out only on the occasion of annual fire dance. The thurible, bell, and the basket containing the invocatory equipment is kept in Kothera[31] the native village of the Bhat[32] priests, so that it can be taken to the temple as and when required.

The *nar*, also called *paswa*, is a resident of Nala.[33] The present *nar* is about sixty years old, belongs to Rajput caste and is a married man engaged in agro-pastoral pursuits. The possession by Jakh has been confined to the family members only. The *nar* is possessed by the deity during worship and invocation. The villagers approach the god in the temple, the *nar* in his village, take the *nar* to the temple site or sometimes invite the *nar* to the worship in their villages or houses for various *uchyanas*[34] (dedication made to god for fulfilment of desires and vows) and their thanksgiving ceremonies. The *nar* is also held in respect and reverence by the local population for his supernatural role in communicating with god, specially to bring favourable rainfall, check excessive rainfall, stop hailstorm and obtain other boons.

The Jakh is invoked on various occasions. The temple ritual schedule consists of thirty-six evocations on days like *amavasya*,[35] Sankranti,[36] Harelka[37] and Dantera.[38] The main worship takes place on the Baisakh,[39] Sankranti[40] and the next day in which the *nar* (human Jakh) of Harmuny Jakh comes to the open-air temple and invokes fire in the form of an ordeal. This annual fire invocation consists of the performance of a ritual dance inside the specially-erected fire altar by the *nar*. By dancing in the fire the human Jakh (*nar*) gets sanctified, purified and attains divination. In the deified state he makes oracles. In this ritual dance, fire is the medium between *nar* and the god Jakh – it is a communicative force between the human and the superhuman, an animating and motivating force symbolizing continuity of life through yearly tests and life-invigorating displays. A detailed description of this annual invocation is given in the succeeding lines.

Annual invocatory rituals are conducted with much religious gaiety, ostentation and reverence. For these occassions a huge crowd assembles at the main open-air temple. The rites, restrictions and preparations begin two days before the Visuvat Sankranti with the imposition of *gothi*[41] (taboo) in the villages of Bhet and Kothera. During the *gothi*, the villagers abstain from anger, desire, quarrel and lead a life of celibacy, purity and noble virtues. No outsider is permitted to enter these villages in this period. Following a strict code of conduct for three days and maintaining a state of purity, the villagers of Bhet and Kothera go to the forest to collect firewood. They cut trees and big logs and leave them for the next year. The logs chopped during the previous year are brought and kept in the terrace facing the open-air temple at Jakhdhar. The fire collection takes place two days before and on the morning of the Visuvat Sankranti.[42] After the collection of logs an altar is erected from the collected logs. This altar, called *moondi*,[43] consists of seven, nine or eleven *hars*.[44] The altar is made in the terrace facing the temple of Jakh and the wooden logs used are mainly of *banj* (*Quercus incana*) and *burans*[45] (*Rhododendrom arboreum*). A large branch of the green *panyya*[46] (*Prunus Cerasoides*) tree with green leaves is also inserted inside the *hars*. It acts as a charm. By midday, when the *moondi* (wooden altar) is ready, the villagers return home and the *gothi* is lifted. During the *gothi* villagers of Bhet, being of Rajput caste, are mainly engaged in cutting and collection of wooden logs, while the villagers of Kothera, being Brahmins, are engaged in worship of Jakh, collection of *melagh*[47] and preparation of food for the priests and firewood cutters. The *das*[48] and *auji*[49] villagers are allowed only on the morning of Sankranti. They bring firewood from the jungle but keep it in a terrace one step lower than the fire altar. The removal of *gothi* is announced by the beating of drums so that the neighbouring villages can also hear them and join in the procession.

On the afternoon of Visuvat Sankranti, a procession starts from village Bhet. The *auji vadak* (drum musicians) leading the way proceed to Kothera, the home of Bhat priests of Jakh deity, collect the *puja kandi*,[50] and set course for Deoshal. The masks of the Jakh deity are taken out from the store and worship ceremony is conducted in the small temple of Deoshal. The procession takes an organized and formal shape from here. In the front are the drum musicians followed by flag and standard bearers of the deity. The masks contained in a basket are carried by the Bhat priest wearing the ceremonial attire. This priest stays at Jakhdhar for the entire duration of the invocation, conducts rituals and returns with the masks after the completion of the fire ritual dance. The procession, consisting manily of male members from the villages of Bhet, Kothera and Deoshal, reaches Jakhdhar by evening, or sometimes, by dusk. The ladies of Deoshal assemble outside their temple and sing *mangal*,[51] bidding farewell to the masks of the Jakh deity.

After the procession, carrying standards and masks of the Jakh, reach the Jakhdhar temple, some of the people go back to their villages and return the next day. The priest and many other people, including the drum-players, stay for the night at the temple site. In the early hours of the Sankranti night, fire is ignited in the *moondi* (fire altar) by the priests and the *moondi* is worshipped in all the four *prahars*[52] of night. On the morning following Sankranti night all masks are washed by the Bhat priest and decoratively displayed, along with the granite statue of the Jakh. By noon, the display decorations are complete and thousands of devotees from near and far off villages assemble. The *moondi* is also burnt by this time and the fire altar becomes a spread bed, a couch of smouldering embers and red hot burning coal pieces. The intensity of heat of this fire altar is so severe that it is not possible to stand near the burning embers.

When the masks of the Jakh deity proceed to witness the annual fire ritual dance, the ladies assemble on the occasion remind Jakh of his relationship with air in their farewell song. The ladies sing *mangal*, enumerating the geneology of the deity and emphasizing his connections with *vayu*. In these ominous songs on the auspicious occasion of annual invocation of the deity the village ladies hail Jakh as the son of air. Some of the lines recounting the genealogical origin of the Jakh are given here.

> O Jakh? We recall your origin;
> We count your genealogy;

You are the nephew of the Nag;
You are the son of the Vayu,
O God you are the Son of the Vayu.

Jakh is invoked for creating favourable wind situations. The association of this indigenous deity with cosmic force air is a clear indication that the local people are aware of the fact that air is an important element constituting the cosmos, a supernatural power relating to fertility, generation and creation.

Thus Jakh is an acknowledged controller of air and worshipped for bringing favourable winds suitable for harvests. The awareness of the importance of the cosmic force of *vayu* is manipulated in the form of relationship between *vayu* and their most favourite God Jakh. In the local cosmogony Jakh deity has been acknowledged as son of *vayu* (air).

The *nar* (human Jakh) of Harmuny Jakh is a resident of village Nala, which is about three kilometres from Jakhdhar. On the annual invocation day during the *gothi*, construction of *moondi* and the worship on days prior to or following the Sankranti day no communication or message is sent by the people of Bhet, priests of Kothera, Deoshal, the assembled crowd and people associated with sacred performances at Jakhdhar to the *nar*. He is entirely directed by powers of clairvoyance, intuition and telepathy. On Sankranti day, when the *moondi* is being prepared, he goes to river Mandakini for a holy dip. On the day following Sankranti, at about midday, the *nar* starts for the Jakhdhar in a procession. In the front are the drum-players of Nala village. The *nar*, accompanied by men and women of Nala village, proceeds to Deoshal and goes to the village temple to worship the Jakh deity. Immediately after the invocation the *nar* is possessed by the god (Jakh) and goes into a trance. With hands lifted up he starts dancing and with praying postures and approaches the Jakhdhar temple. The procession from Deoshal grows bigger as it is joined by drum-players of Deoshal and other villages. From Deoshal to Jakhdhar is a distance of about one and a half kilometres and a steep climb. During the journey the *nar* remains is a possessed state, dancing and making salutary positions towards the Jakhdhar. He is accompanied by the people of Nala, Deoshal and other villages.

On reaching Jakhdhar the *nar* performs three circumambulations around the decorated temple. Then he sits on a flat stone seat located under a small tree in front of the temple. The terraces housing the stone seat and the *moondi* are adjacent to each other, but the ground of the stone seat is lower to the stretch housing the *moondi*. The *nar* sits facing the *moondi*. At this moment the drum-players of eleven villages encircling him play their drum instruments. After the musical invocation, the *nar* runs towards the open air temple, bows to the Jakh, removes his *donkhu*[53] (woollen coat) and upper garments and jumps inside the fire altar. After making few movements inside the fire altar he comes out and goes to the Jakh icon, where water is poured on him. This water is collected by the priests from a water spring located near the temple. After the bath, the *nar* again enters the fire altar and makes few dancing movements and runs towards the Jakh icon. After bowing in front of it, the *nar* tries to go towards the fire altar but is stopped by the priests and other people. The assembled people consult the *nar* and he answers their queries through divination. In this state, he sometimes makes oracles of his own. Then the priest gives him a *deepak* (fire wick), which he swallows. The moment the lamp (fire wick) is extinguished by swallowing, the god leaves possession, the deity leaves the *nar* (*gharik gayi*)[54] and he is transformed back to his normal self, the human form. Then he throws *aksata* (rice grains) as blessings towards the gathering, wears his garments and returns to his village in a procession. The assembled crowd scramble towards the fire altar and try to collect ember and coal ash to carry it home as an auspicious omen of benediction. The priests and people of Deoshal, Kothera and Bhet wind up the decorations, collect the masks in the basket and start the return procession. After keeping the masks in Deoshal and the worship articles in Kothera, the villagers of Bhet return to their village by dusk.

The erection of wooden altar, the ignition of fire and invocation of *agni* by the *nar* in the form of ritual dance in the fire altar without sustaining any physical impairment or burn injuries, in the presence of thousands of people, is indicative of the purificatory virtues attributed to the ignition and invocation of fire. The annual fire dance or the invocation of *agni* by the *nar* in the presence of supernatural Jakh (Jakh icon? masks of temple?) witnessed by thousands of local villagers symbolizes the following:

(i) The spirit medium represents the presence of the Jakh at the rites performed in his name and in front of the masks and granite icon.

(ii) The spectacular or miraculous nature of performance proves the genuineness of the trance and true possession of spirit medium by Jakh.

(iii) The fire instead of hurting, harming or causing injury or mortification of any kind has, instead, acted as a means of expressing and manifesting the true Jakh form and helped him to reach divinity and elevated his status to supernatural diviners.

(iv) The fire has sanctified and purified the *nar*. In its purificatory role the fire has elevated the *nar* from mundane existence to the divine status.

(v) The fire ritual or the fire element is a medium between the human and the supernatural; it is an intermediary between the person and divinity making revelatory oracles.

(vi) The fire is ignited to bear testimony of the elevation of human form to the superhuman form.

(vii) The *nar* returning unhurt, unimpaired and unvitiated from the devastating fire altar appears as a wondrous prodigy of fire and an incarnation holding connections in *dyolok* (atmospheric region) and the *prthvi lok* (earthly region).

It may be observed that the *nar* of Jakh is purified and immortalized by fire ritual for a span of one year, till he re-enacts the ritual and remains in possession of divination powers and oracles so that people can approach him for initiating communication with Jakh or request the deity to heed to their requests at any time during the year.

The moment the *nar* swallows the fire wick and the lamp is extinguished the deity leaves the spirit medium in his human form. This transformation from divine to human is carried out by fire by blowing off the fire wick.

Immediately after the fire ritual dance the *nar* leaves the fire altar, and the people make a scramble for the ash of the fire invocation as it it considered pure, auspicious, creator of prosperity, wealth, good luck and an omen of benediction. This ash is preserved in the house till the next invocation.

Jakh and the Five Elements

The conception of Kedarkhand cosmology is based on the rubrics of the natural settings. Indigenous traditions are manifestations of the human attempt and endeavour to invoke, appease and influence the colossal forces and challenges arising from the natural phenomena of the greater Himalayan ranges. The concept of *nar* and the belief in this anthropolatory worship pattern is a grand design of human dynamism to control the universe, a symbolic human effort to be at the centre of cosmos. The annual invocation ceremony of the Jakh deity is an ideal paradigmatic illustration of the awareness of the perception of *bhutas*, and the logical sequence of their evolution expressed in the oral traditions of Kedarkhand. Let us recapitulate the chronology of the adoration of the elements which is perfectly analogous to their evolutionary sequence.

The main temple of Jakh, Harmuny Jakh, is an open air temple at Jakhdhar. The deity remains below the open sky. The site of the temple at Jakhdhar is a mountain ridge located higher than the local villages and thus closer to the sky. The invocation of the Harmuny Jakh two days before Sankranti is the beginning of the worship schedule. The adoration of sky before any other elements indicates its importance in the ritual ceremony.

The evocation of air is done in the form of a *mangal* sung at the time of farewell given to the masks of Jakh on the occasion of the departure of annual procession. The village ladies singing the auspicious songs recall the genealogy of the Jakh Deity and call him the son of air (*vayu*). In this invocation the favour of air is solicited for generation and creation. The *mangal* are sung on Sankranti day, two days after the first worship of the Harmuny Jakh. So the air invocation takes the second place in the order of worship.

In the indigenous cosmogony the lements are linked by the relationship of cause and effect. The sky (sun rays) and the wind from the atmospheric region, mixed with water, in the form of rain, combine to create fertility, prosperity and richness on earth. The ultimate result of the cause and effect is on the agro-pastoral economy. Though the water or the rain god is invoked several times in the year, during the annual worship schedule the evocation of water comes in the fourth place. After the fire ritual dance, the *nar* takes bath with spring water contained in a vessel, in front of the deity. The whole ceremony is aimed at proliferation of richness and productivity.

The centre of attraction of the entire worship is the invocation of fire by its *nar*. The prodigy evocating fire in the *moondi* represents myth and reality, celestial and mundane, sacrosanct and secular, spiritual and material and divine and human. By linking the atmospheric (*dyolok*) and terrestrial (*bhulok*) phenomena and by uniting the sky and air with water and ground for fertility, prolification, creativity and generation on earth (*srsti*), the *nar* as wondrous prince of fire present *agni* as a super-sanctifier and purifier medium in the cosmos.

The worship schedule symbolically depicts Harmuny Jakh as an embodiment of sky, the masks (of Jkah) as son of air, the *nar* as prodigy of fire, and the fire ritual as purifier of deifeir mediums, the *nar* as controller of rain and thus bestower of fertility and prosperity.

The Jakh worship is an ideal example of nature worship and ritual symbolism of the indigenous cosmogony manifesting the awareness of the evolution of elements in the cosmos and the importance of fire among the elements.

Notes

1. *Garh* is a glensor fort. Raja Ajaipal of Srinagar conquered 52 *garhs* and formed the Kingdom of Garhwal, i.e., the land of *garh* (glens), during AD 1516. Garhwal is pronounced *gadhwal*.
2. The nine regions of India as described in Shaiva scriptures, are Kedar, Manas, Kailas, Himadn (these four are in the Himalayas), Patal, Kashi, Rewa, Nagar and Brahmottar Khand.

3. Five *khanda* are regions of the Himalayas, as per Kedarkhand, are Nepal, Kumaon, Kedar, Jullandhar (Himachal) and Kashmir.
4. White snow peaks of the greater Himalayan snow line in the north.
5. Gangadwar is Hardwar – the mouth of Ganges on the foothills of the Himalayas.
6. Tamasa is river Tons separating Garhwal and Himachal Pradesh.
7. Nandadevi is a peak in the Badhan region dividing Garhwal and Kumaon areas.
8. *Dhol Sagar* is a manual of tunes and melodies for drum musical instruments.
9. Musicians called *aujis*. They are tailors by profession and are called *auji vadak* (drum-players) and musicians.
10. *Manasputra*, the seven sons (*putras*) of Brahma produced from the mind (determination), are the *sapta risis* (seven sages) Marichi, Attri, Angira, Pulastya, Pulaha, Kratu and Vashistha.
11. *Srsti* is the creation – the cosmos – the source of the *bhutas*.
12. Nirankar Gosain is the ascetic who created the universe.
13. Adi Gosain is the first of the ascetics.
14. Shakta are followers of Shakti (Devi).
15. *Jagar* is a lyrical ballad sung in invocatory rituals conducted mainly at night by Jagari, a professional incanter of Jagar engaged in the invocation of deities, ancestors and ghosts.
16. Karna is one of the heroes of Mahabharata – son of Kunti and the Sun god.
17. Narayan is Vishnu, the preserver god.
18. Jakh*ja* to be pronounced like *ja* in Japan. Jakh appears to be a corrupted version of *yaksa*.
19. Mandakini is a major tributary of Alaknanda.
20. Siva is one among the triad Brahma, Visnu and Siva.
21. Shakti is the Goddess Kali (Durga).
22. Kinnar and Gandharva: Yaksha, Kinnar and Gandharva races lived in the Himalayas. Now they are considered demi-gods in the Hindu pantheon.
23. *Nar* is the spirit medium of the deity Jakh. Also called *paswa* or human Jakh. The *nar*, a resident of Nala village, is also sometimes addressed as Jakh *devata* by the villagers.
24. Harmuny Jakh is the name of the main Jakh. It has many affiliatory Jakhs which are invoked in the nearby villages.
25. *Dhar*, in Garhwali language, means a ridge; a small slope or flat portion on the top of a mountain ridge overlooking both sides. Jakhdhar is a ridge where the open aire temple of Harmuny Jakh is located.
26. *Banj* is the name of a local tree. Botanical name of the variety of tree gorwn in Mandakini valley is *Quercus incana*. The open-air temple of Jakh is located under a grove the *banj* trees. The *moondi* is preferably made of *banj* wooden logs as this wood is considered pure. The wood produces coal of a good quality which burns for a longer time.
27. Kedarnath is a famous sacred shrine of Shiva. The mountain peak is named after the temple.
28. Chowkhamba is the four-peaked mountain. Also called Badrinath (Visnu) near the sacred shrine of Badrinath.
29. Eleven villages are Bhet, Kothera, Nala, Devar, Sankari, Bhainsori, Hyunl, Tyuri, Bansu, Rudrapur and Kumera. Jakh is the tutelary deity of these villages. The *auji vadaks* (drum-players) of these villages go to Jakhdhar temple on the occasion of the annual fire ritual.
30. Deoshal is the village of Deoshali Brahmins. The masks of Jakh deity are stored in this village.

31. Kothera is the village of Bhat Brahmins. The *puja kandi* (basket containing worship equipment like the bell, thurible, etc.) in worships/invocations is assigned as per duty roster maintained among the lineage members of the family.
32. Bhat and Deoshali are the names of the subcaste of local Brahmins.
33. Nala is the name of the village belonging to the human Jakh.
34. *Uchyana* is a vow or dedication (*sankalp*) undertaken for fulfilment of a desire by the local people. It is performed by keeping a token amount of cereals of wooden sticks or a promissory amount of money.
35. *Amavasya* is the last day of the dark phase of the moon. Moonless dark night. The junction of sun and moon.
36. Sankranti is the sun's passage from one sign of the zodiac to another. The solar calendar marking the passage of the sun from one sign to another, also marking the change of the month.
37. Harelka is the worship performed for prosperity and protection of good crop. In this worship the goats are sacrificed as offerings to the deity. It is held twice a year.
38. Dantera is worship performed with the new grains of the crop. No animal sacrifice is performed. On this day the Deoshali Brahmin is the *acharya* (presiding priest) of the ceremony and the Bhat priest takes the second position. It is held twice in a year on the occasion of harvesting of crops.
39. Baisakh is the second month of the Hindu calendar year.
40. The Baisakh Sankranti is the major ritual. The invocation starts two days before Sankranti and lasts one day after it.
41. *Gothi* is a taboo imposed on Bhet and Kothera villages. During *gothi* the villagers observe strict schedule, collect fire-wood for the fire altar. The villagers of Bhet are the *sevaks* (attendants) of the Jakh deity. The new name of village Bhet is Narayankoti, due to various archaeological findings there.
42. Visuvat Sankranti is Baisakh Sankranti.
43. *Moondi* is a heap of logs systematically arranged in the form of a fire altar erected and ignited for the fire ritual dance. The *moondi* is about 10 feet long, 8 feet wide, and about 6 to 8 feet high, depending on the number of *har*. (The greater the number of *har*, the higher is the height of the *moondi*.)
44. *Har* is the name given to a pair of 2 layers of logs consisting of one parallel layer and one vertical layer. The base layer of wooden logs is arranged in a parallel position. They are covered by a vertical line of logs. A minimum of five such pair combinations constitutes a *moondi*. Usually a *moondi* consists of 7 or 9 *har*.
45. *Burans* is a Himalayan flower tree. It is of red and allied colours and the king of hill flowers. Botanical name is *Rhododendron arboreum*. *Burans* wood is also used as a substitute for *banj* in preparation of *moondi* but in small quantity, when all the logs of *banj* are not available.
46. *Panyya* tree (*Prunus cerasoides*) is held in supreme reverence in the hills. It belongs to the almond, cherry and plum family. It is also called wild Himalayan cherry. The branches of this tree are brought for all ritual and are considered as sign of good omen. The folklore says that Krishna brought *Panyya* tree from Naglok. The *panyya* has ornamental, herbal and utilitarian value.

    Panyya sticks are used for making *uchyana* for invocation of ghosts, as the special tone of the wood is considered suitable for communicating with ghosts. Its wood is used for making excellent walking sticks. Its seed is used to make wine in various parts of Himalayas, specially Meghalaya and Sikkim.

47. *Melagh* is a collection of cereals mainly consisting of rice and lentils on occasions of ritual celebrations or community feasts.
48. *Das* is the artisan and labour class living in the villages.
49. *Auji* is a tailor. Both *das* and *auji* belong to labour class and are also drum and other musical instrument players. They are original inhabitants of the region but are called *dom* or the impure class and are untouchables. Now-a-days they belong to schedule caste (*harijan*).
50. *Pujakandi* is a basket or coop containing worship equipment like the bell, thurible, etc.
51. *Mangala* are folk songs sung on auspicious occasions by the ladies assembled for the purpose.
52. *Prahar* is a time span of 3 hours. Four *prahars* make a night and eight *prahars* the whole day.
53. *Donkhu* is a woollen coat of half sleeves indigenously made in the villages from the sheep wool and is considered pure.
54. *Gharik* means leaving a person; *gayi* means has. So it means that the Jakh has left.

References

Bahuguna, S.P., 1950. *Virat Hridaya* (Hindi), Lucknow, Alaknanda-Mandakini Prakashan.

Chatak, Govind, 1990. *Bhartiya Lok Sanskriti Ka Sandarbha* (Hindi). New Delhi, Taxshila Prakashan.

Dabral, S.P., 1961. *Uttarakhand Yatra Darshan* (Hindi). Chamoli Garhwal, Vishal Karyalaya Narayan Koti.

Dhasmana, M.M., 1981. 'Syncretic Polytheism in Central Himalayas', In *Himalaya Man and Nature*, vol. IV, no. 8, New Delhi.

——, 1982. 'Himalayan Pilgrimage', In *The Journal of Social Research*, Department of Anthropology, Ranchi, University of Ranchi.

Kedar Khand Granth (Sanskrit/Hindi) incorporated in the *Skanda Purana*, Kedar Khand Granth published by Badrinath Bhaktirasamrita Karyalaya Nandprayag and printed at the Shri Venkateswar Steam Press, Bombay, 1906.

Sankrityayan, R., 1953. *Himalaya Parichaya* (Hindi), Lucknow.

Singh Bhajan Singh, 1980. *Singhnad* (Hindi), Pauri Garhwal, Bhajan Singh Kotsara

Vidyarthi, L.P., B.N. Saraswati and M. Jha, 1978. *The Sacred Complex of Kashi*, New Delhi, Concept Publishing Co.

7

(55)

Perception of Bhutas in Garhwal

D.R. Purohit, Poornanand & Richa Negi

The folk beliefs of Garhwal, on the basic constitution of man, differ from the *Pauranic* tradition. Two origin myths of Garhwal narrate the constitution of man and the cosmos. The first myth, found in Lata village on China border in the lap of Nanda Devi range, is the most plausible of all Nanda myths of Garhwal.

According to this myth, in the beginning there was only water, and water everywhere – having an *a priori* existence. From the whirls of water originated Shakti, the goddess. She longed for a companion, and started churning the waters. First came up twelve seeds of grain, then twelve species of grasses and plants which were kept safe in *patal Lok*, the underworld. Next came up the Kapila cow, then Kalp Vriksha, Dev Kanya, the pitcher of nectar, and the pitcher of poison. It was followed by Brahma. The Goddess wanted to woo him as her husband, but he refused saying that he was borne of her. Then came Vishnu, who also rejected her on the same grounds. She then rubbed her thighs, and out came Ishwar Raja, Siva. Siva also rejected her prayer, but with a concession that they could marry after an interval equal to twelve generations. Shakti became so infuriated on his refusal that she spit upon his thighs and up grew his genital from there. It continued growing up to sky with such a speed that the Goddess had to stop it by creating dense smoke around and above it. It stopped but the sweat which seeped down in the process gave birth to two cells of algae on the right and left of the genital. The cells were broken and inside them were found two frogs, Dendkhi and Mendkhi. The frogs started woozing out saliva at an enormous speed, giving birth to bubbles. The goddess then created a fish of silver, put life into it and asked it to break open the bubbles. Out of many bubbles broken, the two bubbles revealed two celestial beings, Nal and Nalini, the brother and the sister. In order to test their celestialness, she threw upon them her *agni-patt sara* (the fire cloth), and *hasanda jyundal* (smiling sacred rice). The test was successful.

Nal and Nalini grew as adolescent. But they started having an amorous relationship. The goddess then separated and sent them to far north and south. There they planted their incestual sin upon the cows, buffaloes, wild animals, birds and natural vegetation. The remaining sin was left upon a stone. After twelve years they returned and decided to marry. Nalini started bearing children now.

When the first child was born, it slipped to Naglok and got transformed into various parts of Naglok. Its head was transformed into sky; its eyes, the stars; its bones, mountains and valleys; and its flesh, the soil.

The same was repeated with the second issue which slipped into Martya Lok. There Nal found that Ishwar Raja was the king. Ishwar Raja loved to have human beings as his companions/subjects. Therefore Nal wanted to create man. He first tried to make the body of man with various metals, but failed. Ultimately, he made it of ashes, phlegm, dust, and mud and succeeded. But the man would not hear. So ears were planted on his body. Many words were tried to get a response from this man. At last he answered to the word *ann*, food. Nal thus created everything that was needed for human existence – grains, oxen, fire, wind, cow, sleep, measurements, insects, etc.

The third issue was lost into Swarg Lok, the ether, which was ruled by Anchali Raja; Nal created nine planets, *yagya*, etc.

In this way the myth provides explanation for every object of the universe. But it does not explain the constitution of the human soul and the five *bhutas* separately. On the basis of the myth and popular beliefs and practices, the following points have been explained.

The Gross and Subtle

Folk myths of Garhwal nowhere give the mathematical details of the constitution of each *bhuta* (elements of nature). However, a recognizable pattern of the gross and subtle is found in the form of the concrete matter and the all powerful souls of gods, goddesses, man, animals and birds. All such souls are believed to be the subtle forms of the *pancabhutas*. Finding expressions in their human vehicle, they assume all powers of a gross form. The case of *ran bhuta* (soul of man dying at battle), and *gharya bhuta* (soul of a man dying prematurely with wishes left unfulfilled) is an evidence.

Thus all Bhumyals, Bagdwal, Latu, Heet, Khetrapal, Bheldeo, are the subtle forms of earth. All goddesses and Dropadi, Jakh, Narsingh are the subtle forms of fire. Bayal, an invisible procession of divine spirits represents air. Shankar and Nad-Budh Bhairav are the subtle forms of sky as they are the presiding deities of *dhol*, Garhwali folk drum. The myth of the *dhol* also says that in Dwapar, Vam Dass Drummer of Mandhata had a *dhol* called *gagan*, sky. Chhaya is the soul of water.

Characteristic Features

The beliefs of the folks of Garhwal about the cosmos and the human world are strongly patterned. There is incest among the human, animal and vegetal world because Nal and Nalini did it first. Ishwar Raja's agreement with Shakti is the cause of not marrying into the same clan for at least twelve generations. Strikingly, not a single act of the universe exists which has no explanation in the myth.

Ritual and Social use of *Bhutas*

When souls of gods and goddesses are invited to the community, they are given a gross forms of ensigns animated with the help of the following: sacred ashes of the shrines of Trijugi-Narayan and Kalimath (fire), soil of the all sacred shrines, like Tholingmath, Mathyana, etc., and soil under the bed of a lion (earth), water from Ganga at Hardwar and Vasudhara, Gangotri, Yamunotri, etc. (water). The sky element is omnipresent in the form of aerophonic and membranophonic instruments. Besides, there is a practice of fire and water rituals. *Jal Jatra* (water procession), is a common ritual of tree worship. The bonfire in the dance arena is for ritual worship, and is later used as a test for the powers of gods who jump into it for the purpose. In profane rituals, the use of all four elements is a must without which the spirits cannot be aroused.

Following the Indira Gandhi Centre for the Arts thesaurus project, a number of words concerning the five elements have been collected for understanding the folk aesthetics of Garhwal. Since the work is still in progress, I have presented in the Appendix, by way of example, a few related words, such as smell (an attribute of earth), sound (an attribute of sky), burning (an attribute of fire), etc.

APPENDIX

Thesaurus of Folk Aesthetics

The Garhwali dialect, according to Grierson, is a later growth of *Khash* or *Darad* language (*Linguistic Survey of India*, 1914). Dr. Suniti Kumar Chatterjee in the *Origin and Development of Bengali Language* also supports Grierson's view. This view was held for a long time till Govind Chatak came up with a more convincing theory in this *Garhwali Bhasha, Aik Bhasha Shastriya* and *Vyakaranic Adhyayan* (1959), where he propounds that Garhwali dialect originated from Shorseni Apabhransh.

Nothing has so far been written on the folk aesthetics of Garhwal. While serious efforts have been made on the dictionary of Garhwali words. The first work of Jazat

Chand Ramola, considered to be comprehensive, is available only with 'a' and 'aa'. Next, the dictionary prepared by late Baldev Prasad Nautiyal could print only 'a' and 'aa' alphabets. This work is still thought to be the most comprehensive and authentic. Unfortunately it is still lying unpublished in the custody of his son. The only dictionary which has so far been published is by the late Jay Lal Verma's *Garhwali Bhasha ka Shabdkosh* (1982), published posthumously.

Since all critical works on folklore of Garhwal have been either in Hindi or English, no pattern of poetics in folk idioms has emerged so far. The scholars have only been using the tenets of Sanskrit poetics to the folk literature. However, the corpus of this folklore is so rich with aesthetic words, motifs, symbols, metaphors, idioms, proverbs and mythic structures that a sustained and concentrated effort alone will be able to document it completely.

This chapter has only tried to collect random words under the following broad categories : mythopoetic, sensory, figurative and emotive.

The first characteristic feature of aesthetic words and idioms of Garhwal is its synthetic quality. It suggests its growth from the intimate interaction of the humans with the objects of nature. Still holding the passion and energy of natural symbols, just word or expression is capable of drawing a complete metaphor. Thus a sensitive being is a *kafuwa shareel*, like the consciousness of a *kafee* bird, and a heart is a *neeli paraan*, the heart of a *neeli* bird.

The second feature is the multiplicity of synonyms, homonyms and homographs. For example, there are scores of words for a single expression of smell:

kikran is burning of woollen stuff.
kutran is burning of cotton.
kumran is burning of human hair.
kaunkhan is smell of rotting of grains.
khikraan is burning of chilly.
chiraan is smell of urine.
bhujyaan is smell of roasting grains.
kachyaan is smell of half-cooked things.
mankhyaan is smell of humans.

The same richness is found for the expressions of temperature, taste, touch and sound. Dozens of words are used for various sounds:

araat is sound of being smothered.
kaklaat is sound of noise.
kanaat is sound of light groaning.
kiraat is sound of crying of a baby in pain.

kilkanu is sound of shrieks.
khaklat is sound of water.
khikchaat is sound of free laughter.
gablaat is sound of gutteral speech.
gamgyaat is sound of fast water current.
gumnaat is sound of whispers.
ghungyaat is sound of fast wind or engine.

Homonyms are also found in plenty. The word *bathaun* is used for air, telling, talks and a vegetable.

The most striking feature is the use of motifs in structural unit of the sentences. The motifs work with force and efficacy on the reader/audience. These words serve the purpose of imparting an aura of the past to the present in rituals and dance and in mythifying the present.

rui ki gholyansi, sutalya doodh : coziness of cotton, milk feeding with pot

chalaunya si teer, pathaunya si beer : like a ready arrow, and ready warrior

wonsi ku jharwalu – bata ku gadhwalu : flapper of dew and pioneer of journey

mati jaise ann – dhungyun jaise dhann : grains plenty as soil and riches plenty as stones

alu khaye mass – chhale peene khoon : ate hot flesh and drank unclotted blood

rang si dhalaki – fool si alasi : transformed like a colour and withered like a flower

chaukhamba tiwari – chhatish awash : an arched palace and multiple of chambers

bara gaun tai lagai dheet – bhanja tai lagai peeth : feast dozen villages and discard your own nephew

A major portion of the words is onomatopoetic. The sound of the words brings in the association of the theme. Words like *humankar, dumankar, jalankar, udankar,* are redolent of the sounds of Vedic *mantras*.

Mythopoeic

agnipatt sado	mythical cloth with Goddess Shakti having properties of fire
ardhanga	disguise of the goddess as Sita
umana	nakedness of the first man and woman,

	Nal and Nalini
ausar	festive period of mask dances
ubhed, manauti	vow of offering
kaguli	letter used by gods
kutneti	mythical female in *pandwani* who enamoured Arjun
khanvai	shaman/diviner.
khali sodhan	preliminaries of *devadasi* dance
khankar budya	clown of Gopichand drama
khet milya	encounter of characters
khelwari	short dramas performed during the mask dances
ghani hvwege ghungryali lathi hvwege chunkyali	an expression used for the beauty and movements of the one-year-old Nanda
chaitola, hastola	dance performances in Malari valley
chalu-palu	provisions for the rituals
chol bhatta	ritual of bringing gods into human company by offering them rice and *dal*
janyati	wedding guests
jangooru	shaman, diviner
jat-aukhyat	heredity
tuno-totake	witchcraft
thantu nachaun	to rehearse dancing with the ensign of goddess
tharpada(v)	to consecrate
dhiyan bhatta	feast offered to married sisters at the time of conclusion of a professional ritual
patter bhatta	feast given at the time of final winding up of masks
manglaun	to invoke
jagan purush	clay effigy of *yagya purush*

jas	blessings of gods
jamman, nyoja-nisan langota	ensign of god or goddess
jeunra	death god
jagari	ballad singer
talwar	monodrama on myths and legends rendered through dialogues and songs
deora, jat, vanyat, jugat	cyclic procession of gods and goddesses
deori	devouts participating in the religious processional ritual
deoangasi	made of the celestial element
deokhali, deokhala	arena for dance-drama of gods
dhari	devouts bearing the ensign of the god or goddess
dhavari	loud call
na:r, pashwa, patter, dankrya	vehicle of god or goddess
nakchhdi roop	perfect copy of beauty
Nathu Panday	a humorous character in folk interludes
naikwart, palkwart	a kind of dramatic performance by a particular community of Garhwal
payan	leave an identification mark at the place of departure
patter padhaun	interacting with the masked characters
patter kudi	hut made for masks
pothlya	two clownish characters in Gainda and Moru Dar episode of Pandwani
panwada	heroic ballads
banatoli	place where the ballads of Jakh god are sung for one night

budulu	a prominent character both sacred and humorous in mask dances of Jakh
baidi-baida	two choric characters harbingers of gods in mask dances
bhalda	narrators of Nanda, Narsimha
bhanibansi	director-cum-singers in mask dance-drama
bharat	story
mwar	a pioneer of masked characters
makhawa	clown
mirgwalla	sweat and dirt of the body of Shakti
rath	procession
Lata	legendary character in Nanda myth
vindara	amphitheatre
sirtu	whole-night performance
humankar, dumankar, nirankar	the first words used in the recital of origin myth
ransu	narrative tale
santa	class

Figurative

adat, larat	the sound of being choked
kakadat	the sound of regular complaints
kaklat, kiblat	combined noise of females
kataktal, kitaktal, kitanau	sound of thunder
kanat, kanaun	sound of a sick man
karat	sound of wringing pain
kirat, kilat	sound of pain of baby
killa	noise
kilaroli	combined noise of children
kilkanu	crying

kumanat, gumnat	inaudible whispering
kainsal	cymbals
khabdat	sound of removing domestic articles
khaklat	sound of water
khamnat	sound of neck bells
khikhchat	ludicrous laughter
gamgyat	sound of water current
gablat	sensation of lice or bug on the body
gaungjyat	echo of water current
gugrat	howling of leopard
gidkanu	sound of clouds
ghaghrat	sound of the slabs of a millstone
ghugrat	howling of a dog
ghungyat	sound of wind and engines
chachrat	creaking sounds
chunchyat	sound of rodents
chhamnat	sound of ornaments
Chibrat	sound of the movement in the bush
jajlat	sound of earthquake
tatadat, taprat, tabrat	sound of a fall
tal	beat
thatrat	shuddering
damnat	sound of falling grains
ninyare	cricket
pataktal	sound of strike on the head
pipdat	sound of breaking open the pods
faftal	sound produced by bathing of a bird
bardat	muttering
bhimnat	buzzing

damdyat	sound of heavy foot steps
dandyat	crying sound of an animal
runak	dim sound
sinsyat, sunsyat	sound of water and wind
sulgari	whistling

Sensory

ang malkana	twiching
anmil, anmale	discordant
kachyonda	hack
kachana, kachyan, pairaun, pairwar, synnd-pati	make-up
kirmodi si dall	file like the fruites of kirmod
kutmani	bud
kungali	tender
kauvyar	mime artist
kanchua	frock coat
khankryala jonga	
mungryali feeli	a powerful man
khitkani si	erotic laughter
kot, kothali	inner apartment
gabhar	central action
galthu	dull character
ghinduron si rath	like the procession of sparrows
chakha	moment
chakandaṛ	prankish character
chakhuli	bird
chaunru	rectangular place for audience
chamachham	full rhythm

jhallar	impulse
jhukmuk, jhusmuns	dawn
janaka-janaki	movement of a very heavy thing,
jhaloor	nose ornament
jhumala, limli, khantada, jhulada	raiment
dhaunpeli, dhamel, chufuly, chufali	locks
dhaunkalyo	farce
neuo	girdle
nakal-chhakal	imitation, copy, acting
naikyan, pater, naiky:n	traditional female dancers
deocheli pathuva	female ornament of wrist
bathaun	air
bathen, bigralli, band, swani	beautiful women
malyo bhidako	crowd
mull hansan	burst of smile
bhanbhani ritu	nostalgic days
bhukki	kiss
bhentagati	meeting
mokharu	mask
taprat	flurry quandary
tatu ko timanya	ornament of breast
tandu-bhandu	paraphernalia
thamka, kaub, saraun, san	gesture
thandu-mathu	slow pace
dari	crowd
dhal-panyal	potentials for art and acting
rasyan	literary joy
rungdya bhanun	music piercing the heart

vensar, bulak	nose-ring (eliptical)
bhujaawali nath	nose-ring (circular)
sunangan	golden
hidra	moving crowd

Emotive

anmani	restlessness
asand, khari, nisyad	crisis
alokan	background
anasurt	unknowingly
aglyar	pioneership
urda	gale
uryoun, misaun	to set in motion
uthaun	to raise the pitch of drums
umal, jhallar	impulse, psychic drive
kankryalo	full of valour
kandura, kansuna, kanduda	evesdropping
kwansu dil	tender heart
kalkali	compassion
kablat	sensation of restlessness
kansu, jhala	interpretation through the beats of drum
kudwak, kutwak	ominous speech
kunas	an expression of awe
kurodh	anguish
kauthgyar	festive crowd, spectators
kau-bau	dilemma
khand-mand	nemesis
khuded, khud	nostalgic, nostalgia
khotu milaun	rehearsal

khaulu, khali	arena
goga	rumour
ghan	catastrophe
chaunla janu	to possess
chass, chasak	pain in heart
chhagal	concluding beats of drums
jama	state of mind
jaltyara	jealous
jikudi, jitama	heart
jhidjhidi	stir through spine
tanku	turban (*bhotiya*)
dabkhan	staggering
daundi-chaundi	declaration through drums
dhab	spirit
dandol	chain of thoughts
dutti	scandalous female character
dund	scandal
thakchat, thakart	catharsis
thad, thaad, thal	fair
theero	shock
dhargas, dhito	bold
dharmani	dance arena
dhandh	wonder
dhami	drummer
nigure, nithur	callous
nisparai	desolate
par	act
pan	temper
paito, paitasar	preliminaries

pancharanu	to challenge
fadu	thread of story
fadu milaun	connecting the links
baram jagnu	intuition
baramtal	tension
baduli	hiccups in remembrance
badeen, jhumariya	female bard dancer
barpala	duty shifts in cultural performance
bavarya, ularya	over romantic
bijog	sorrow
bisaun	resting period in drum beating
biblandi karuna	crying pathos
bukara, bukari, bokaran	burst of cry
bainda	whimsical
baugi	indifferent
bhavan, bhaman	feeling of loneliness
bhaun, dhal	tune
bharmana	fantasy
manswant	human presence
mayalu, mayalku, mayaldu	affectionate
mandan, khali	dance ensemble
maya	love, passion
bharamana	fantasy
raijanu	prosper
ramkadi-chamkadi	lustrous carriage
rathen	to be stunned by spectacle
rasbaso	full of aesthetic pleasure
rood, roodi	summer, drought
rangmathu	exhilarated

raibar — message

rauns, chapchapi — empathy, pleasure, satisfaction

rithaul — chain of thinking

lad — sentimental love

laudyabaikh — womanish male

sabryu:n — souvenir to compare

sumrana — memories

saraun — full of rhythm and rhyme

swal duhraun — response of dialogues

sikasar, sakasar — copying

sirokhanu, siraun — vow of offering

suwa — darling

saimani — greeting word used by the low caste for the higher caste

saunjadya — playmates

sodhnu — narrate in detail

hakdak — wonderstruck

harihatt — intransigence

hungara — unintelligible dialogue by masked characters

hirr — shudder

gyan baul, vairagya, nirvane — renunciation

8

The Visvakarma Worldview

Jan Brouwer

This is the first outcome of a study which focuses on the interface between the as yet unexplored field between worldview and patterns of thinking on the one hand, and life-styles and environmental situations on the other.

For all practical purposes, the study was split into a pilot study and a main research project. The pilot study, which is nearly completed, approached the main topic with the pan-Indian concept of *pancabhuta* as its leading theme. This caused a critical view of existing research tools, concepts and their original bedding, the academic disciplinary divisions, dimensions and discourses of analytical write-ups. In short, it raised a fundamental issue of methodology.[1]

This project explores a rather limited aspect of Indian reality, namely, the much neglected worldview and lifestyle of the "makers of the world" or the craftsmen called Visvakarmas in Karnataka. Indigenous thought is marked by dichotomous as well as comprehensive abstract categorisations, a lack of one-to-one identifications, as well as a lack of multiple exclusiveness. It follows that our approach should be multi-disciplinary and multi-dimensional.

The multi-disciplinary character of the approach means that narratives and speech is left to be studied by narratologists or folklorists, and material and social discourse not to sociologists or indologists. Such divisions are artificial speech and narratives are sensitively embedded in the material and social discourse.

This study is convential insofar as I study a single, relatively small community: the artisans of the Visvakarma caste in Karnataka (South India). However, at the same time the focus is on the ideological, historical, economical, and political relationship between them and the others.

To sum up, the project's argument is *twofold*:

(i) to help the respondents, in this case the Visvakarma artisans, to become more knowledgeable agents themselves and not to displace their knowledge in favour of so-called updated technology befitting the market forces or a welfare state, this reducing the indigenous comprehensive sphere of (technological) knowledge;

(ii) to consider Visvakarma speech, narratives and material expressions of thought neither as random selections from various local tool boxes nor concoctions of the ignorant.

Having presented the argument and outline of approach, I shall now proceed with a few words on our sources, focus, and analysis. I take my inspiration from structural anthropology, semiotics and empirical sociology, while recognising the analytical distinction between the informants' *ideal* and *actual situation.* It has to be acknowledged that there is an arbitrary relationship between the informants' interpretation of their ideal and the abstraction of their actual situation.

The Analysis of Three Sources

The method of analysis considers narratives and the material culture, i.e., myths, the crafts, its tools, workshops and products as systems of communication. They are messages, modes of signification or forms (vide: Barthes, 1989 (1972): 117-142).[2] Thought can be expressed in speech, myth or material, each of which has its own historical limits and conditions of use. The same type of analysis can be applied to each mode. A furnace is a furnace; a furnace in the smith's narrative is no longer quite a furnace as a it as a furnace which is the womb of the Goddess. It is decorated and adapted to a certain type of usage. Narrative and material carry a message which cannot possibly evolve from their own 'nature' for anyone can be arbitrarily endowed with meaning. It is given a particular signification irrespective of the mode of representation. For the Visvakarmas, the furnace is a manifestation of the Goddess. It signifies the Goddess, or more precisely, for the smith the furnace is deified. The furnace (signifier) expresses the Goddess (signified). However, on the analytical level the furnace is loaded with the Goddess: the furnace and the Goddess existed before they united and forming the sign: it is a meaning. Following Barthes, I call the signifier of this order (i.e., the secondary order of speech, myth and material (in contrast to the primary order of language (*langue*), the form and the signifed the concept (Barthes, 1989:126). There are functional implications such as that of the part to the whole of the furnace and the anvil, or furnace, anvil and the workshop and craftsman.

In the narratives, into the queen, maid, prostitute, river, princes, first drained off contingency, the female figure will attract the attention: the cosmos which is composed of a male and female constituent part. The queen, as form has a shallow, isolated and impoverished meaning; as the concept of the female principle, it is tied to the totality of the cosmos.

The fundamental character of spoken, mythical or material concept is appropriated: the female figures precisely concern a given form of the Visvakarma. The concept can have many signifiers: queen, maid, prostitute, daughter of a king, river, furnace, tools, which actualise the agreement of the predicate. The repetition of the concept, through different forms, allows us to decipher the narratives or material, which aims at the discovery of the meaning. The concepts are constituent elements of the texts or contexts (workshops, crafts) and the concepts have to be named.

The manifest meaning of a narrative, etc., is what the narrators say about it, e.g., it explains the origin of the caste, the existence of sub-castes, their degenerated condition today. In other words the legitimating function of the myth, etc. has its manifest meaning. The manifest meaning is, however, distorted by the concept, because the form of the narrative is already constituted by a linguistic meaning. The signifier has two aspects: the full meaning (queen, prostitute, furnace, etc.,) and one empty (female constituent part of the cosmos). The furnace is a furnace, but also a manifestation of the Goddess. There is alteration gathered up in the concept. The method of deciphering requires switching from the position of audience to that of anthropologist.

In language the sign is arbitrary: nothing compels the acoustic image furnace (naturally to mean the concept furnace (De Saussure, 1966: (1931)). The sign here is unmotivated. In narratives and material, however, the choice can never be fully arbitrary and has to contain some analogy. There is always partiality in the analogy of the meaning and the concept. The form drops many analogous features and keeps only a few: the hollowness of womb and furnace: the product which comes out of it; the colour (black) of furnace and the Goddess (Kali). Moreover, a complete image could exclude the myth. The images work with flaws as to lend credibility to it. In the Fort Store,[3] the guilty figure is not identified; in the myth on the origin of tools,[4] the source of fire is not given; in the workshop, the water is not named. Finally, the motivation is chosen. From the vast repertoire of divine characters, in this case, Kali and Siva are chosen as signifiers.

For the Visvakarmas these expressions of thought are fundamental, and their narratives and materials are reason.

In the case of the crafts lexicon, the *adurubasha* will not be considered on the level of primary order of language, but on the secondary order of speech, narrative and material.[5]

As for the historical reconstruction of the artisans' terms of migration and settlement, their relationship with the environment (both ecological and economical), the analysis of the crafts lexicon considers the linguistic background of the terms, their usage and their speakers.

As regards the cognitive aspects of the artisans, the same approach as outlined above will be applied. At this stage of the data collection, I can only indicate or be tentative and conclusions cannot yet be drawn. Therefore, let me illustrate the approach. I postulate a relation between two terms, a signifier and/or signified. The relationship is one of equivalence as both objects belong to different categories. For example, in the crafts lexicon *pudi* stands for 'gold'. In Kannada *pudi* means 'powder'. In the crafts lexicon, *bilipudi* stands for toddy. *Bill* (K) 'white' and *pudi* (K) 'powder'. We have thus identified the signifiers, viz., gold and toddy for one signified *pudi*. The reference here is to solid gold which in common parlance is a symbol for life. From earlier work (Brouwer, 1987), we know that solid gold is used to make ornaments to be used on the liminalities of the body, i.e., the liminalities of life. Ethnography is full of examples, including my own (Brouwer, 1988:124) where toddy (palmwine) (which is a white liquid) is offered to the Goddess Yellamma. She is – as her name indicates – the Goddess of the border. In other words, toddy marks the border of (village) life. Thus, we have here the analogy between the two signifiers and the signified. It provokes two questions which cannot yet be answered. Which term does the lexicon give for liquid gold? What can we say about the opposition between *bilipudi* 'white powder' (toddy) and *karipudi* 'black powder' (arrack)? The technical difference between toddy and arrack may be relevant here. Toddy is a natural product and arrack is a cultural product. The signification of the earlier analogy is life. The conclusion could be that the Visvakarma view life or the living state as the natural one in contrast to death or the dying state which is seen as cultural. Further research should reveal different signifiers for the signified *kari* 'black' and those for death or dying state.

It thus seems that the crafts lexicon is a multi-ordered semiological system. That which is a *sign* in the system becomes a mere signifier in the next.

The analysis of the connections between the different orders of the system will reveal the Visvakarma view of Self and Society in its most basic way.

A subsequent feed-back to the analysis of narratives and materials will then explain the logic of the cognitive choices. At the same time, the analysis may reveal whether the concept of *pancabhuta* plays a determining role in the cognition of the artisans, and if so, how.

As De Saussure (1931/1966) has demonstrated, language is an exemplary semiological system. It is of the first order, while narratives and materials is a second order semiological system, for it is constructed from a semiological chain existed before. The crafts lexicon falls into this category of systems, but it itself is multi-ordered.

The Five Elements

The Five Elements – sky (ether), water, fire, wind and earth – are called in Sanskrit *akasa*, *ap*, *tejas*, *vayu* and *prithvi* and in Kannada: *akasa*, *niru*, *benki*, *gali* and *manu*. In Visvakarma scholarly interpretation of the Visvakarma ideology, both in writing and spoken, the authors/scholars use the Sanskrit terms. The Visvakarma craftsmen, both in speech and narratives, use the Kannada terms. Among the lay Visvakarmas, mostly craftsmen, the knowledge of *pancabhuta* as a concept is rare, but certainly not absent. On this level, the use of the Kannada terms, or the lack of completeness of this knowledge, probably indicate absence of knowledge of the Sanskrit literature (as far as the concept is concerned) and could thus be an original knowledge. On this level, the concept is often materially expressed either directly or through a variety of signifiers. In other words, the craftsmen many know the expression and the code, but not the interpretation.

On the level of Visvakarma scholars, the knowledge of the concept may be original or taken from the (*brahminical*) Sanskrit literature. Thus, on this level, the originality does not lie in the concept itself or in the interpretation *perse*, but in the interpretation and the concept's signifiers in a particular (cultural) ideological or narrative context. Here, the point cannot be the difference between Great Tradition and Little Tradition, or between *brahminical* and non-*brahminical* theory, but the concept as a tool to express Visvakarma ideology. In contrast to the lay level of craftsmen, the material expression is absent here and replaced by interpretation. However, the signifiers of the two levels are not always the same.

Ethnographical Perspectives

Three Indian Traditions

I shall now place the aforementioned two levels in a wider context. In present India, three different traditions can be distinguished viz., the Scriptural Tradition (ST), the Traditional Practices (TP), and the Modern State (MS).[6]

In the Scriptural Tradition, various works deal with the Five Elements; they are explained and/or applied theoretically in the philosophy. This, what may be called, the classical view on the Elements is not our immediate concern. For our purpose, the second tradition (TP) may be divided into Visvakarma craftsmen, other artisans, and others. These three groups of the population may have different views on, and practices in terms of, the Elements. However, within the groups of Visvakarma artisans also different views may prevail.

The Visvakarmas

The world of the South Indian smiths has neither been studied much in detail by ethnographers nor by historians. In historical studies, the smiths have not received the same attention as agriculturists, priests, or even weavers. Those scholars who have made crafts and craftsmen central to their studies focus especially on contemporary technical aspects of the crafts (Untracht, 1969; Fischer & Shah, 1979; Krishnan, 1976; Strandgaard, 1976; Mukherjee, 1978; Blankenberg, 1985). In these studies, the tacit object of the study is to displace the artisans' knowledge in favour of so-called updated technology befitting the market forces or a welfare state, thus greatly reducing the indigenous comprehensive sphere of (technological) knowledge. Even more sensitive studies of particular crafts, notably pottery (Dumont, 1952; Srinivas, 1959; Saraswati, 1963; Ishvaran, 1966; Behura, 1978), did not help the artisans to become more knowledgeable agents themselves. This was mainly caused by the mono-disciplinary approach of the authors.

Furthermore, the social position of the Visvakarma artisans have generally been treated in the anthropological literature as anomalous, aberrant and not fitting a model with much of the debate focused on the issue of right and left hand castes.

The Visvakarma caste comprises ironsmiths, carpenters, coppersmiths, sculptors, and goldsmiths. They are manufacturers who disturb an existing natural order to obtain material which they transform into cultural artifacts meant to be static and permanent.

Their ideology comes to us in three forms, viz., origin myths oral or written, printed handbills with coded schema's and coloured pictures. It shows a single bodily image of the Lord Visvakarman, the mythological ancestor of all Visvakarma craftsmen. The latter are the living replicas of the Lord. The single body, the Virat Visvabrahma or universal essence is equated with Prajapati. From the five faces of this Brahma, the five archetypical craftsmen emanated: Manu, the ironsmith; Maya, the carpenter; Tvashtri, the coppersmith; Silpi, the sculptor; and Visvajna, the goldsmith.

The Visvakarma ideal is thus concerned with autonomy and completeness, while it gains significance through the homology between Lord Visvakarman and the Visvakarmas of the social world. The five archetypical craftsmen have no relationship with one another apart from belonging to the same body in this ideal image, there is absolute separation between the five craftsmen; one does not depend on the other and together they are self-contained. Painted or printed pictures show this Visvakarman with five (coloured) faces and ten arms holding ten different, often violent, attributes. While below Visvakarman there is a picture of the cow and the tiger and the line *ahimsa paramo dharmah*, which means 'non-violence is the (our) supreme way of life'. Thus for the artisans, the centre of the moral universe lies with them and not elsewhere as we read in much of the available anthropological and sociological literature. The Visvakarmas have stepped out of the Hindu fold, like Christians, Buddhists, Virashaivas, but unlike them, they have at once stepped back and formulated their own cultural ideology without rejecting the Vedic and classical Sanskrit literature. We can arrive at a better prospect for understanding the whole of Hindu society by focusing on the rhetoric and discourse of Self and Society as provided by the Visvakarmas.

The Visvakarma Views on *Pancabhuta*

The Scholarly Views

According to Visvakarma scholarly interpretation, each archetypical craftsman is associated with one of the Five Elements as given in Table 1:

Table 1
The Five Elements and Five Craftsmen according to Scholars

1.	Manu	ironsmith	*prithvi*	Earth
2.	Maya	carpenter	*ap*	Water
3.	Tvashtr	coppersmith	*tejas*	Fire
4.	Silpi	sculptor	*vayu*	Wind
5.	Visvajna	goldsmith	*akasa*	Sky

However, each Element is intrinsically connected with each other inasmuch as half in each belong to the self same substance and the other half being made of the other Element at the rate of 1/8 of each of the other Elements.

Furthermore, according to the same sources, the Five Elements are associated with series of external and internal objects. Only a few of these associations are known to me now: *earth* includes ether, heaven direction, mid-directions; *water* includes herbs, greenary; *ether*, soul; *fire* includes wind, sun, moon, (nine) stars.

Following Visvakarma exegesis, an evolution is presented thus: from *aum* came *akasa*, from *akasa* the *vayu*; from *vayu* the *agni*, from *ap* the form and *prithvi*, while at every stage there is an addition of *guna* to particularise the Element, viz., sound to *ether*; *touch* related to wind; *form* related to fire, the essence *rasa* related to water, and *smell* related to earth. The information regarding the properties, associations and relations of the Elements seems far from complete.

The scholarly view is also found in so-called handbills, which are schematic representations of Visvakarma ideology. They are available at certain Visvakarma *mathas* or at major festivals of Visvakarma sponsored temples and shrines. As regards the Five Elements the scholarly view corresponds with the handbills in one respect, viz., the association of each archetypical craftsman with one of the Five Elements.

The data given above thus present two problems:

(i) In the scholarly interpretation, the ideal Visvakarma represents a totality of five crafts and five elements. This single body thus consists of Five Elements. Concomitantly the single bodily image represents five different crafts each of which is associated with one element. Apparently, the Visvakarmas are aware of this problem for one of their swamijis has particularised the elements for each craft. However, to understand this complex interpretation, it is necessary to decipher the codes of the entire handbill. Needless to say it is beyond the scope of this paper to elaborate this, but I shall engage myself in this analysis in the monograph to be prepared as final report of the project.

(ii) The scholarly exegesis demonstrate an equality of all the five craftsmen and an equality, the actual crafts in the world are significantly different from one another in terms of autonomy, completeness and use of violence. At the same time the craftsmen's interpretation of the Five Elements in their crafts show a qualitative difference. A similar discrepancy between ideal and actual situation has been found in the Visvakarma material and social discourses.[7]

The Lay Views

In the actual situation of the crafts, the three smiths (iron, copper, gold) hold a similar view on the presence of the Five Elements in their crafts as given in Tables 2 and 3:

Table 2
The Five Elements and the Three Smiths

Crafts Elements	*(ironsmith/coppersmith/goldsmith)*
akasa	"the static, cold, empty, unused furnace"
niru	"to control the fire"
benki	"to heat the metal"
gali	"to kindle the fire"
manu	"to make the furnace"

The carpenters and sculptors have a different view presented here in Table 3.

Table 3
The Carpenter's and Sculptor's View on the Five Elements

Crafts *Elements*	*Carpenter*	*Sculptor*
akasa	blue/black paint	black ghee
niru	to season wood	to select stone
benki	to make paste to bend wood	to make ghee
gali	to destruct wood	to destruct stone
manu	to use at base for making polishing powder	to protect stone

Although the above views (Tables 2 and 3) are true statements, they relate to a certain abstract level. On a lower abstract level a more refined picture emerges. In ironsmithy, the earth (*manu*) is stated "to rust the iron"; in carpentry the earth is not only used to prepare the applicant, but also to preserve wood in underground holes; in coppersmithy the earth is not only the furnace, but also the clay of which the moulds are made.

The craftsman's information on the Five Elements provides at least one important clue to the understanding of the Five Elements in the handbill. In Table 4 the two relevant sets of data are put together.

Table 4
Five Elements, Five Crafts and the Craftsman's View

Craft	*B*	*W*	*C*	*S*	*G*
handbill	earth	wind	fire	water	sky
craftsman's view	rusts iron	season's wood	destructs *pancaloha*	cracks stone	empty furnace

B = Ironsmith *W* = Carpenter *C* = Coppersmith
S = Sculptor *G* = Goldsmith

In other words the elements are associated with the crafts in the handbill in such a way that the *bhuta* is that particular element which is a danger to the particular craft:

(i) the earth causes the iron to rust; (ii) the wind kills the wood; (iii) the fire destroys the holy alloy; (iv) the water cracks the stone; and more subtle, (v) the empty furnace is destructive for the goldsmith. Thus, the Five Elements of the handbill have to be read in their destructive capacity. Further, research on the handbill is needed to discover the codes of the creative capacity of the elements.

In the following section I shall place the concept of *pancabhuta* in the wider context of the Visvakarma artisans.

Pancabhuta: Self and Society

In the foregoing sections, we have seen how the Visvakarmas classify themselves (body), their crafts (assets and process) and the relationships between themselves (archetypical craftsmen and elements) in terms of the Five Elements. The question thus arises whether they also classify the rest of the world in the same terms. To answer this question one has to consider the crafts lexicon or "secret language" of the Visvakarmas.

The crafts lexicon covers at least the following areas:

(i) categorical terms : such as place, time, good, bad, pure, impure, right, left, gift etc.;

(ii) craft-related terms : such as those for raw-materials, tools, assets, processes of manufacture and delivery of products etc.;

(iii) terms referring to people : such as names of castes, sub-castes, tribes, ancestors etc., and

(iv) terms relating to customs : such as those for non-vegetarian food, alcoholic drinks, matrimony etc.

All members of a craftsman's family know the lexicon albeit in different degrees and as per different categories, for example, the male members know more craft related terms, while the female members know more terms related to customs and habits. Those who have left the craft for modern occupations have either a very limited knowledge of it or no knowledge of it all. The goldsmiths seem to have more elaborate lexicon than the ironsmiths.

Discussing the clan names of Indian castes, Levi-Strauss concludes that "we have here groups conceived in terms of a cultural model" (1976:120). His description shows that many Indian tribes are human groups conceived in terms of a natural model, for clan names are plants and animals and many Indian castes are human groups conceived in terms of a cultural model, for clan names are manufactured objects. The

Visvakarma seem to fall in line with the other castes, but not completely. Although it is too early for any definite statement, there are some clues in the crafts for lexicon which suggest that the Visvakarmas conceive society not in terms of a cultural model for none of the other castes are named by manufactured objects. Instead the others are conceived in *temporal terms*, notably a few directly related to death. In this list there are, however, a few exceptions, viz., Bestas, Idigas, Muslims and Vaishnavas are named after an animal, timber or parts of trees respectively. The Bestas are a Scheduled Tribe, the Muslims are not Hindus and the Vaishnavas are not Shaivas. Thus, from the Visvakarma point of view, outsiders in relation to the castes are classified by terms from the natural order. The Idigas are no exception here for they are Telugu caste Hindus. They are toddy tappers and named by a term for firewood. Thus, among the terms of the natural order, it is a particular kind which purposes to (be) destroyed, i.e., not to live. In other words, Society is conceived of as a cultural order and its outsiders in terms of a natural order.

The Visvakarmas conceive themselves in terms taken from their crafts. In other words, in terms of a cultural order. But they are all manufactured objects and *spatial* terms. Here too is one interesting exception; the ironsmith. In this list he is named as a bird (a herom). The exception of this list too is named by a term from the natural order.

Thus the Visvakarmas view society in temporal terms and themselves in spatial terms, while exceptions to this classification are named in terms of the natural order. Terms of the cultural order such as manufactured objects are not used in the names for others. Where *death* is amply represented in the terms for society, *life* is not represented in the terms for self. But the self is represented by the concept of the Five Elements.

Notes

* The data on which this chapter is based, were collected during six months of fieldwork for a pilot study on the ironsmiths of Karnataka commissioned by the Indira Gandhi National Centre for Arts, New Delhi. I am grateful to this Institution for their continuous support.

1. The basic ideal of the present case study (pilot study) and research project is to understand the informants' capacity to order his own world. This means to recognize Indian realities in terms of its own concepts. In other words, our search is one for indigenous categories, which eventually may lead to an indigenous science with Indian perceptions and kinds of analytic relations.

2. The analysis I propose here is basically inspired by the semiotic approach to myths presented by Barthes as early as 1972.
3. In the Fort Story, all Visvakarmas, pure and united lived in a solid, magnetic fort, which could not be destroyed by anything. However, the fort is besieged resulting in a mixed marriage, a fire and escapes, and the origin of endogamous sub-castes (different and new descent lines). For an extensive analysis of this story, see Brouwer, 1987b, 1988.
4. The origin and imagery of tools and workshops have recently been discussed in a paper presented to the seminar on "Sources for History of Science and Technology", Jawaharlal Nehru Centre for Advanced Scientific Research, Indian Institute of Science, Bangalore, January 6-12, 1992 (Brouwer, forthcoming).
5. What I have called the Crafts Lexicon is named by the Visvakarmas *adurubasha*. When the informants speak English, they talk about their "secret language". However, the name for this language or code has two connotations. *Aduru* means 'deceit' as well as 'iron-ore'. *Basha* means `language'. It may thus be translated as 'language of deceit' or 'language of the ironsmiths'. Whether it is a language or only a lexicon is difficult to say at this stage of data collection.
6. Heesterman was one of the first to recognize three Indian traditions since at least the late eighteenth century. The Scriptural Tradition of the Sanskrit literature and the domain of the Traditional Practices were now juxtaposed by the tradition of the Modern State first in its colonial and later in its sovereign form (see: Heesterman, 1985).
7. The handbills elaborate the ideal by association of each archetypical craftsmen with a large number of attributes among which the Five Elements (See Brouwer, 1978b and forthcoming).
8. The material discourse considers the crafts in isolation. Distinguishing the spiritual from the temporal plan, it leads to the discovery of a complementary opposition of two categories of crafts. To mark the crafts' disconnection from the world, the participants view the crafts processes as transcendent acts and have 'ritualised' or 'universalised' the raw materials, processes of manufacture and the finished products. Where their ideal concept of the universe consists of a male and female constituent part, the flaw is here visible by the introduction of the concept of neutrality and the two types of craftsmen — the specialist and the generalist. The unavoidable use of external agents in the world are then either accepted as necessary connections or denied by making them incidental.

   In the social discourse, the ideal caste as a unitary concept, leads to the dichotomy of caste in the world. The complementary opposition of two categories of caste is expressed in both spatial and temporal terms. The existence of various and different Visvakarma sub-castes demonstrates a discontinuity between caste and sub-castes of the world are then traversed by a neutral, mercantile realisation to which the ideal also breaks down. *Vis-a-vis* society, two types of sub-castes emerge: separate or single craft and comprehensive or multi-craft.

References

Barthes, R., 1989 (1957). *Mythologies.* London, Paladin Grafton Books.

Beck, 1973. The Right-Left Division of South Indian Society. *Right and Left. Essays on Dual Symbolic Classification,* Rodney Needham, (ed.), Chicago, University of Chicago Press.

Behura, N.K., 1978. *Peasant Potters of Orissa. A Sociological Study.* New Delhi, Sterling Publishers Pvt. Ltd.

Blankenberg, F.P., 1985. *Implementation of rural technology projects in India.* Ph.D. thesis. Almelo, Technical University Twente.

Brouwer, J., 1977 (1978a). *Handicrafts and Craftsmen.* Some aspects of the social relations of the sandalwood and rosewood carvers in rural and urban settings, Malnad Region and Mysore City, Karnataka State, India. ICA Publication No. 20, University of Leiden, Leiden.

——, 1978b. *Structural analysis of a Visvakarma handbill collected in Karnataka State*, India. Paper presented to the Xth ICAES, New Delhi.

——, 1987a. An exploration of the traditional division of labour between the sexes in South Indian crafts. In *Invisible Hands. Women in Home-based production.* A.M. Singh and A. Kelles-Viitanen, (eds.). New Delhi, Sage Publications.

——, 1987b. The Story of the Magnetic Fort. The Leiden In *Tradition in Structural Anthropology.* A. de Ridder and J.A.J. Karremans, (eds.) Leiden, E.J. Brill.

——, 1987c. A Matter of Liminalities. A study of women and crafts in South India. In *Men in India.* Vol. 67 No. 2.

——, 1988. *Coping with Dependence: Craftsmen and their Ideology in Karnataka (South India).* Leiden, Ph.D. thesis.

——, 1990. Material Expressions of Thought (Aspects of Ironsmiths in South India). In *Techniques et culture* 15. pp: 105,129.

——, 1991. The Artisans of India and Visvakarmas of Karnataka. In *The Quarterly Journal of the Mythic Society,* Vol. 82. Jan-Jun '91, Nos. 1-2.

——, 1992, forthcoming. *The Makers of the World, Craft, Caste and Mind of South Indian Artisans.* New Delhi, Oxford University Press.

Dube, 1959. *Indian Village.* London, Routledge and Kegan Paul.

Dumont, L., 1952. A remarkable feature of South Indian pot-making. In *Man,* June, pp. 81-82.

Fischer, E and H. Shah, 1970. *Rural Craftsmen and their Work. Equipment and Techniques in the Mer Village of Ratadi in Saurashtra, India.* Ahmedabad, National Institute of Design.

Heesterman, J.C. 1985. *The Inner Conflict of Tradition. Essays in Indian Ritual, Kingship and Society.* London, University of Chicago Press.

Ishvaran, K. 1966a. Goldsmith in a Mysore Village. In *Journal of Asian and African Studies.* Vol. 1 pp. 50-62.

Krishnan, M.V., 1976. *Cire Perdue Casting in India.* New Delhi, Kanak Publications.

Levi-Strauss, Claude, 1976 (1966). *The Savage Mind.* London, Weidenfeld and Nicolson.

Mukherji, Meera, 1978. *Metal Craftsmen of India.* Memoir No. 44, Calcutta, Anthropological Survey of India.

Saraswati, B.N., 1963. Caste, Craft and Change, In *Man in India,* Vol. 43, No. 3, pp. 218-24.

Saussure, F. de, 1966 (1931). *Course in General Linguistics.* Edited by C. Bally and A. Sechehaye in collaboration with A. Reidlinger: translated by W. Baskin. New York, Mcgraw Hill.

Srinivas, M.N., 1959. The case of the Potter and the Priest. In *Man in India,* Vol. 39, No. 3.

Strandgaard, Ole, 1976. *Stensmeden I Gadag. Nogle Forelobige Noter on Traditional Kunst i Dagens India.* Copenhagen, National Museum.

Untracht, Oppi, 1968. Metal Techniques for Craftsmen. *A Basic Manual on the methods of Forming and Decorating Metal.* New York, Doubleday & Co.

9

The Birhor Universe

Ashim Kumar Adhikary

Men has a primordial urge to know his own self, his place in the universe and his relation to it. Man, unlike other animals who respond to the demands of the physical world primarily by means of their sensory receptors and motor effectors, is not satisfied with just living life but also grasping it, knowing it, perceiving it meaningfully. Man is a symbolizing animal and he perceives his world symbolically. To understand man we need to understand his perceptions and classifications of the objects and phenomena of his universe in and around which he lives.

The culture of pre-literate peoples is homogeneous and is guided essentially by the oral tradition or the collective memory of its members (Saraswati, 1970). The perceptions of their cosmic and phenomenal world can hardly be grasped by a deductive and systematic analysis. They are to be understood through a careful study of their practice by an inductive analysis. The vision of cosmic order is reflected in the social and cultural organization of the pre-literate peoples.

In this chapter, an attempt has been made to delineate the nature of perceptions and categorizations of the elements and objects of the universe in an oral cultural tradition. The perceptions and categorizations will be studies in the context of the cosmogonic myth and everyday activities.

Birhor Economy and Social World

The Birhors belong to the Mundani group of tribes and are concentrated in the central-eastern India. In Orissa they are found mainly in the districts of Sundergarh, Sambalpur, Keonjhar, Dhenkanal and Mayurbhanj. In these regions they are locally known as Mankidi, Mankria or Mankar-khia Kol because of their habit of eating and sharing monkeys. In the Oriya dialect *mankar* means monkeys, and *kkhia* means the habit of eating. The self-ascription of the people is, however, Birhor, and there is no perceptible difference between them in different regions.

Though broadly branded as hunter-gatherers, the whole gamut of the Birhor economy in the above-mentioned areas of Orissa involves the exploitation of forest resources and the maintenance of an essential economic articulation with caste peasants and the market economy of the larger society. The Birhors collect jungle products and exchange them with the neighbouring settled Hindu peasants for their day-to-day livelihood. The jungle resources mainly collected by them are from the *bauhinia* creeper that grows profusely in these regions. From the barks (*chhakkam*) of these creepers, various kinds of ropes and rope-products are made. Various minor forest products are also procured and exchanged in the neighbouring society. Hunting of wild game is another of their economic activities. But hunting is pursued occasionally and the animals hunted are primarily used for consumption. Sometimes they also sell live monkeys and skins of *langur*. Though hunting does not contribute much to their economy, they keep up a spirit of hunting and continue this mode of production as a cultural norm.

In the context of their life-situation the Birhors cannot operate the clan-lineage based segmentary system of social structure, characteristic of the Mundani group of tribes. They now organize their subsistence activities, primarily in terms of two groups that are referred to by them respectively as *orha* (household) and *tanda* or *tola* (band). *Orha* serves as their basic production and consumption unit, and revolves around the nuclear family of husband, wife and unmarried children. Most of them, however, comprise of partial or broken families and show a flexible nature.

There is no central authority to regulate band-formations among the Birhors. The band has no territorial affiliation, and its formation is not seasonal. It is a regular phenomenon and the Birhors always move and live in bands of several related households. Though the Birhor bands are flexible in nature, they always comprise of marriageable groups. The role of exogamy, the principle of reciprocity as well as the autonomy of individual households to move from one band to another help maintain interaction and communication over a wider region. They divide their patrilineal clans and lineages into small operational groups and align themselves in such a way as to maintain an effective scale of society and to deal with the probable scarcity of marriageable spouses.

Structure of the Birhor Universe

The Birhor of Orissa broadly divide their universe into two parts — *rimil* (sky) and the *utaye* (earth). They conceive the earth as a round-shaped flat surface and the sky, a hollow concave overarching it. This structure of the universe appears to be somewhat like a cone, and is similar to the structure of their leaf-huts.

Some of the Birhors, however, say that there is a world beyond the sky and another below the earth. They do not have any specific terms for these worlds, and seem to have varying notions about them. Some call the world beyond the sky *sarag* (heaven), and say that the departed souls live there. Some say that the world beyond the sky is inhabited by human beings like those on earth but the men there are all cultivators. Water of their fields permeates through the sky on earth as rain. The Birhors do not have much to tell about the world beneath the earth. They simply describe it as a dark region full of water. These ideas seem to have been taken from the neighbouring Hindu peasants.

The Birhors divide the *utaye* into *disum* (forest-clad hilly regions) and *muluk* (regions other than the forest-clad ones). Specifically speaking, by *muluk* the Birhor refer to the villages and markets. The Birhors consider *disum* to be their own country and *muluk* to be the country of 'other people'.

A careful study of meanings of their social interaction reveals that the Birhors constitute a morally-ordered *gemeinschaft*-type of social-cultural world in *disum*, their own territory in the forest, and a rationalist-utilitarian *gesellschaft*-type of social-cultural world in *muluk*, the territory dominated by the caste-peasants and market economy.

Natural Phenomena and Supernatural Spirits

The Birhors think that whole universe is created and presided over by Sing Bonga or the sun and his wife Chandu Bonga. Sing Bonga resides in the *rimil* and from there rules the entire universe. Though the Birhors assume that the union of a male and a female essential for the procreation of every object and phenomenon, they do not always explicitly narrate the origin of the phenomena in those terms. Sing Bonga is regarded by the people as the supreme deity. He is extremely powerful and the creator of all things on this earth. He is basically good and thought to be benevolent. He does not interfere in the domains of other gods and goddesses, though he is omnipotent. He is worshipped by the people once a year usually in the Bengali months of Paus-Magh (January-February), and a white cock and a white he-goat are sacrificed. Chandu Bonga is also worshipped in the months of Paus-Magh, sometimes along with Sing Bonga, and sometimes on different days. But in her case a black hen is sacrificed.

Though the Birhor cannot give an idea of the appearance of the deities, they seem to make a correlation between the sex and colour of the sacrificed animal and the deity worshipped.

Dharti Mai, a female deity, presides over the *utaye*. She looks after almost all the natural resources and the creatures on the earth. In brief, she provides food to all creatures and looks after their well-being. She is worshipped usually in the Bengali month of Agrahayan (November-December). A black hen or a black she-goat is sacrificed for her worship.

The Birhors also talk of two other deities – Lugu Haram and Burhi Mai. Some of the Birhors consider these deities as the offspring of Dharti Mai. Lugu Haram, a male deity, presides over the east, while Birhi Mai, a female deity, presides over the west. Both deities are worshipped together annually, preferably in the month of Paus-Magh.

Lugu Haram and Burhi Mai have seven sons, each of whom presides over a particular natural phenomenon. For instance, Hanuman Bir is regarded as the presiding deity of the animal species *langur* (*Presbytes entellus*). He is worshipped with red fowls. Bandra Bir presides over monkeys (*Maccacus rhesus*). Red fowls are sacrificed to this deity. Nanda Bir presides over the wind, while Paban Bir or Hoyo Bir presides over rain and storm. Black cocks are sacrificed to these deities. Bagh Bir presides over tigers and cocks of mixed colours are sacrificed to him. The bear is presided over by Hundar Bir. Babsa Bir presides over thunder and meteor. Both Hundar Bir and Babsa Bir are worshipped with cocks of mixed colour.

The Birhors identify two categories of ancestral spirits – Hapram and Churgin. The Hapram are classified into Bura Burhi and Chowrasi. The Burha Burhi are the spirits of the near ancestors whose names are remembered by the people, while the Chowrasi Hapram refer to those ancestors whose names are not remembered. The relationship of the living with their Hapram is both contractual and ethical. Every Birhor family has an ancestral shrine called *asthan*, the seat of Hapram. The members of the family protect and worship it regularly, and carry it whenever they shift their camps. Hapram are thought to mediate between the supernatural deities and the living. They look after their descendants and guide them in a crisis.

Though the Hapram live in the supernatural world along with the Bonga, the Birhors make a distinction between these two categories of supernatural spirits. Hapram are placed just below the Bonga. For the worship of a Hapram the animal is sacrificed by beating (*kutam*) its head, while for the Bonga it is beheaded (*bonga*). If the Birhors show negligence towards their Hapram and do not propitiate them, calamity may fall upon them. It is not because the Hapram are angry with them but because the people fail to conform to the normal rules of relations with their ancestors who constitute an integral part of their moral community. The *asthan* is a sacred place, and is highly susceptible to pollution. Briefly speaking, the living people feel it is their duty to look after their Hapram who, in turn, take care of their descendants. They are bound by a perpetual reciprocal relation. According to custom, when a man dies his son buries his body and constructs a leaf-hut over the grave. After two or three days he has to call back the departed soul (*jiu*) to rest in the hut. An *asthan* (sacred seat) is prepared for the soul. The son then gives him food and drink. The belief is that if the son does not do this the soul of his father will remain a *bhulah* (wanderer) and would not be able to enter the supernatural world to live with other ancestral spirits or Hapram. The spirits of the dead continue the individuality of the living persons and have the same names and disposition as they had before death. The supernatural world of the Hapram is an extension of the social world of the Birhors.

The Churgin includes spirits of the dead who wander about and live in uninhabitable places on earth. The Birhors identify eight such spirits: Daini, Pangri, Churni, Draha, Khut, Bhulah, Bhulah Chandi and Baghat. The classification of these spirits is made primarily by the nature of death as well as the nature of their habitat and disposition after death. This category of spirits is placed below the rank of the Hapram. The Birhors seem to have a constrained relation with these spirits who are considered basically malevolent.

However, these evil spirits are not kept completely out of communication. The recognition of malevolent ancestral spirits and the custom of offering food and drink to them in different ritual contexts helps maintain the structural equilibrium. The Birhors ceremonially invoke these spirits and offer oblations. They are worshipped at the boundary of the settlement primarily to placate their wrath, and are requested not to interfere with the acitvities of the living.

All the Birhors cannot get Hapram-hood. To achieve it one needs to conform to the prevalent norms and customs that emphasize personal conduct as well as maintenance of good relations among relatives. If a Birhors dies unmarried, he cannot get Hapram-hood. Marriage is an important social phenomenon, and it gives a man direct access to his Hapram, and raises him to the status of manhood or, more precisely, 'birhor-hood'.

The Birhor broadly classify the animals into three distinct categories and arrange them in a hierarchical order. This classification shows not only their attitude towards the animals but also the nature of the relation they have with them. In the first category are cows, buffaloes, goats, fowls and the like. All these animals are of the domesticated variety and do not belong to the jungle. These are first sacrificed to their deities and then taken for consumption. The second category includes *langurs*, monkeys, rabbits, porcupines, squirrels and the like. These animals are consumed by the Birhors without any ceremonial slaughtering. In the third and the lowest category are dogs, tigers, bears, snakes and the like. The Birhors do not eat these animals and believe that neither god nor any other human being takes their meat.

The Birhors maintain a symbiotic relationship with the natural phenomena and live in peaceful co-existence. They believe that even the ferocious animals do not inflict harm if they are not annoyed or harmed. One of my informants of about 50 years of age told me that he had never in his life seen any case of snake-bite, nor any case of death from the attack of tigers. On many occasions I came across snakes moving around the settlements of Birhors and noted that they simply drove them away with mild scoldings as if they were pets. The children appeared to be sportive at the sight of snakes in their camp-sites rather than being afraid. However, there are instances of attacks from wild animals. Though such cases are usually explained as expressions of anger of supernatural deities or as consequences of the violation of some social norms, they are often explained as a result of breach of a normal rule of behaviour with the animals. The Birhors do not cut the branches of the trees like *uli (Mangigera indica), matkom (Basia latifolia), sarjom (Shorea robusta), taraf (Buchanania latifolia), triil (Diospyrosmelanoxylon)* when they start blooming in the jungles during March and April. Even the trees like *kadam daru (Anthrocephalon Cadamba), hesa daru (Ficus infectoria)* and *bari daru (Ficus bengalensis),* which offer little by way of subsistence, are treated carefully when they blossom.

The Birhors gear their activities keeping in view the prominent environmental and natural phenomena. They divide their calendar into three seasons–*rabang* (winter), *shitang* (summer) and *da* or *jargi* (rainy) corresponding to the natural phenomena of cold, heat and rains.

Days (*singi*) and nights (*ninda*) also correspond to the normal presence and absence of *singi* or the sun in the sky. The Birhors distinguish four parts of a day – *sheta* (morning), *tikia* (noon), *ayub para* (afternoon), and *ayub* (evening). *Sheta* starts with the barking of dogs when the sun peeps through the eastern horizon. The literal meaning of *sheta* is dog. When the sun is above the head, it is *tikin,* and when the sun comes down towards the western horizon, it is *ayub para* (the coming of evening). *Ayub* is the time when the sun is no longer visible but its rays still illuminate the earth. In all these cases the Birhors usually point out the positions of the sun in the sky with their fingers.

Concept of Self and Some Essential Elements

Though the Birhors are ascribed by others in the locality as Mankria, Mankidi, Mankirdia or Mankar-Khia Kol, they distinguish themselves as Birhors from all other people who are categorized as *diku* (alien or foreigner). The term Birhor is a summation *bir* (jungle) and *hor* (man). Collectively the term Birhor means 'man of jungle'. However, as to the origin of the people, there is a story among the Birhors of Orissa.

> Once there was a Kherwar king in Chotanagpur who had two sons. After the death of the king his sons started quarrelling over the throne.

> The elders of the state came forward to mitigate the dispute. They asked the princes to run a race on horseback and told that the throne would belong to the man who would win the race. Accordingly there was a race, and the younger prince won. The older prince was delayed because his turban got entangled in the thorns or a bush on his way. The younger prince got the throne while the elder one took to a wandering life in jungles. The present Birhors are the descendants of the elder prince.

In this story it is noticed that among many other things, the emphasis on their association with a glorious past. Many of them, even today, feel proud if they find an opportunity to identify themselves as *nagbasi* Kherwar, i.e., Kherwar of Chotanagpur. The story also speaks of their traditional association with the jungles.

The manner in which the term *hor* is used in contrast to other human groups indicates that it is primarily a category of human beings – the category *hor* is meant for 'we', and *diku*, for 'they'. It is found that some of the Birhors can specify 23-24 different ethnic groups within the broad category of *diku*. All these ethnic groups are referred to in terms of their occupations. Some of them are also reckoned in terms of their place of concentration or peculiar idiosyncratic personality or habit. The Birhors use the term *horhon* for Mundas, Santhals and other Mundari tribes. By this the implication is that they are not *hor*, but people like *hor* or very close to *hor*. They are not 'we' but like 'ourselves'.

The Birhors of Orissa do not have clear conceptual categories distinguishing man from not-man. But a distinction between man and not-man becomes apparent in the way and the manner in which they confront the various natural phenomena in the context of their life-situations. The assumptions are mostly unstated, and may be grasped through an inductive analysis of their practices, and by asking the respondents about the meaning of their behaviour in the context. The Birhors, however, consider every natural phenomenon and object in the universe having a life (*jiu*) which is created by Sing Bonga. They do not view man and nature as separate. Life is the common factor commenting the relationship between man and other phenomena and objects in nature.

S.C. Roy (1925) narrated a story of creation of man and earth prevalent among the Birhors of Bihar. The story is very similar to the one found among the Santhals.

> In the beginning all was water. There was only one lotus (*salki*) plant with its head above the waters. Sing Bonga or the Supreme deity was then in the nether regions (*patal*). He came up and sat on the lotus flower. He commanded the tortoise (*horo*) to fetch some clay from the bottom of the ocean. But it failed.

> Sing Bonga then told the crab (*karkom*) to bring up some clay. It too failed. He then ordered the leech (*lendad*). The leech dived into the ocean and devoured its fill of clay. Coming up to Sing Bonga the leech vomitted out the clay into the hands of Sing Bonga. Sing Bonga then pressed it between its hands and threw bits of clay in each of the four directions of the ocean. Instantly there arose land mass on the surface of the water, and thus developed the earth. Sing Bonga then levelled the moist and uneven earth by means of *mer*. In the course of levelling, earth came to be heaped up at places which became the hills and mountains.
>
> Sing Bonga scattered seeds on the moist earth from which sprang up various kinds of trees all around. The winged-horse known as Pankhraj was then created by the supreme deity. After that Sing Bonga created a figure of a man out of clay, and left it to dry. But Pankhraj trampled it under its feet at night. Sing Bonga then created a dog and another figure of man that were left to dry with their faces turned towards the direction from which the wind was blowing. By evening the clay figure of the dog dried up. As the wind entered its nostrils it became endowed with life. The dog then guarded the figure of the man from the horse. When the clay figure of the man dried, Sing Bonga endowed it with life (*jiu*) by blowing wind into its nostrils.

In this story there is the concept of primeval ocean from which life came forth. There is a preponderance of watery substances in the process of conception and birth in the animal kingdom. Water is viewed as a fertilizing agent. Seeds and bulbs and eggs of insects are lifeless in soil until thers is rain.

Life is often equated with wind force. In the story, the clay (*hasa*) figure of the dog becomes endowed with life when the natural wind (*hoyo*) enters its nostrils. So, also is the case of the figure of human being that was given life by Sing Bonga by blowing wind into its nostrils. The earth not only sustains lives but forms the very constitution of man and other creatures in nature. That *hasa* (clay) constitutes the *hormo* (body) of human being, and the *hoyo* (wind), the (*jiu*) (life) is often verbalized by the people.

With these perceptions of some of the basic elements of life and nature, the Birhors also have a notion of the life-process. Though they consider SingBonga and Dharti Mai as the creator and the protector of lives on earth, they are aware of the natural biological process of physical union between a male and a female in the procreation of an organism. Male sex is called *sanre* and female, *enga*. In their traditional method of fire-making they use two sticks – one, called *sanre*, used perpendicularly, and, the other, *enga*, used horizontally on the ground. Fire is produced when the male stick is drilled into the groove of a female stick. It is to be noted continuous wind is to be blown with the mouth on the meeting point of the sticks during the process of drilling for making a fire.

Fire is called *singel,* that has also life and death. On occasions of *thathi* ceremony after a birth and *hoyon* ceremony after a death, the old fire is ceremonially extinguished and a new fire is lit. On occasions when animal sacrifices are made in a Birhor family two fire-sticks or *guglus* are lent out as the belief that it might bring misfortune or even death to its members. The Birhors believe that by slaughtering animals, they give their *jiu* to their deities. So, fire which is sacred and forms an integral part of life should not be parted off during an animal sacrifice.

The birth of a child is regarded as the creation of a new *jiu* (soul). They say that Sing Bonga is always creating new *jiu* and sending them to earth. Once a soul is created by Sing Bonga its gets entangled into the cyclic order of the life process. The sun or Sing Bonga is the ultimate source of life. It creates the *jiu*, hardens the *hormo* and also protects them. In their perceptions there is an implicit assumption that sunrise and sunset symbolize the phenomena of life and death. It is observed that the Birhors bury their dead with the faces turned in the direction of the east.

Death, to the Birhor, is an important stage of life when some perceptible change occurs in one's life and physical activities. Though the nature of death among the Birhors decides their fate in after-life, they do not believe in a complete cessation of life. It is a phenomenon of transition and is often termed as *gach enaia*, i.e., to die, to depart, or to go out of sight. There is a continuity between the worlds of the living and the supernatural, and death mediates the two.

Conclusion

It is evident that the Birhors perceive many more visible and invisible things in the natural and supernatural domains than described in the preceeding pages, and maintain a kind of intimate relation with them. Though they seem to have some empirical knowledge about the utility of many plants and jungles, and are aware of the regular courses of many natural phenomena, they do not think that they can control and regulate them. They think that the ultimate power lies with the presiding supernatural deities with whom they need to maintain a ritual relationship. There is a significant relation between the human world of the Birhors and the natural and the supernatural universe they conceive of.

It is observed that the elements and objects the Birhors encounter within their life-situations or inherit from their ancestors through myths, stories and legends, form an integral part of their oral cultural tradition. All these elements are, in a way, within the limits of their own space and time that are concrete and not abstract notions. *Disum* is the centre of their moral life. Their divisions of a year are correlated with the perceptible natural phenomena of cold, heat and rain. Days and nights are directly related to the positions of the sun in the sky. Earth and wind are considered to be the basic elements of the constitution of man and other animals. Water, specially its moistening nature, is also thought to be an essential element in the development process of life and organism on earth. Heat, emanating specifically from the sun, is considered essential for the hardening of the constitution of the human body that is made up of soft clay, and there is reflection of such a notion in their myth of creation.

The sky is the place of Sing Bonga or the sun. The other world that the Birhors perceive is on the other side of the sky and is somewhat similar to theirs.

Sex, colour, and sometimes, shape, habitat, personality and temperament are used by the Birhors as criteria for classification of objects and elements and for the grasping of their social relations. There is no distinction between animate and inanimate things, and the entire universe is endowed with life. Their Supreme Deity is not an abstract concept. He comes out of primeval ocean, and is entangled in the cyclic order of the life-process of birth and death. Like the Birhor he also needs a female partner. The perception and classification of the objects and phenomena of their universe revolve round the axis of their self and society.

References

Adhikary, Ashim Kumar, 1984, *Society and World View of the Birhor*, Calcutta, Anthropological Survey of India.

Durkheim, Emile and M. Mauss, 1963, *Primitive Classification*, London, Cohen & West (English edition).

Roy, S.C., 1925, *The Birhors: A Little-known Jungle Tribe of Chotanagpur,* Ranchi, Man in India Office.

Saraswati, B.N., 1970, *Contributions to the Understanding of Indian Civilization*, Dharwar, Karnataka University.

10

Bhuiyan Primal Elements

Pradeep Mohanty

The presence of key words for the five natural elements forms an intrinsic part of the linguistic repertoire of any cultural group. This is essentially a means to cull together the fundamental and holistic articulation of that group with the multifarious expressions of nature. Language is the culling together of these expressions for communication. It may therefore be permissible to conclude that expressions for the five elements must be found in all languages of the world.

The presence of five elements as part of the worldview is known from time immemorial in the Indian tradition, more particularly in textual-based ones. The occurrence of the five elements in non-textual based traditions, such as tribal traditions, is less known. This chapter traces the presence of the five elements in the tradition of the Bhuiyans of Orissa which form an integral part of their socio-economic and magico-religious lives.

Of the various aboriginal tribes inhabiting the State of Orissa, the Bhuiyans of Keonjhar are anthropologically the most interesting. They are one of the few tribes whose different branches represent various stages of cultural evolution from the more or less primitive cultures of hill or Pauri Bhuiyans to the Hinduized Bhuiyans of the plains. The Bhuiyans are extensively distributed over the States of Bihar, West Bengal, Assam and Orissa, with vastly varying populations.

In Orissa, they are found chiefly in two different stages of cultural development, i.e., the most primitive hill or Pauri Bhuiyans of Keonjhar, Sundergarh and Dhenkanal, and the more advanced Bhuiyans of the plains of Bamara and Gangapur. This chapter is based on the fieldwork carried out among the Pauri Bhuiyans of the Keonjhar district.

The Five Elements

Earth

The word *bhuiyan* seems to have been derived from the Sanskrit term *bhumi* meaning land. Hence the Bhuiyans designate themselves either as the autochthones or owners of the land. They have a legend supporting their association with land. This legend recounts how the Bhuiyans took one of the jars presented to them by the Dharam Devta (sun god) at the time of the creation of the earth and opening the jar how they found it was full of earth. So they treated earth to be their wealth and called themselves Bhuiyans. They thus developed strong ties with the land, which was considered to be the most sacred and revered, more than even the mother. The oath taken in trials is only by touching the earth and it is believed that if one utters falsehoods while holding soil in his hand, he will soon die.

Earth is associated in almost all the Bhuiyan rites, rituals and festivals. Basumata, one of their chief goddesses, is believed to live under the earth. She is the first deity to be worshipped first in all the festivals. Many of the Bhuiyan gods and goddeses are made of terracotta. Every year before the start of shifting cultivation, one of the main components of the Bhuiyan economy, the earth goddess is worshipped with a sacrifice to ensure good crops.

When a Bhuiyan marriage is fixed, at the time of the betrothal ceremony, the bridegroom's close relatives visit the bride's house for a celebration. After the celebration, the bride's parents present a terracotta figurine of the bride to the bridegroom's parents, which symbolizes that they are taking the bride with them. This also means that their relationship will never break as the bride's figurine is made of earth – one of the most revered elements of the Bhuiyan culture.

Fire

The Bhuiyans attitude to fire is one of great reverence. The sacred fire in the village dormitory is never extinguished. It is believed that if the fire is allowed to go out, it may bring disaster on the village. In many villages the dormitory fire is used to light the felled trees for forest clearing. Fire is worshipped at all festivals. It plays a vital role in the Bhuiyan life-cycle of birth, marriage and death.

In every Bhuiyan household a sacred fire is kindled at the time of the establishment of the household. This fire is never used for cooking and other mundane purposes. It is fuelled with certain kinds of wood and is kindled in a special manner – by rubbing the sticks – and is never allowed to burn out. In this fire the householder makes offerings to the gods and the ancestors.

Fire also epitomizes the principle of cosmic order. It is considered fundamental to the whole universe – all that lives has fire in it. Hence fire is regarded as an epitome of the fundamental principle of life which implies an ordered relation of all the things in the universe with one another and with the ultimate source of life.

Water

Water plays a very important role in the magico-religious life of Bhuiyans. In all major festivals, the ancestors are worshipped with water near the river bank. When a child is born he is given a ceremonial bath, and so also after a person dies. Guests and visitors are seen off up to the bank of the river. A person possessed by ghosts or by any evil being is taken to the river bank to relieve him of the evil spirit. This indicates the power of water to eradicate and destroy the evil. The cause of this attribution of power to water lies in the belief that water has a close affinity to these evil. Some evil beings are said to reside in water. It is believed that some real and mythical creatures dwell in water, some of which are good and others bad.

Water is believed to possess the power of anti-evil. This power of water is utilized by the Bhuiyan sorcerers against the evil beings. It is also considered to be one of the mediums for transference of sin or impurity to the enemies, and, accordingly, used for such purposes.

Sky

The Bhuiyans regard Dharam Devta (sun god) to be one of their supreme deities. For the Bhuiyans the sky and the sun are synonymous. It is regarded as a genial creative power which fosters the growth of plants and the development of all that makes for happiness. It is also seen as a fierce destructive power that blasts and consumes all the noxious elements – spiritual or material – that are a menace in the life of humans, animals and plants.

Many Bhuiyans believe that Dharam Devta and Basumata, two of their most important deities, are husband and wife. Almost in every religious ceremony, Dharam Devta is compulsorily saluted, and without this no religious act is regarded as complete. Whenever liquor is taken, a few drops are first poured on the ground with the prayer *Upere Dharam Devta Tale Basumata* as a common incantation expressing reverence to the supreme deities. While taking a vow either the name of the sun god is uttered or a fistful of earth is held. It is believed that nothing can be kept hidden from the sun god who keeps a watch over all beings and so any lie or falsehood in his name is certain to bring trouble to the offender. The sun god and the earth goddess are always viewed as benevolent deities.

Air

The use of the term 'air' in the Bhuiyan culture is confined only to the healing practices. The Bhuiyans have their own indigenous ways of curing diseases. Whenever a person falls sick, he is taken to the *dehuri* (religious head) of the village. The *dehuri*, by the act of blowing air, heals the person from the disease.

Thus the oral tradition plays a crucial role in non-textual based ones, such as tribal traditions. From the above discussion it is clear that the five elements – earth, fire, water, sky and air – form an integral part in the socio-economic and magico-religious lives of the Bhuiyans of Orissa.

11

Primal Elements in the Santhal Musical Texts

Onkar Prasad

In traditional vision, man is a replica of the cosmos. He is constituted of five basic elements — sky, air, fire, water and earth. His life-cycle, mode of thought and pattern of behaviour are all governed by the cosmic laws. This primal vision of man is found to be fully integrated both in textual and oral traditions. While in the textual tradition it has been very systematically and analytically presented, in the oral tradition it remains unexplored. In this chapter, folk songs collected from among the Santhals of Bolpur-Sriniketan in 1991 have been dealt with.

The study centres on some of the basic postulates such as whether the Santhals in their primal thought follow an evolutionary scheme with regard to the basic elements, i.e., sky, air, fire, water, earth,[1] whether the Santhals view themselves as constituted of five or four basic elements and whether the primal elements are referred to in songs connected with cosmogonic practices of the Santhals.

The Santhal Myths

Archer (1974), who made an extensive use of the Santhal sung-poetry to understand the life and culture of the Santhals observes:

> Santhal poetry is Santhal life;
> Santhal life is Santhal poetry
>
> [Archer, 1974: 346]

This observation, showing the embeddedness of the Santhal life in their sung-poetry, suggests that methodologically it would not be wrong if the sung-poetry of the Santhals, connected with cosmology, is studied as evidence of their thought and feeling. It is worth mentioning here that songs dealing with the cosmology cannot be fully understood without some knowledge of the myths behind them (Bowra, 1962).

The two Santhal myths of origin, originally collected by Skrefsrud (1887) in the Santhali dialect and later translated into English by Bodding (1942), are given here.

MYTH 1

Towards the rising of the sun (the east) was the birth of man. At first there was only water, and under the water there was earth. Then Thakur[2] Jiu created the beings that live in water, the crab, the crocodile, the alligator, the raghop boar fish, the sole prawn, the earthworm, the tortoise and others.

Thereupon Thakur said : "Whom shall I now make ? I will make man". Then he decided to make two of earth. He had just finished making the two, and when he was going to give them souls (life) the Day-Horse[3] came down from above, trampled them to pieces and left. Thakur became awfully grieved by this.

Then Thakur said : "I will not make them of earth; I shall make birds". Then he made the two Has Hasil birds[4] pulling (the material) off from his breast. He placed them on his hand; they were looking very beautiful. Thereupon he breathed on them, and they at once became alive and flew upwards. They moved about flying, but as they could not find a place to alight anywhere, they therefore always alighted on Thakur's hand. Then the Day-Horse came down along the gossamer thread to drink water. When he was drinking water he spilt some froth of his mouth and left. It floated on the water; thereby foam was formed on the water.

Thakur then said to the two birds: "Do alight on the froth." They did so. When they had alighted they moved about over the whole sea, the froth carrying them along like a boat. Then they implored Thakur : "We are moving about, that is so, but we do not find any food."

Then Thakur Jiu called the alligator; he came; and the alligator said to Thakur: "Why did you call me Thakur?" Thakur said to him: "Would you be willing to bring up earth?" The alligator answered him: "If you tell me to do so, I might bring it up." Then having gone down in the water he went on working, bringing up earth; but all was dissolved.

Thereupon Thakur called the prawn. He came. Having come he said to Thakur: "Why did you call me, Thakur?" Thakur said to him: "Would you be willing to bring up earth?" The prawn answered him: "If you tell me to do so, I might bring it up." Then he went down in the water; having gone down he went on working, bringing it up in his claws; all the earth was dissolved.

Thereupon Thakur called the raghop boar fish.[5] He came. Having come he said to Thakur: "Why did you call me, Thakur?" Thakur said to him: "Would you be willing to bring up earth?" The raghop boar fish answered him: "If you tell me to do so, I might bring it up." Then having gone down in the water he bit (the earth); he was bringing some of it in his mouth and some on his back; all the earth was dissolved. Since that time the boar fish have no scales on their body.

Thereupon Thakur called the stone-crab. He came. Having come he said to Thakur: "Why have you called me, Thakur?" Thakur said to him: "Would you be willing to bring up earth?" The crab answered Thakur: "If you tell me to do so, I might bring it up." Then having gone down in the water he went on working, bringing it up in his claws; all the earth was dissolved.

Thereupon Thakur called the earthworm. He came. Having come he said to Thakur: "Why did you call me Thakur?" Thakur said to him: "Would you be willing to bring up earth?" The earthworm answered Thakur: "If you tell me to do so, I might bring it up, provided the tortoise stands on the water."

Thereupon Thakur called the tortoise. He came. Having come he said to Thakur: "Why have you called me, Thakur?" Thakur said to him: "No one is able to bring the earth up. The earthworm has promised to bring it up, provided you will stand on the water." The tortoise answered Thakur: "If you tell me to do so, I might stand." Then he stood on the water.

When he had taken his stand, there Thakur chained his four legs in the four directions. The tortoise became immovably quiet on the water. Then the earthworm went down to bring up the earth; he reached the earth. Now he had put his tail on the back of the tortoise and with his mouth down below he began eating earth, and this he brought out on the back of the tortoise. Then it was spread out and fixed like a hard film. He continued to bring up earth; he brought up enough for the whole earth.[6] Then he stopped.

Thereupon Thakur caused the earth to be harrowed level. By continual harrowing some was heaped up on the implements; these became mountains. Then, when the earth had been brought up and levelled, the foam that was floating on the surface of the water stuck to the earth, and as Thakur sowed *sirom* seed[7] on this foam the *sirom* plant sprang up first (before all other plants). After this he let the *dhubi* grass[8] be sown and then next to come up was the *karam* tree,[9] thereupon the *tope sarjom*, the *labar atnak*, the *ladea matkom*,[10] and after this all kinds of vegetation. The earth became firm. In all places where there was water, there he let sods be put, and in all places where water was bubbling up, there he let it be closed up by pressing pieces of rock down on it.

Thereupon, having made a nest in a clump of the *sirom* plants, the two birds laid two eggs. The female bird sat on the eggs, and the male bird looked for and brought food. Continuing in this way they hatched the eggs : "O mother! Two human beings were born – one boy and one girl". Then both of them sang :

O dear dear, on the sea,
O dear dear, these two human beings,
O dear dear, have been brought into the world,
O dear dear, these two human beings,
O dear dear, where are they to be put?
O dear dear, you two please tell him,
O dear dear, the great Thakur Jiu,
O dear dear, the two have been brought into the world,
O dear dear, these two human beings,
O dear dear, where are they to be put?

So they implored Thakur saying: "How shall we two support these two human beings?" Thakur gave them some cotton and said to them: "Whatever you two eat, press the juice out of these things and make a place on the cotton wet therewith, and put this into their mouths to suck." By sucking and getting food in this way they grew and commenced to walk. But as they were growing the anxiety of the two birds increased. Where to put the two when they grew up?

So they besought Thakur, and he said to them: "Do fly round and find for us a place for them to stay. Then they flew towards the setting of the sun; they discovered Hihiri Pipiri. Having returned they told Thakur of this. He said to them: "Do take them there." Then they took them along carrying them on their backs. They put them down and left them there. What became of Has Hasil, this the ancestors of old have not told us; therefore we do not know.

The names of these two human beings were Haram and Ayo.[11] Some people call them Pilcu Haram and Pilcu Budhi.[12]

MYTH 2

The sons of man (i.e., the Santhals) say, it is told, that at first this earth did not exist; it was sea, and it was dark; but the spirit of Isor (god) was flying round over the water, and Isor was alone. (The expressions used show that the narrator must have been in contact with Christians.) From heaven above, it is told, Isor came down along the gossamer thread to bathe; having bathed he again passed along the same gossamer thread upwards to heaven. It is told that Isor or Chando (the sun) has no parents; and when the sun rises we call this to be born, and about the setting of the sun we say: "Now he has entered the body of his mother; but the parents of Chando or Isor are *sarag* (heaven) and *patal* (nether world)." As he was coming down and passing up one day, some thought came to his mind; he had just put his clothes down and had had his bath. Then he created those that stay with him; he created Jolmae rani (the water-mother queen), Kalibhanj rani, Bintoria rani, Jhimoli rani (the earthworm queen) and several others that stay with him. Thereupon he created the five – the six – Jaher era (the lady of the sacred grove), Gossae era (the goddess of the sacred grove), thereupon Maran buru and Mahadeb to stay with him.

When he afterwards came down to bathe and was sitting there rubbing himself, he rubbed out who knows how much dirt from his collar-bone; he was pressing this with his fingers and of this he made two very beautiful birds and put them down near his clothes. When he had bathed he brought up with him a little water in the hollow of his hands and was sprinkling this on his clothes; some water spattered on the two birds and this became their gift of life. They at once flew upwards. And, it is told, as he saw that they were very beautiful, he sang (in corrupt Bihari):

> The Has Hasil birds are flapping their wings,
> Up to heaven, father, they went,
> In the heavens they are strangely flying round.

And, it is told, because he has also told us of this wonder, we sprinkle flour-water (refers to part of the ceremonies at the name-giving festival), and after this the midwife tells us the race and *sept* or country. When the two birds became tired of constantly flying, from high up they caught sight of Mahadeb floating on the water; then flying down they alighted on him, because they did not find any other place to alight on. Everyday they alighted on him, and by constantly doing this they worried him, and by letting droppings fall on him they covered him with filth.

Then Mahadeb thought: "Why did you Thakur Jiu, make these two birds? Look here, by constantly alighting on me they have been troubling me, and by dropping dirt they have also covered me with filth. I shall, at once tell Thakur Jiu this." He did so and said this to him. When Thakur Jiu heard this he said to Mahadeb: "Wait, let them alight for a while and also let them drop filth; we shall first have a talk about these two." Then he called together those he had created first and told them all about the two birds. He said to them: "Well, I have made these two birds, where shall we place them? For we have no place for them to stay." They then said: "To give these two a place to stay we shall bring up earth." And they said: "Well, whom shall we get hold of to bring up earth?" Again they said: "Who is master of the water?" They said: "Raghu boar." (the same as raghop boar); they asked him and sent Maran buru to fetch him. Here they sing to a buan melody :

> O dear, dear, do go to him,
> O dear, dear to Raghu boar.
> O dear, dear, he will bring up the earth.
> O dear, dear, he will make the earth appear,
> O dear, dear, he will bring up the earth.

Then Maran buru called and brought Raghu boar. They asked him: "How is it, are you master of the water?" He answered: "Yes, I am." They asked him: "Would you be willing to bring up the earth?" He said: "Yes, because if you tell me to do so, I might bring it up." Then, it is told, they decked him up like he was at first; when they had done this, he became very glad and started singing to a *sohrae* melody.

> Father, deck me out, Father, give me a cloth round loins;
> Father, like the large prawn. Father, let me become grand.

Then, it is told, the boar at once with a great display entered the water; who knows how far away the earth was, he went along and reached there and took some earth on his back. When he was carrying it up, all the earth was dissolved and flowed away. He brought only some *dal* (*Panicum stagninum*): this they kept. They said to him: "You were unable to bring up the earth." He answered: "Quite so, Father, it has not been done through me." Then they asked him: "Who is, beside you, a master of the water?" He answered: "The master of the water is the sole icak'." (a name for the large prawn). Then they sent Maran buru to fetch him. Here follows a song like the first to a *buan* melody, only with sole icak' for Raghu boar.

The prawn was brought, and now follow the same questions and answers. They then said to him: "Come then, give up your head." For some reason or other they asked for and kept his head. The prawn entered the water, reached the earth, used his two claws, and took earth on his back; but it was all dissolved and flowed away; but in one claw he brought along the roots of the *dhubi* grass and in the other claw the roots of *sirom*. This they also kept. They asked the prawn: "Above you who is master of the water?" He answered: "Above me is Dato kuar master of the water." (Dato kuar, the crab prince, is another name for dhiri katkom and heard in Karam binti). They did not give the prawn his head back; therefore prawns have no heads even now-a-days.

Maran buru was asked to fetch the crab, and here follow the same questions and answers, and the same result. In one claw the crab brought the root of the *karam* tree, in the other claw the root of the lotus. They also asked for and kept his head; therefore crabs have no heads even now-a-days. They asked him who was master of the water above him, and he named Kachim kuar (the tortoise prince).

Maran buru was sent and fetched him. (They sing the same as previously, only with Kachim kuar as the name.) When they asked him whether he would bring the earth up he answered: "No. Father, I shall perhaps not be able to bring it up; but if somebody will bring it up I might keep it." Then they asked him who was master of the water above him, and he answered that it was Jhimoli. Maran buru was sent to fetch her. (Again they sing the same song with Jhimoli named.)

When Maran buru had brought Jhimoli rani (the earthworm queen), and they asked her whether she would bring the earth up, she answered: "Yes, I might bring it up, but who would keep it?" They said to her: " We have got a person who will keep it." Then these two took counsel together, and Jhimoli said: "When I bring it up perhaps enemies will eat me?" They arrange to prevent this; they made the stem of the lotus hollow and made her enter into this; they made Kachim kuar lie on his stomach on the water of the sea and placed the posterior of Jhimoli on the back of the tortoise. Jhimoli commenced to eat down in the water and was punging excrements on the back of the tortoise. She punged a tremendous heap. Then when Kachim kuar became tired of lying on his stomach, he suddenly moved, and all the earth was dissolved and flowed away. Then they said: "Oh, oh, the earth was brought up, but as the tortoise did not remain standing, it was lost." And they said: "Let us chain him." Then, it is told Chando from somewhere brought a chain; they fixed an iron post and chained his four legs. The Tortoise then said: "Don't chain all my four legs; let me have one leg free, so that I may scratch myself with it. They therefore let one leg be free." It is told, when Kachim kuar sometimes scratches himself, the earth is moved. They tethered the Tortoise to the iron post, and as the Earthworm again ate earth she punged excrements on the back of the Tortoise, and this time the earth remained there.

When the earth had been brought up, they yoked the bull and the cock together to level it. They harrowed its level, and where here and there rubbish remained, these places became mountains or hills.

In the earth which was brought up they sowed grass and planted the root of the *karam* tree, and they arranged a garden to plant different things, fruits of all kinds and trees. Among all the trees the *karam* at once became very high, and when the Has Hasil birds saw this they left Mahadeb, flew to the *karam* and alighted there. They found their food in pools, but came to the *karam* to rest.

As time passed they had intercourse with each other and found a clump of *sirom* grass to lay their eggs. Having made their nest in the clump of the *sirom* grass they got two eggs. As they were sitting on these they became fecundated, and a voice was heard from their inside. Being frightened by this the two birds left sitting on the eggs. Maran *down* 10 buru then said to them: "As you know, I saw that you had laid eggs there; why are you not sitting on them?" They told him: "We were sitting on the eggs; but there is a kind of sound in them; fearing this we are not sitting." Maran *down* 10 buru then said: "Well then, come along, we shall hear whether you are telling me the truth or not." Then they all went there and listened. The voice was like this (a song, *buan* melody):

O dear, dear, in the sea,
O dear, dear, *dal* grass came into existence
O dear, dear, on the *dal* grass.
O dear, dear, *sirom* came into existence;

O dear, dear, on the *sirom,*
O dear, dear, the Has Hasil birds are making a nest

When Maran buru heard this he said to them: "O, don't be afraid of this; sit diligently on the eggs, you two." And by their continued sitting on the eggs two human beings came into existence, and they sing to the same melody:

O dear, dear, with what to support the two
O dear, dear, with what to keep the two?
O dear, dear, with milk to support the two,
O dear, dear, with cream to keep the two.

Maran buru told Chando this, and Chando gave Maran buru milk and said to him: "Do support the two human beings, and take care of them." Then Maran buru was given over to the two, and he supported them, until they grew up. He taught them to work and instructed them. But where the two birds went and what happened to them, we do not know. But where the Has Hasil birds were born, and where they laid eggs, and where the two human beings were born, this place we call Hihiri Pipiri.

These two myths, which differ slightly from one another in their account of cosmogony, are expected to be helpful in understanding the songs under discussion.

It is worth noting again that the usual song-form of describing the matters relating to cosmology is the *karam*[13] but they are also described in other forms of Santhal songs viz: *baha*[14], *dasae*[15], *don*[16], *lagre*[17], *sohrae*[18] etc. However, a study of the latter forms of songs, specially the *don,* would be more meaningful than the former in understanding the way the Santhals perceive the primal elements in different contexts of their ritual practices and also their underlying principle of cosmogony.

The Cosmogonic View

As revealed through a *don* song rendered during marriage, this universe was invisible in the beginning. There was darkness all round and it was foggy everywhere. The universe could be seen only after the sun produced light out of anger.

Song 1

Sedae ma dinre
Jolomoy ma jugre
Candoe tahekana serma cetan
Nutre tahe tahe
Kurha re tahe tahe
Cando aris lena
Aris akan tey marsal keda

Long ago
The sun was above the sea in the sky
The sun became angry
By living in the dark
And by living in the fog
His anger produced light.

As the Santhals believe, in the beginning of creation there were nothing except the sky and the ocean. Whereas the sky had the sun, the moon and the stars, the ocean had some aquatic animals like the earthworm, the turtle, the fish, the crab, etc. When the supreme being wanted to create man, he could not do so. Instead, he created the two celestial birds. But the birds had no place to sit on except on the head of the supreme being. They had found the space below the sky full of water. This belief of the Santhal is reflected through a *don* song rendered at the *manjhithan*[19] on the day of the Karam festival.

Song 2

Dakma cetan re
Serma lata re
Has hasi cerekin
Rak' homorok
Tokarikin aboka
Tokarikin japida
Has hasi cerekin udau langayen
Thakurak bohok rikin aboka
Onde gekin japida
Has hasi cerekin jiwetgeya

Water is above
It is below the sky
The two, the Has and the Hasin weep
Where will they sit ?
Where will they sleep ?
The Has and Hasin are not tired of flying
They will sit on the head of god
They will sleep there
The two, the Has and the Hasin are alive.

In a another *don* song rendered on the occasion, the primeval birds are later described to have been sitting on the white foam floating on the cosmic ocean.

Song 3

Umin maran jolompjre
Dak'ma talare
Pondge photo dombol dombol

Nelkin mese daina
Koyok kin me
Photo cetanre barya cerekin nelok kana

In the middle of water
Of that very vast ocean
The white foam undulates,
See O sister !
Look at the pair of birds
Parching on it.

According to the Santhal myth the white foam referred to in the song is nothing but the froth from the mouth of Sin Sadom (Horse of the Day) on which the birds were told, by the Supreme Being, to alight. It is said that the Sin Sadom would come down to the sea along the gossamer thread to drink water. The belief of the Santhals is expressed through a song rendered in the late evening or at night of the second day of the Sohrae, known as Bongan.[20]

Song 4

Serma khonak sin sadom
Jolamoy tey phedok kan
Nui sona sadom dore
Tokoe ren co ?
Sin cando ren kanae dak
Nui phedok kan
Dak nu katet gecoy
Ruar calak kan

The celestial horse of the day
Descended on the sea from the sky
To whom this horse of gold belongs?
This belongs to the sun
It descends to drink water
It returns after drinking water.

In a *don* song rendered during marriage, the sky is described to be without water and the earth without soil in the beginning. Later, as the Santhals believe, the air lifted the water up into the sky and the earthworm lifted the soil up that, finally, resulted in the formation of the cloud and the earth respectively.

Song 5

Sermare dak banu
Dhartire hasa banu
Sange dharti sajaw banu
Hoe doe rakap keda sermare dak
Lendon hasae rakap ket

Sangi dharti sajaw ena

There was no water in the sky
There was no soil on the earth
Truly the earth was not fully arranged.
The air lifted the water up into the sky
The female earthworm lifted the soil up
Thus, the earth was properly arranged.

When the earth was created, it was not dry but marshy. It became dry only after the air was created by the Bird King. This vision of the Santhals of the physical nature of the world is found in a *don* song rendered at the *manjhithan* on the last day of the Karam festival.

Song 6 *Laha pahil dharti losot ge*
Thol thole tahekan
Cekate dharti rohor ena.
Losot' hawet lagit ponkhiraja
Hoy may benaw ket
Ona hadar hoy tege rohor ena

In the beginning
The earth was marshy
How could the earth become dry?
To make the marshy land dry
The Bird King created the air
With that hard blowing air
It became dry.

In some songs the Santhals express their quest to find the origin of the earth and man. As they believe, the earth was created first by the earthworm with the help of the turtle. Later, their first ancestral couple Pilcu Haram and Pilcu Budhi sprang from the eggs of two celestial birds, a goose and gander. Thus, the Santhals do not consider earth and man to be direct creations of god. If the sky and earth stand for god and nature respectively, then man is on the side of nature and hence a product of the earth or nature (Mahapatra, 1984:61). This belief of the Santhals is revealed through a *Don* song sung just after the Karam festival.

Song 7 *Tokoe jonom dharti*
Tokoe jonom pirthimi
Tokoe jonom dharti
Manewa hor
Horo jonom dharti
Lendet' jonom pirthimi

Has-hasi cere jonom
Manewa hor.

From what did the earth originate ?
From what did the earth originate ?
Form what did man of this earth originate ?
This earth originated from the turtle
The soil originated from the earthworm
A pair of swans gave birth to man.

In a *dasae* song, like man, the cow and the spirit are thought to have originated from the earth itself. In this song the direct role of the Supreme Being in the creation of the terrestrial animal is again being denied. The earth is also believed to be the perennial source of creation not only for living beings but also for non-living beings – the spirits dwelling in the nether world. The song is rendered during *dasae daran* (begging expeditions) of the Dasae festival.

Song 8

QUESTION *Oka redo ho guru ho*
Gaiko janam len guru ho
Gaiko janam len
Toka redo ho cela ho
Bonga upal len cela ho
Bonga upal len

O Preceptor, where did the cows come from ?
O Preceptor, where did the cows come from ?
O Disciple, where did the spirit come from ?
O Disciple, where did the spirit come from ?

ANSWER *Dhiri rarure guru ho*
Gaiko janam len guru ho
Gaiko janam len
Sinje buta re cela ho
Bonga upal len cela ho
Bonga upal len

O Preceptor, the cow has originated from the stony place
O Preceptor, the cow has originated
O Disciple, the spirit has originated from under the *bel* tree
O Disciple, the spirit has originated.

The Santhals believe that world-creation is followed by the world-destruction. The latter is, however, not the ultimate reality, for it leads to the renewal of the world-order. This belief of the Santhals is revealed in a *baha* song rendered on the first day of the Baha celebration. The song refers to the event of the *sengel dak* (fire-rain) that continued for five days and five nights[21] at the instruction of the Supreme Being and was later, according to a myth, followed by the raining of water, which is symbolic of a new birth order resulting from the catastrophe-like fire-rain as mentioned above.

Song 9

More sin more ninda
Sengel dak doe jari leda ho,
Manwa toka redo ben tahekan
Menak menak dhiri dander
Menak menak dhiri kahar do
Ona relin tahekan
Ona relin sunduc tahekan

For five days,
And for five nights
O man, where did you live ?
Where were you hiding ?
We (two) were hiding in a cave
We (two) were hiding in the cave
We (two) were hiding there
We (two) were hiding there.

Primal Elements Constituting the Human Body

In Santhal thought, a human body is considered to be constituted of three fundamental elements of the universe – air, earth and water. But in Santhal songs available to me, only two of them, i.e., air and earth, are described as essentials of human body. Reference to water is made in metaphorical terms, viz., 'water like the spring of life', etc. A *don* song rendered at the time of performing the ritual of Cumaura[22] during marriage illustrates this point.

Song 10

Hasa hormo ho hoe livi
Jian jhardak do chilkau kana
Jivi ban hilok do hasa dhurire mesaw abon
Jian jhardak do mesaw cabak

The body is soil
And life is air
The water of the spring of life overflows.
The day the life goes out
We turn to soil
The water of the spring of life also sinks into the earth.

In another *don* song, water is again referred to in metaphorical terms like the one mentioned earlier. Moreover, of the other two elements — air and earth — air assumes the greatest importance for a human being to survive and is thought to be located in the chest of the human body.

Song 11

Saru sakam dak do saru sakam dak
Nasiak koce tege duru coa
One onaka gecon koram hormo
Hoe ho nundun lenkhan
Hormo hiri coa dharti rege

The water on the *arum* leaf
Drops down with its slight bending
Similarly with the coming of the air
Out of the chest
The body falls upon the earth.

The exigency of air for the survival of organic life is further emphasized in *sohrae* song rendered on the day of Jale[23] when the villagers move from house to house to collect tolls.

Song 12

Hoy hoyte dare bancak
Hoy hoyte horko bancak
Hoy hoy tege daina
Jiwet' menak bon
Hoy gebon ader jonak
Hoy gebon odok ka,
Hoy cabak' khac ge boeha babon tahena

A tree survives with the air
Man survives with the air
O sister, we are alive for the air
We inhale the air,
We exhale the air,
O brother, we will not survive
If the air is exhausted.

Another *don* song categorically refers to earth as one of the constituents of the human body.

Song 13

Serma renan ninda sisir
Cando rakap lenkhan ban tahena
Manwa hasa hormo horo goc lenkhan do
Hasa dharti rege mesaw loa

The night dew of the sky does not exist
With the rising of the sun
Likewise after death,
The earthly body of man
mixes with the earth.

However, if man is like other products of the earth, water is one among the three basic elements that constitutes man. In the following two *don* songs, one rendered after the Erok[24] (sowing festival) at the *manjhithan* and referring to air and water; and another rendered after the Hariar[25] (sprouting festival) and referring to earth and water, the paddy-crop, a product of the earth is considered to be constituted of air, earth and water. Hence this derivation of the Santhals with regard to the paddy-crop may equally stand for man.

Song 14

Wealth, Wealth
Where is your mother ?
Where is your father ?
My mother and father
Are wind and rain
My milk is water trickling.

[Archer 1974 : 22]

Song 15

Wealth, Wealth
O mother wealth
Where was your birth ?
I was born
In the soil
I was born
In the splash of water.

[Archer 1974 : 22]

From the two songs 14 and 15, associated with agricultural rites of the sowing of paddy seeds and transplantation of paddy seedlings, it is revealed that for the work of gestation and germination accomplished by nature, the union of wind and rain and water (sky ?) and earth is inevitable.

In yet another *don* song rendered just before the Erok festival the paddy seed is described to be weeping for its marriage with the earth which is necessary if the earth, which returns to sterility when left to itself, has to be made reproductive. But this is not possible unless the rain from the sky mixes with the earth and makes her wet.

Song 16

The paddy is weeping
The paddy is asking
When will be my wedding ?

When the water of the sky
Drenches the earth
Then will be your wedding.

[Archer 1974 : 22]

It becomes explicit from songs associated with agricultural rites that water is most essential for production. If it does not rain during the rainy season, the peak period for agricultural operation or even after it is over, it would mean a lack of cooperation between the sky and the earth and would result in hunger for all. To bring about the union of the sky and the earth the Santhals observe a cosmogonic practice – the marriage of frogs called Rote Bapla. It is believed that this act of ritual mimesis will bring rain. This occasion is marked with the singing performance of *lagre* music and dance.

Song 17

In the sky the clouds rumble
O god, on the earth dust flies.
O god, the ears of the corn dry up
The hearts of men are breaking
O god!

The song indicates that the union or marriage between the sky and the earth is possible only through the mediating function of water. This function of water is further observed in the context of marriage specially when the rite of *sindaradan* (act of affixing vermilion to the bride) is observed. In song 19 the mediating function of water between the groom and the bride – the male and the female – can be clearly marked.

Song 18

More goten ul sakam,
Mimit' lota dak
Chitkaw amkan com banco,
Hordom bondi yidin jonom jonom

Five Mango leaves,
And a pot of water,
I do not know
If you really sprinkled water over me
I do not know
If you really wetted me or not
But you made me a prisoner
For entire life.

The Analysis

In this chapter I have been trying to give an overview of the Santhal vision of their phenomenal world of unseen and seen nature. The sources have been Santhal songs presented in different contexts of their ritualistic observances. It is observed that some songs, having a dimension outside the present, give an insight into the unseen reality of primeval time. In some songs, for example, it is told that in the beginning there was darkness all around and thus nothing was visible (Song 1), everywhere there was water below the sky and above the earth (Song 2), there was no soil on the earth and the earth was not fully arranged (Song 5), the earth was marshy (Song 6), etc. All these perceptions of the Santhals about the primeval time refer to the beginning of the world with abstract principle[26] such as chaos and asymmetry.

Further, as revealed through some Santhal songs, the sky, water and soil had their existence before the terrestrial space was created by the earthworm (Song 3 and 7), air was created by the Bird King to dry up the terrestrial space which was marshy in the beginning (Song 6). Man was born when the earth became inhabitable (Song 7), and god rained fire for five (or seven) days when the descendants of the primordial couple were not living in concordance with the laws of the cosmos (Song 9). All these perceptions of the Santhals relating to evolutionary cosmology help in establishing the following chronology of earthly creation.

(i) creation of the sky (*serma*), the cosmic ocean or water (*dak*) and earth (*hasa*)
(ii) creation of the aquatic animals including birds[27]
(iii) creation of land
(iv) creation of air (*hoe*)
(v) creation of trees and plants
(vi) creation of man, and
(vii) creation of fire (*sengel*)

As it appears in the process of dealing with the evolutionary cosmology through their songs and myths the Santhals follow a specific scheme.

It is also observed that the Santhals relate themselves to the basic elements which are thought to constitute the universe. In their vision a human body is constituted of the three basic elements – air, earth and water. But in songs available to me it is described to be composed of mainly two basic elements – air and earth (Songs 10, 11, 12 and 13). In these songs the entire body is said to be constituted of *hasa* (soil). *Hoe* (air) that makes the body move is said to be located in the chest. Reference to water, the third element, is made in metaphorical term. Life is viewed like the flowing water of a spring. But if the implicit statement of the Santhals made through the origin myth – that man is a product of nature – be accepted and if an analogy be drawn between man and other products of nature specially the plants (thought to be constituted of air, earth and water), then the same is equally valid for man and justifies indirectly the perception based on their inductive experience.

Further, from the study of some *don* songs associated with agricultural practices of sowing the paddy seeds and transplantation of paddy-seedlings it is clear that the Santhals visualize a relationship among the cosmic elements analogous to male-female paradigm. This perception is clearly marked in the dramatic enactment of the marriage of frogs held to draw sympathy of the cosmos through the union of the sky and the earth. But the dichotomy like air-water (Song 14), seed-earth (Song 16), sky-earth (Songs 18), male-female (Song 14), dry-wet (Song 16) etc., has, by principle of cosmogony, to be negated through the union of contraries[28] for the return of fertility of the land and/or the woman. But this can be achieved only through the mediating function of water that brings together the sky and the earth, the male and the female, etc. Apparently because of this significant function water has assumed the property of sacredness in Santhal culture and is, therefore, considered auspicious in various contexts of rituals like marriage, etc. It is noteworthy that in contrast to water, the fire in the *baha* myth is described as an element of destruction.

It is interesting to observe that majority of the songs that deal with the creation and the body element are *don* songs of the marriage. This seems to be natural because the marriage-ritual symbolizes union of contraries without which any creation or recreation is impossible. Moreover, as observed by Mahapatra (1986), marriage is the occasion on which the Santhal song of cosmology is recited. The entire song is meant to put the occasion in a wider, universal context of society and tradition. Marriage as an institution, as he adds further, is referred to the beginning of human creation and the particular occasion of the marriage is sought to be viewed in the larger context of the creation of the world, the dawn of human civilization, the emergence of the Santhal community and its migration in historical times (Mahapatra 1986 : 146).

Besides, on its own, the *don* is rendered on many other occasions like the Karam, the Erok, etc., the *karam* is a usual song-form to deal with the history of world-creation. But the purpose of singing *don* after the recitation of the *karam* is to convey the message that creation is not a process of automation but must be preceded by the union of opposites. Erok is a celebration of sowing the paddy seeds, of introducing them into the womb of the earth. The rendering of *don* on this occasion does symbolize or mean a celebration of the union of the seed and the earth (Song 15).

Finally, a *baha* song referring to the continuous fall of fire symbolizes destruction, but only a part of the truth presented in the song. The destruction is not final. In the *baha* myth, of which this song forms a part, it is said that the fire-rain is followed by the fall of water to restore the world-order. Thus it may be said that the Santhals, in their thought, follow a basal principle of cosmic order, viz., creation, destruction and recreation.

Notes

1. In Santhali, sky, air, earth, water and fire are called *serma, hoe, hasa, dak* and *sengel* respectively.
2. Lit., 'the lord'.
3. The Sin Sadom is mentioned here. The Santhals connect the name with the sun.
4. Has is the Hindi name of goose or swan; Hasil is the female. Other Munda people have a similar story; the Mundas have only one egg, from which both the first human beings came.
5. The Santhals know a fish called so; this is the *Silurus glavis*. I do not know the English name.
6. The foreign influence in the story seems to be evident.
7. *Sirom* is *Andropogon muricatus.*
8. The *dhubi* grass is *Cynodon dactylon.*
9. *Adina cordifolia*, Hook.
10. *Sarjom* is *Shorea robusta*, Gaertn.; the prefix *tope* is used in the meaning of 'cut off', or 'short'; *atnak* is *Terminalia tomentosa*, W. & A.; *labar* means "highly coloured". *Matkom* is *Bassia latifolia*; *ladea* means 'crooked' or 'bent'.
11. *Haram* is the common word for an old or elderly man; *ayo* means 'mother', a word borrowed from an Aryan language.
12. Pilcu Haram and Pilcu Budhi are the common designations of the first parents. *Haram* is the common word for an elderly man; *budhi* is the common word for an elder, especially married woman, it is an Aryan word; *pilcu* means small or tiny.
13. It is known after the festival is held in the name of a sacred tree, the *karam* (*Adina cordifolia*). The festival is organized by an individual Santhal with the object of bringing prosperity and pleasure in life. A specialist known as *karam-guru* is invited to recite the songs of *karam* on the occasion that deal with the history of world from creation and through ages according to Santhal tradition.
14. This form of song is named after the flower-festival, the Baha, that is organized in the month of Chait (February-March) to celebrate the beginning of the Santhali year.
15. It is named after the festival Dasae, celebrated in the month of Asin (September-October), when the Santhal boys have completed their course in medicine.
16. It is known after a dance performed during the marriage ceremony, the *bapla.*
17. It is rendered specially on the eve of the Corok *puja* (hook-swinging festival), but can also be sung on other festive occasions.
18. It is known after the festival Sohrae, held when the harvest is over in the month of Paus (December-January).
19. It is a sacred place in a village street erected in honour of the spirits of the predecessors of the village headman. The place consists of a raised mud-platform at the centre of which is a post with a stone at its base.
20. It is the second day of the Sohrae festival on which every head of the household offers sacrifices to *abge* (sub-clan spirit), *hapramko* (ancestral spirits) and *orak bongas* (household spirits) once a year to ensure their continuing protection.
21. In a different *baha* song instead of five days and five nights, god is said to have rained fire for seven days and seven nights.
22. It is a rite performed by the bride's mother during the marriage before the new husband and

wife enter the house. At the door, the bride's mother waves the winnowing fan three times over the heads of the couple scattering the articles such as *dhubi ghas*, paddy and *adwa caole* behind their backs.

23. It is the fourth day of the Sohrae festival on which the Santhals move from house to house of the village to collect tolls and perform that act of mimicry.
24. It is an agricultural festival which is held in the month of Asar (June-July) before the sowing of the winter paddy. The festival is concluded by singing and dancing in the village-street.
25. It is an agricultural festival which is performed in the month of San (July-August) when the paddy seeds have sprouted new shoots. The festival is held before transplantation of the paddy-seedlings.
26. In philosophy, specially Greek, as L.H. Gray (1971) writes, cosmogonies are divided into three classes: (i) those beginning with a spiritual principle, (ii) those beginning with an abstract principle, and (iii) those beginning with a material principle. Overlapping of these three principles to some extent may be found in any culture.
27. The goose and the gander, to which the Santhals refer in their myth of creation, prefer to live in water most of the time. They seem to be originally aquatic creatures, which were later domesticated by human beings as terrestrial creatures.
28. Union of contraries, as Pierre Bourdieu (1977) writes, does not destroy the opposition (which it presupposes), the reunited contraries are just as much opposed, but now in quite a different way, thereby manifesting the duality of the relationship between them at once antagonistic and complementary, *neikos* and *philia*, which might appear as their own twofold nature if they were conceived outside that relationship.

References

Archer, W.G., 1974. *The Hill of Flutes: Life, Love and Poetry in Tribal India*: New Delhi, S. Chand & Co, (Pvt.) Ltd.

Bodding, P.O., 1942. *Traditions and Institutions of the Santhals.* Oslo Etnografiske Museum, Bulletin 6.

Bourdieu, P., 1977. *Outline of a Theory of Practice*, Richard Nice (trans.). Cambridge University Press.

Bowra, C.M., 1962. *Primitive Song.* London, Weidenfeld & Nicolson.

Chattopadhyay, K.D., 1978. *Tribalism in India.* Delhi, Vikas Publishing House.

Gray, L.H., 1971. "Cosmogony and Cosmology (Introductory)", In *Encyclopaedia of Religion and Ethics*, James Hastings (ed.), vol. 4, pp. 125-26.

Mahapatra, S.S., 1984. "Structural Approach to Santhal Myth", In *Tribal Language and Culture.* Visva-Bharati, Department of Oriya, pp. 55-61.

Mahapatra, S., 1986. *Modernization and Ritual: Identity and Change in Santhal Society.* Calcutta, Oxford University Press.

12

A Santhal Myth
Five Elements

Kanak Mital

This chapter draws upon the IGNCA thesaurus project under the Loka Parampara programme (Appendix). It is the first in-house project of the life-style study of the Santhals of Santhal Parganas and was taken up in 1988. The two dictionaries, in several volumes, on the Santhals by J. Campbell (1953) and P.O. Bodding (1929), form the base of the thesaurus. The beginning of the thesaurus was made from this point and it is webbed around the elements. Taking language through which man expresses himself, the meaning of the Santhali word *banam (aam* or *am* = self, you; *bana* = draw towards) is studied. *Banam* is thus called an instrument which draws the best towards you or yourself; it also communicates its ethos towards the universal phenomenon.

> *gota duniyam banag a boge aah em hatau aa*
> I will search the whole world for the best thing for you.

All love songs are sung accompanied by the *banam*. It is through the *banam*, its sound and rhythm, that the best for the loved ones can be obtained. This aspect comes out clearly in the myth of this musical instrument.

> Once there lived an old couple. They had seven sons and a daughter who was the youngest of all. The sons used to go for hunting and the daughter cooked meals for them. Some time later the couple died. So all their sons and daughter came to a forest to live. There they lived in the same way as they used to live earlier, the sister cooking the meals and looking after the house while the seven brothers went hunting. One day while their sister was cutting *sin arak* (leaf-vegetable), one of her fingers got cut, and the blood of the wound got mixed with the vegetable. She cooked it and served it to her brothers after their return. They found the vegetable delicious. They asked their sister how the

vegetable became so tasty, and found that her blood had got mixed with it. The eldest brother wondered that if her blood could make the food so delicious, how tasty would her flesh be. So he decided to kill her and share her flesh with his brothers.

One day, he found his sister climbing a tall tree. They did not want to lose the chance. They spread thorns around the tree to prevent her from escaping. Then the eldest brother shot her with an arrow. Others followed, except the youngest one who loved his sister deeply. The eldest brother noticed that his youngest brother appeared to be reluctant to participate in what they were doing. So he threatened to kill him if he failed to carry out his command. At last the youngest brother was made to follow the command of his eldest brother. Their sister fell dead. Her body was cut into seven pieces and each brother was given a piece. Everybody ate the piece of the sister's flesh except the youngest one who left the place. He went, with his share, to a pond, and wept bitterly. Seeing this, the fish, the crab and all other creatures in the pond came out and sympathetically asked him the reason for his sorrow. He narrated the whole story to them. After having heard him, they suggested not to eat the flesh of his sister and instead to put it inside the mound of white ants.

After some time, there grew a beautiful guloic tree. It gave beautiful flowers. A melodious sound was heard from the tree. A *jugi* who very often used to come for picking up flowers heard its melodious sound and was astonished. So one day he cut a branch from the tree and constructed a musical instrument, the *dhodro banam*. Since then the Santhals construct the *banam* out of the guloic tree.

[*Santhal Music*, Onkar Prasad, 1985]

The entry point for the preparation of the multi-lingual thesaurus on the Santhals was initiated through this myth of the *banam*. The myth shows the relationship of the group (man/Santhal) and its environment (nature), out of which the instrument was born. The Santhals have a strong belief in the magical powers of this instrument which acts as a medium between themselves and the supernatural, with whose blessing, they claim, they can achieve the impossible. Thus, the myth reflects the whole man-nature relationship. The anatomy of the human being is conceived by the Santhals in the various parts of the instrument and is divided into head, ears, neck, chest and stomach.

The head is always on the top like the space or the sky. Thus, the *bohok* (head) represents space. Neck and chest are connected with respiration. Thus, *hotok* (neck) and *koram* (chest) represent air. The stomach is considered as the fire bag representing hunger, and the womb an organ of discharge. Thus *lac* represents both fire and water. The *banam* as a whole represents body or earth. The string, the most important part of the instrument, unites all parts of the *banam* and interlinks the elements together, representing a whole, i.e., earth. The string is considered as the breadth of the instrument and the body. It is the life-giving force of the instrument and the human body, without which both would be lifeless and dead. Earth, being female, is a symbol of fertility.

Body Parts	Santhali terms	Equivalent elements
head	*bohok*	space/ether
ears	*lutur*	ether
neck	*hotok*	air
chest	*koram*	air
stomach	*lac*	fire
body	*banam*	earth

Banam is considered, by the Santhals, as an extension of their physical self. They look upon it as a living being as is apparent from its morphology. The instrument is used to establish communication with the non-living entities. Considering the *banam* as an embodiment of their self, they hold similar attitude towards other elements of their environment. This attitude towards their ecology forms an integrated part for a peaceful and meaningful coexistence.

An attempt has been made to analyze terms pertaining to one element, i.e., water. It is interesting to note how the community conceives this element, uses it in daily life and has different manifestations attached to it.

Water (*dak*) plays an important role in the life of a Santhal. From the terms available, it is evident that when a child is born, it comes out into the world from water (womb, *lac*). The midwife who helps the delivery is called *dak dudulica* or *dak dula budhi*. By a birth not only the parents but the whole village becomes unclean. Before the purification ceremony, the villagers oil themselves and bathe. A ritual is performed by the midwife by sprinkling water on the gathering. At marriages good omens are judged through water. The main ritual of marriage (*dak bapla*) is performed in water. The whole house and village becomes unclean by death, as it does by birth. The funeral pyre is lit only after the potful of water is broken. Again, as at birth, the purification ceremony is performed by the whole village bathing at the village pond. Drinking of *handi* (rice beer) at each of the above-mentioned occasions are varied. Different drinks are offered at different occasions to the *bongas* (guests). Food prepared at the three major occasions of life are – *neem dak* (at birth), *gur dak* (at marriage) and *sauri dak* (at death).

APPENDIX

Conceptual Plan of Loka Parampara Projects

Indira Gandhi National Centre for the Arts has initiated a number of projects under its programme of life-style studies in its Loka Parampara section. These projects are launched to concretize the conceptual plan of the Centre which encompasses the study and experience of the arts at all levels.

The Centre seeks to adopt a new approach to evolve an alternate model for studying life-styles. Such an approach is based on the premise that life is not fragmented into single dimensions or isolated units, and nor can one model replicate in full a complete picture of the cultural life of a given community. This approach considers culture to be a multi-dimensional system in demarcated or defined space. Such studies aim to draw attention to the inter-dependence of nature and man. Where man is in nature, inter-dependent and inter-related, the ecological balance is mentioned by a consciously-articulated belief of relationships. Thus, the five elements – fire, water, earth, air and ether – though physical necessities, are given a symbolic significance. The natural environment, which comprises of soil (earth, rocks), water resources, flora, fauna and sources of energy (thermo and solar), acquire great significance. Life is punctuated by defining special moments in daily, monthly and annual cycles, where the inter-dependence and inter-relationship are tactfully or explicitly stated. Social structure, kith-kin patterns evolve and the cosmology develops myth which is manifest in a worldview, and insight, vision, knowledge, technology and manual skills are inter-wedded in symbiosis. These multi-disciplinary studies hope to bring out the inter-dependence of man and nature, especially as reflected in what are called the arts. They hope to underpass the intrinsic relationship of life-function and art, and to re-establish the study of rural arts in the socio-cultural context. Naturally, inter-action between levels of society and amongst regions will be logical.

Subsequent steps will be taken to investigate man's view of himself and the understanding of the body system. Preventive and curative indigenous medicinal systems which have evolved and developed drawing largely upon water, vegetation and animal resources of the region, will be studied. Besides this, a body of myths are intrinsic to the system, both as knowledge and therapy, physio(somatic) and psychic. A large number of rites, rituals and shamanistic practices are part of this world, i.e., ethno-medicinal. They are valid from the point of view of physio-psychical efficacy and others which may appear as superstition to outsiders.

The social structure of the group, individual and society have finally to be placed in the framework of time – daily, monthly, annual – computed in terms of the movements of the sun, moon and stars. All human activities are regulated by the movement of these planets in the sky, specially, the physio-biological rhythm of women and the rites and rituals used to punctuate the rhythm. The vegetation, crop-pattern is also regulated by this movement and thus sowing, reaping of particular crops, correspond to the astronomical lunar or solar calendar. The myth-rites and rituals are the uppermost layers of this relationship of body-rhythm, nature-rhythm, cultivation-rhythm and astronomical cycle.

Most collective or domestic rituals, which comprise arts, crafts, regulation of vegetable, animal life, place of pilgrimage, in statis and flux, can be observed along this multiple stave system of body nature, annual crop cultivation (myth, art and crafts) placed in annual cyclic time, measured along equinox of the sun or movement of moon or of other planets. This is universal. The solar and lunar calendar is the most fundamental device of tribal, rural, urban continuum and interaction, even within single communities. In circumscribed time, for that specific duration, all spatial and level hierarchies are broken and equalization or reversal of roles takes place. Artistic manifestation is intrinsic to this life-style and the punctuation of rhythm through rites and rituals and festivals is common. Space is consecrated or enlarged. Finally, the life-cycle from birth to death, rebirth provides another framework of time where physical and metaphysical, sacred and profane, coalesce and interpenetrate.

This study of man-family and man-society wil bring out the position of individual and community, organization of society as well as acceptance of individual in the collective. Further, the fairs and festivals aim at creating in circumscribed space and time, the experience of cosmic space and time. Its outermost manifestation – verbal, kinetic and aural – is called art and ritual. Inseparable from the above are crafts in a society. Each of them has a utilitarian as well as symbolic function. The form and design are conditional and governed by the worldview, myth and the ritual which each article reflects at given moment. The study of the crafts include natural inorganic and organic resources, life-cycle and its physical/cultural and mythic world. When taken out of this context and alienated the article acquires the status of a pure and decorative art object for museums. Equally important and more fundamental is the transmission of skills of these crafts from one generation to the next. This includes inculcation of skills, identification of raw material, nature of soil, composition (terracotta, clay), rocks, stone, vegetables, trees, bark and metals and minerals, as well as actual making of an object.

Placing man at the centre, the study will attempt to examine his physical, social and cultural parameters in defined space and time. From this will emerge a holistic and comprehensive picture, which will be webbed together with the basic elements – water, fire, air, earth and ether. Graphically, the model may be represented as a cultural sphere with life inside and manifestation outside on the surface. This may be identified both as indicator of life and as a starting point of understanding the webs of cultural areas which may be placed in an orbit of daily, monthly and annual time cycle.

Guidelines

The study of man can be conducted in various ways: by studying him directly, by studying his environment, material and human aspects, and the art forms he creates, and by studying man's conscious awareness through an investigation of his vocabulary.

Language articulates at best the community's perception of the self-consciousness. Thus a beginning will be made to understand this self-consciousness by articulating through the language its vocabulary of the five universal elements — water, fire, air, earth, ether. This methodology will be applied in both circumstances, i.e., relation to the body of man and his natural environment. The corpus or thesaurus of words will provide an insight into the community and man's perception of the world and its relationship with him as a physical and mental being. Conversely, the worldview is reflected in both life and art.

Keeping in mind the general outline of the studies as mentioned, the structure of the pilot projects in the section are given here. All the projects will be studied through six modules. The first four modules will be common to all the projects, while the next two, though same in structure, will be specific to each project.

Module I : Multi-Lingual Bibliographic Module : Preparation of a comprehensive list of primary and secondary source materials related to the project. Acquisition of books, articles, newspaper cuttings, etc., and any other written material on the subject concerning the project.

Module II : Module on Physical Environment : A detailed geological survey of the land, its flora, fauna and climate to be collected from the Imperial Gazetteers and other government records and the latest available data. Indigenous administrative terms to be listed in the context of the above. Various government reports on population to be acquired and scrutinized.

Module III: Cartographical Module : Preparation or acquisition of a list of secondary source, cartographic material related to the project and the region is essential. Collection of maps, atlases, books as cartographic source material for preparation of maps on the area and its environs may be done on the following themes — administrative, relief and drainage, distribution of population, climate (rainfall and temperature), flora and fauna, land use, minerals, soil, migration, distribution of various musical instruments, materials acquired (if any) for manufacture.

The time frame for modules I, II and III will be six months. In the case of module III the time limit may be increased if necessary.

Module IV: Module on the Basic Elements and Life-style : Specimen collection of vocabulary related to the five elements and preparation of a thesaurus of vocabulary related to them, is to be compiled. The vocabulary will be compiled by asking questions in relation to the body, physical environment, climate, plants and animals.

The second part of the module will be the compilation of the same terms and concepts (vocabulary) in relation to life-style, daily routine and special occasions.

The third part will be the collection of words/terms and their metaphorical use in describing the music, musical instruments, dance, drama, clothes, textiles, decorative arts, etc. Secondary sources will be scanned if available and list prepared of the indigenous terms.

Module V: Module Specific to the Project Theme : This module is project-specific and will bring out the specific vocabulary in the community to be studied in relation to grains, vegetation, crops, food, vocation, livelihood, etc. The main aim of this module will be to see how some elements are inter-related to the above-mentioned parameters and the life-cycle of the entire community.

Module VI: Main Theme of the Project and its Various Manifestations (human interaction) : This module is project-specific. Some terms/concepts and the use of words in relation to the main theme of the project along with the gender roles. The time cycle and the seasons will be taken into account in this module.

The time frame for modules IV, V and VI will be six months. Further abstraction of the project will be done after the data have been analyzed and interpretated.

13

Five Elements in Santhal Healing

N. Patnaik

The Santhals believe that as long as the balance between human beings and nature and supernatural beings is maintained there would be harmony, peace, health and happiness in life. It is their belief that any sinful act, incest and infringement of social customs makes anyone who commits such an offence suffer from illness. Otherwise a human being has a natural right to live up to old age in good health and die a natural death.

The evil spirits, whose number is legion in the Santhal world, are enemies of men and bent upon harassing them and eating up their vitality and causing illness and death. There are *bongas* (supernatural beings) and witches in large number in the Santhal habitat and they only know how to make someone unwell but do not know how to make well.

There are priests in every Santhal village to propitiate the deities and there are medicine-men and magicians to neutralize the effects of sorcery, evil eye and witchcraft. The institution of *ojha*-ship and training given on herbal medicine and healing practices is very elaborate and well-established. The *ojha* is a diviner, sooth-sayer, sorcerer, exorcist and magician and an expert in herbal medicine. He knows all the methods of home remedies, like *sekao* (fomentation), *iskir* (massage), *soso* (marking with the juice of marking nut) and *tobak* (marking the affected part with a pointed sickle made red hot). He also knows the divinations of purging the evil spirit out of the body of ailing persons.

The Santhals take preventive and precautionary measures against certain diseases. In the month of January-February (Magha), all men of a village observe sexual abstinence and on a day, fixed earlier, sacrifice a black female kid and a black pullet at the end of the village and bury them there. They also take vows to offer sacrifices to the *bongas* living on the village boundaries the next year, provided they keep good health throughout the year. After the ritual, some medicinal pills, comprising different kinds of medicinal herbs are ground and mixed with *handia* and distributed among the villagers. Then sanctified rice-water is sprinkled in every house by the *ojha*.

They wear different kinds of amulets, on a string, round the neck, waist or elbow. Medicines are kept in a receptacle which is sealed. Another form of amulet contains ancient stone beads. It is used to keep cholera and smallpox away. It is believed that the amulets can save a person from epilepsy, bronchitis and cough, and are often tied on children.

The Santhals rarely suffer from diseases of the teeth. They regularly clean their teeth with a tooth-stick made of *sal* twigs. They do not eat anything and do not drink even water before cleaning their mouth and brushing their teeth with a *datanni* (tooth-stick).

The sanitary habits of the Santhals are remarkable. They like open air and their villages are not congested. The houses are built on fairly high lands and sufficient space is left between the houses. They have very broad streets and the houses are set apart from one another. The houses are put up round a courtyard and all rooms open to the courtyard. No house appears to be crowded. They do not have any windows in their houses. Every house has only one door. Generally they cook their food outside, but have a fire place inside also, where food are cooked during rains and in winter. Since there are no proper outlets the smoke from the oven gets trapped inside the room. The fowls are kept inside the living room at night.

The herbs and ingredients used in medicine are available in the locality. The Santhals can identify many medicinal herbs and are able to use them without consulting the *ojha*. But the *ojha* and other practitioners keep stock of these medicines and supply them to the patients whenever needed. However, the common people have no knowledge of the invocations, incantations, spells and magical formulae which are the prerogative of the *ojha*. Only he knows how and on what occasion such *mantras* and *jharnis* can be used for remedial measures.

As regards the preparation and application of medicine, the following procedures are observed. Some medicines may be given in their natural form. An example of this form is the use of *bael* fruit. Some medicines are soaked in mustard oil or water. Some medicines are boiled and the boiled water is given to the patients. The common procedure for the preparation of medicines is to grind the ingredients on a flat stone and mix it with other ingredients. Medicines are given on empty stomach in the morning, repeated at noon and in the evening. In the case of bone fractures, splints are used in the bandage. The splints are made of cut pieces of *sar* (*Sacecharum Sara*). Medicinal steam-bath is also given as a remedial measure for certain maladies. In certain cases, particularly carries of the teeth, the worms (*tejos* or main god, as the worms are called) are removed.

The administration of medicine takes into account the day it should be done. For the Santhal not all days of the week are auspicious. A fairly large number of remedies are treated on Sunday morning before easing the bowels or attending morning ablutions. Sunday is generally considered to be a good day, and, so, the remedy to be most efficacious is administered on this day.

Not all types of water are suitable for the preparation of medicine. In some preparations, carefully-collected dew is used. To collect the dew, a clean piece of cloth is dragged over the grass in the morning and then squeezed out. Dew, thus collected, is supposed to have a mysterious quality that makes the medicine efficacious. Similar qualities are attributed to hail water. Hailstones are collected in time and kept in a bottle for future use. The vessel used for the preparation of medicine is always a new, unused earthenware pot which is used for preparing and administering the remedy. The earthen vessel is considered to be cleaner than other types of vessels. The girls who help in the preparation of medicines are always unmarried. The precaution is probably more to ensure that the girl has not been exposed to the influence of the *bongas* than with their virginity. It is believed that a married woman could be under the influence of her husband's *bongas*.

Yet another interesting point has something to do with the association of women that a sacrificer, on the night previous to the day of sacrifice, is to be kept away from women. The same restriction is observed before the preparation and administration of medicines to cure barrenness in women.

The Five Elements

The concept of the *pancabhuta* extant among the Santhals are found in the local folk sayings, literatures and oral tradition. A few sayings which convey some ideas of the *pancabhuta*, similar to those mentioned in a funeral hymn derived from the *Rigveda*, are:

> *Hasa Halam Hasare Mitaua*
> The earth-made body will mix with earth.
>
> *Hay jijiban Hayare Mitaua*
> The air-laden life merges in air.
>
> *Nan Halam Tha Sengal Langitha*
> This body is for the fire.

Santhal literature is very rich, but its cataloguing and compilation has not yet been done exhaustively. The literatures are in Hindi, Oriya, Bengali and Roman script. Some of them are in Ol Chiki. The two sources which make a mention of the five elements in the most abstract manner are *Hital*, published by the late Pandit Raghunath Murmu, who invented the Ol Chiki script, and an unpublished manuscript by the late Ram Dayal Majhi.

Pandit Raghunath Murmu's book *Hital* gives an account of the five elements. Stanzas 15 to 21 are quoted below. It is in the Ol Chiki script.

Maranburu Kate Mid Tha Etemte An En Jahirain
Kate Mid Tha Kenya Tem An En

It may be so that you as Maranburu turned left.
It may be so that you as Jahirai turned right.

Serma talare an thatam tarak Janpam En
Hudur ate Bilit Barandu Gurlau Achur En

The force of these rotations met at the mid-sky.
As a result the whirlpool was born with thundrous sound.

Achur Achur Bilid Barandu Khanak Am An En
Sin Bonga Ar Epil Engel chand Dhartiks

As a result a new world was born and
Sun, stars, moons, were also born.

Serma Marsal Enada Aanga Sirij En
Ana Barandu Rege Atha Jatak thab En

They took their respective places in the path of that rotation.
The sky was lighted with the birth of sun.

Elan thale thatam Sin bonga Rem Am Kad
Taa thale thatam Dharati taan rem Am Kad

You generated fire in the sun and you cooled the earth.

Dharati Chetan Sin Yinda Hulan Achur En
Taya Khan Haya, Hasa Dhiri tha Kam Benao En

There came day and night thereafter on earth and
therefore air, soil, stone and water were created.

Dharati Chetan Jiyi Sirij An Adam An Ked
Hansa Hansali Jiyi Dukin Barandu Anaga En

Out of these elements came up life with health and
happiness which living beings (Hansa and Hansuli) enjoyed on earth.

These stanzas indicate that the human body is made up of the five elements which, when balanced and in harmony with one another, bestow well-being on mankind and other living organisms.

Ram Dayal Majhi better known as Dayal Baba, came from Basipitha in the Udala subdivision. He was a Santhal and, according to his people, died at the age of 120 years. His grand-daughter's husband, Sida Hembram of Beguniadiha of Udala subdivision, has a manuscript of Dayal Baba. Some of the extracts from this are given below. These are regarding *halma galahan* (constitution of the body).

1. *Ata Serma Haya Situn*
2. *Jarage Japud San Salam Anan*
3. *Serma Daletem Ajam*
4. *Taker Dalete Halam Am Ana*
5. *Haya Daletam Urum*
6. *Hayad chapu Gun Anan*
7. *Situn Sengal Marsal Anan*
8. *Manmi Halmare Med Anan*
9. *Med Daletem Yenyel Kana*
10. *Jarege japud tha Kana*
11. *Anatege Alam Rasa Anan*
12. *Helem Jaj Jharam Urun (Ma)*
13. *Rasa Alam Urum Gun Ana*
14. *Ata Da Aan Kana*
15. *(tha) Dhare Dhiti Gata Aman Akan*
16. *Ana Dege Manmiya Mun Akan*
17. *Ji Gun Dale Mena Akan*

The literary translation of these lines follows. However, further studies are required for the analysis and explanation of these abstract ideas.

1. Earth, sky (ether), air and brightness (fire).
2. Unceasing rain – all such creations appealing to mind and soothing to body.
3. Space (heaven) enables us to hear.
4. Space created resounding which helps in hearing.
5. Air or wind gives you feeling and realization of things.
6. Air is endowed with the quality of touch.
7. Fire emits light.
8. Man has eyes.
9. Eyesight enables you to see.
10. Rain gives water.
11. The watery substance in tongue is due to rain.
12. Therefore the tongue can taste sweet, sour, hot (chilli).

13. The watery substance of the tongue has the quality of taste.
14. The earth on which living organisms sustain life by air, water, warmth, light (fire), ether and earth is a wonderful place.
15. There is soil (earth), stone and vegetation all round and they help life to grow healthy and contented.
16. The man had nose which has given him smelling sense; and
17. The air all around helps this sense to function.

There are many other such sources – some printed and others as manuscripts. Some of them are in memory of Santhals who had personal contact with the saintly persons, reformed, thinkers and writers. There is an urgent need to locate these, and retrieve them and prepare an annotated and classified bibliography on the subject of the five elements.

14

The Angami Fire and Water

Vibha Joshi

We begin with the assumption that the rationale of a people's activities can be located in their cosmological system. Broadly speaking, cosmology refers to a set of concepts people have about the universe around them. It comprehends their relationship with nature, and the object of this conceptualization is, to quote Durkheim and Mauss (1963: 81), "not to facilitate action, but to advance understanding, to make intelligible the relations which exist between things". People relate to the world outside themselves and transmit and modify the cosmology of previous generations. As auspicious/inauspicious or a pure/impure status may be ascribed to the various entities of the cosmos depending on the type of power – benevolent or malevolent – they are thought to possess and their relative position in the hierarchy. In this context they become instruments for forecasting or divination.

The influence of this cosmic reality on human beings can be understood in relation to the gender assigned to these and the time and space they occupy. The cosmic world is seen in a time-bound framework having a direct relationship with human processes. Thus, cosmology deals with people's conceptual systems – how people organise their views of the cosmos; how reality is ordered; and how they order their relationship with it. A cosmological understanding maps out the indigenous knowledge of the people, and it is in this knowledge that various phenomena are explicated.

This chapter focuses on the concept of fire and water, two of the five basic elements which are thought to constitute man in the Indian Sanskritic textual tradition, among the Angami Nagas of north-eastern India. The five elements – sky, air, fire, water and earth – are basic to life. All cultures in the world have specific terms for these elements and assign certain properties to them. For this chapter, I have chosen two elements fire and water because their effects are easily visible in both positive and negative senses and these find a place in the Angami thought regarding preservation of body.

Let us first look at the way these two elements are dealt with in general thought.

As a vital principle, water allows people to ward off illness and to keep death away. In the *Vedas* water is associated with the origin of medicines, which may be because water makes the plants of pharmacopoeia grow, or because of its intrinsic qualities. In a more positive sense, water is said to give vigour, make old men young and prolong life. Water can be ambiguous, it may fulfil a positive function. It bathes, dissolves and purifies. Essential to human life and necessary for the growth of plants, it symbolizes a generative or life-giving quality very similar to creative power. On the other hand, it can be hostile to man. There are catastrophic rains and floods; people drown in rivers and seas. These may not be taken as simple accidents but as manifestations of evil powers allied with the liquid element (Rudhardt, 1987: 356-58).

Fire with its warmth and light, fulfils a vital requirement of human life. Yet the same element can wreak destruction. Both positive and negative functions are united in fire's role as an instrument of melting, refining, and purifying. In a religious context, fire has come to play a very large role in cult, myth, and symbolic speech. Some elements of fire worship and the use of fire in ritual and in symbolism are rooted in and developed out of practical experiences of human beings.

Methods for maintaining and transporting fire survived from olden times, so it was seldom necessary to kindle fresh fire. Conversely, life and fire were so intimately connected that widespread custom dictated that the household fire be extinguished when someone died. The development of hearths, altars and stoves as well as the collection of fuel of different kinds was influenced by practical and ritual considerations. Fire is widely used in cooking, to keep away dangerous animals, to flush out forest games, to clear forests and to harden implements (e.g., point of spears). In religious rituals basic distinction is made between the purer 'perpetual fire' and the 'new fire' that is kindled with great conscientiousness and awe (Edsman, 1987: 340-46).

In the light of the above, let us see the various ways in which the Angamis perceive the elements of fire and water, the properties that are assigned to these and how they are reflected in their ritual processes. Firstly, let us delineate the use to which these two elements are put in daily life and compare them with their usage in specific rites that are performed during the ritual of Sekrenyi.

A background information on Angamis will help in the understanding of the importance which is given to these two elements.

Angami Nagas are hill people depending basically on cultivation and livestock-rearing. Angamis are one of the only two groups of Nagas out of the seventeen who practice wet rice cultivation on terraces made on the hill slopes. This allows them to cultivate the same plot year after year. They depend, to a very small extent, on slash-

and-burn cultivation. Angamis were traditionally warriors, the Angami men spent majority of their time in warfare with hostile villages and taking heads. Since 1879, when the British succeeded in annexing their territory, the inter-village feuds have come to an end. With the introduction of Christianity in the region several Angamis changed their faith – approximately, 70 per cent have embraced Christianity. Angamis are patrilineal and patriarchal and practice clan exogamy.

The description of the usage of water and fire in the daily lives of the Angamis which follows here, basically relate to their traditional life-style and is taken from J.H. Hutton's (1969) monograph on the Angamis.

No myths or legends associated with fire (*mi*) and water (*zu*) have been recorded among the Angamis. But a notion of bad fire does exist in a neighbouring group, Memi, who consider fire which burns up the house as bad fire. Clean fire is required to start the fire again. This clean fire is either brought from another village or a new fire is kindled from the fire stick (*ibid.*, 341).

The Angamis traditionally built a fireplace with three stones. Before building a new house, the man of the house builds a fireplace. When the construction of the home is complete and only thatching is left, the fire is to be brought from the house of a Kika Kepfuma, that is, a man who has performed the Lesu ritual and has thus earned a higher social status and the right to put horns on his house. If there is no such person in the clan of the house builder then fire is brought from the house of any person none of whose children have died. This fire is taken inside the new house by the owner who wears a ceremonial dress and carries a spear (*ibid.*, 52).

The symbolism is very clear. Fire is brought to carry good luck from the person from whose house it is brought to the new household. In the fireplace only wood is burnt and if possible it is not allowed to go out. If required it could be relit with matchs, it did not necessisate the use of firestick. It was considered a serious offence to put out a man's fire (*ibid.*, 56). Even now, in Angami villages the fire in the hearth is not allowed to go out completely.

Construction of a three-stone hearth also culminated the traditional marriage rituals. On the third day of the marriage the bridegroom sends three stones to form a fireplace through a messenger to his house. On the morning of the fourth day the bride makes the fireplace. On the following day the bride and the groom go to the field and, on their way home, bring a small piece of firewood. This completes the marriage ceremony (*ibid.*, 223).

At childbirth, the mother is kept separate from rest of the household and a separate hearth is built for her in the same room as the general hearth (*ibid.*, 214). This is still practised among the non-Christian Angamis. The building of a separate hearth relates more to the liminality of the status of mother and the polluting effect which the process of giving birth may have on the household hearth.

At the time of an illness, especially an infectious one, fire was burnt in the doorway to ward off the spirit of illness. This act perhaps reflected the destructive aspects of fire – fire that could consume everything, destroy houses, burn *jhum* fields, and destroy the disease-causing spirit.

Angamis know only one way of making fire, through a firestick called *segomi* (*sego* = wood; *mi* = fire). A piece of wood is split at one end, which is slightly notched to keep the thong from slipping. The two parts are kept wedged apart, usually with a stone. A thong of about two feet in length is made from a split bamboo. The shreds whittled from the bamboo, thatch and dry moss or cotton wool are placed in the fork of the stick and beneath it. One foot is placed at the unsplit end of the wood and the thong drawn under the fork in the notch and pulled swiftly to and fro until spark catches in the tinder, a little blowing produces a flame. This way of producing fire is resorted to only during the Sekrenyi ritual and while performing a personal ritual to ward off bad luck. During Sekrenyi omen is also read while making the fire. Fire in this way is made only by men. It is considered a male activity and a firestick is an invariable part of the items that are traditionally buried with the corpse of a man.

Fire is used primarily in three ways by the Angamis, first is the domestic fire used for cooking, second the ritual fire which is lit at a particular occasion, and third, the Angamis use fiire to clear the *jhum* patches. Angamis practice *jhuming* to a very limited extent. Another use of fire is to ward off illness-causing spirits but it is not known whether this tradition still continues.

Let us take a view of the various ways in which water is utilized by the Angamis. Here we can distinguish between the water used for irrigating the rice terraces[1] – which is the principle mode of cultivation and source for subsistance – water used for washing – both ordinary and ritualistic use – and water used in making *zutho* – the traditional rice-beer which was the principal drink.

Water was thought to possess special cleansing properties. During the head-taking days, the warrior who brought a head to the village was required to wash his hands and mouth with water. He was supposed to throw away not only the water used for washing but also all the water found in his house. Only after this was he allowed to eat or drink. On the following day the warrior was required to go to the village spring with a spear and a shield and bathe (*ibid.*, 238-39). Thus any bad luck which the warrior might have come in contact with or the bad luck of the man whose head was brought was washed off ritually.

Somewhat similar procedure was adopted in case of a lasting illness. In such a case a man was supposed to dig where there was no water visible on the surface until he found water (usually near a water spring). This he would fence over. He would then kill an unblemished cock, wash and cook it with this water. He would continue to drink this water till he became well (*ibid.*, 99).

Rice-beer was usually drunk instead of water. While drinking it was a practice to set aside something for the spirit. Either a finger was dipped in the cup and touched to the forehead, or a little of the drink was tipped on to the floor, or both offerings were made. Hutton says that this activity was not connected with any particular deity and perhaps was associated with a man's own *ropfu*, who might be described as combining the characteristics of a familiar, guardian angel, and the notion of a man's individual destiny (*ibid.*, 97-98). This is practised even now and in all probability the offering is made to the guardian spirit (*ropfu*) of the man. The Angami medicine men are often seen offering rice-beer in this fashion to their tutelary spirits.

These are the various ways in which the Angamis utilized fire and water. If we take the positive ritualistic aspects they assigned to the elements fire and water, we find that the cleansing aspect of water and fire are brought out in the one of the most important rituals of the Angamis, Sekrenyi. The festival is not merely a prayer for bodily health but to ensure a healthy functioning of the society.

The term Sekrenyi literally means 'sanctification festival' (*sekre* = sanctification; *nyi* = feast; *thenyi* = festival). The festival takes places after the harvest and falls on the twenty-fifth day of the Angami month Kezei (January-February) and lasts for five to seven days.

The Angamis follow the lunar calendar known as *khruphr* (literally, 'to read the moon'; *khru* = moon; *phr* = to read). The festival date is fixed between the new moon day and the no moon day during the month of Kezie (January-February). The festival is celebrated on different days by the various Angami villages.

Some variations exist in the method of celebration. Certain ceremonies performed by one group of Angamis are absent in the other groups. The description[2] of Sekrenyi which follows is basically the western Angami (Khonoma village) way of celebrating it. I also had an opportunity to witness the southern Angami Sekrenyi celebrations in Kidima and Viswema villages during fieldwork in January 1991. I have included my observations in the description of the festival.

The rituals performed are basically for good health of the men who performed the role of a hunter and a warrior in the traditional system. This notion of good health pertains not just to the physical body of the observer of the ritual, but also the metaphysical one. The Khonoma villagers conceptualize the body as having both physical (*umo*) and metaphysical (*uphu*) aspects.

A week before Sekrenyi rice-beer is prepared by each household. Some of it is kept separately, to be used only by the men during the performance of the ritual on the first day. This rice-beer is not shared with anyone and only the performer of the ritual may consume it. During the festival men remain chaste and do not share the hearth and their meal with women.

Sekrenyi Festival

Two days before the Sekrenyi festival, *themuo keza* and, *kide* rituals (*genna*) are observed.

Themuo keza literally means a dividing of meat (*themuo* = meat; *keza* = to divide). On this day several animals – cows, pigs, dogs – are killed and divided among the members of an household or the families who have contributed to the purchase of the animal.

Kide: On the day of *kide* wooden spoons are made, which are to be used for Sekrenyi cooking, pots are cleaned and oak wood pegs are made for making the ritual fireplace. On this day two cups made of plantain leaves are pinned on the front wall of the house and rice-beer is poured into these. It is probably an offering to the ancestors.

DAY ONE

Uphu Mesa The male members (followers of *kru nanyu*) of the village go down to their respective *khel* wells before the sunrise – as early as 2.30 a.m. to 3 a.m. These wells are cleaned a day before the ritual and no woman is allowed to draw water from them. Near the well, the men wash themselves and their hunting implements.

Mi-Ki literally means 'pulling the fire'. After coming back from the well, a fire is made in the traditional way by the head of the family or the clan, outside of either the joint family house or the clan house. In the lighting of fire it is believed that if the spark is first produced to the right of the stick the year will be a good one for men, and if to the left, for women. From this fire a new fire is kindled in the kitchen hearth, which is to last till next Sekrenyi.

Utho-Phi A cock is strangled by each male member of the household. The position of the legs of the cock at death is observed. If the right leg crosses over the left (*peza ba*) it is a good omen for human health. If the left leg crosses over the right (*pevi ba*) the omen is good for harvest in the coming year. The entrails of the cock thus killed are taken out and predictions are made by the priest. This practice is followed in most western villages and probably the northern villages as well, with the exception of Rusoma, a northern Angami village, where it is the *themu* (traditional medicine man) who inspects the entrails and makes predictions. After this, the liver of the cock is cooked in the Sekrenyi pot. The pot is either purchased especially for this occasion or is kept separately and is used only for Sekrenyi cooking every year. The cooking is done with little rice, ginger and some chilli. Half of the cooked liver is thrown away 'as if given to the enemy', with a curse:

> *A ngumvu miabu hacieha, krie di puomecu puometou si ebiaeie euo*
>
> May you eat this meat, may your body not function properly and when
> I throw the arrow let it pierce through your heart.

After this the men eat a small piece of the cooked liver to reinforce the curse. Rice-beer specially kept for the ritual is drunk in a cup made of plaintain leaf. Before taking a sip the man tips the drink to both left and right side. It is an offering to the spirits (*terhoma*).

Among the southern Angamis it is *misu kizie*, a combination of the western Angami *uphu mesa, miki, utho-phi*, except that an omen is read at the time of making the fire. The bamboo string used for making the fire is broken and the length of the ends are observed. If the left end is longer it is considered a good omen for health in the coming year.

DAY TWO

Thi-Sie An effigy (*thi-sie*) symbolizing game, is put up on a long bamboo pole. The priest shoots the first arrow reciting a prayer for the welfare of the whole village. This is followed by the youth shooting the arrows one after the other. Predictions are made on the basis of the part of the effigy which is hit by the arrow. If the arrow hits the body of the effigy, it foretells good hunting; if it hits the head, it foretells success in war.

Among the Southern Angamis the second day is called *krienyi*. On this day pots, which were used for Sekrenyi cooking, are cleaned after sunset and kept away for the next year.

DAY THREE

On the third day of the festival, young boys and girls go to the jungle to collect wild vegetables. They also collect stems of the *tirhu-the* plant, the pith of which is used for making beads.

Chuti-tho It pertains to making beads of bamboo and *tirhu-the* plant. These beads are used for decoration of the youth houses or *kikremia*.

The southern Angamis call it *nuosotho*. On this day a chicken is killed in the name of the child by its mother, an extension of the birth ritual.

DAY FOUR

Lhie The next day is the day for festivity (*lhie* literally means 'festive'). The youth sing folksongs as well as a special song known as *sokre-sene*, which is sung only during Sekrenyi (as told and observed in Kidima, a southern Angami village).

In Kohima village the youth celebrate *thekra-chi*, i.e., they sing and dance the whole night. In case of a death in the village before the festival date has been announced, the festivities are cut down a little and there is less singing. It is also the last day of *kide* in the southern areas hence it is also called *kide yongu*, after which no more rice-beer is poured into the plaintain cups.

On the fourth or the fifth day of the festival, the traditional dress is worn by the villagers and a grand procession is taken out. The head of the Kruna nanyu ('followers of traditional religion'; *kruna* = ancestor; *nanyu* = religion) gives a call to the villagers from the main *thehuba*. The members of respective *khels* begin the procession and meet at the main *thehuba*, from where a combined procession is taken out. In some villages young women do not take part in the procession while in others they do. After singing and dancing, rice-beer is drunk communally.

On every evening of the festival, bonfires are lit either outside the house of a clan elder or inside the *kikramia*. Around this young men and women sit and sing folksongs. The first day rituals are carried out only by the followers of traditional religion but the later festivities may be joined in by the Christians as well. For the songs and the dances, traditional dress is worn by the youth and procession is taken out in the village. The different *khels* join in at the main *thehuba* (meeting place) and go around in circles singing *sokre-sene*. The processions are led by the priest or the eldest man in the village. In between the dancing, war cries are given out and some enthusiastic folks may perform a little war dance with spears and guns in the centre of the circle. A number of gun shots mark the celebrations on this day.

On the first two days of Sekrenyi, songs are sung almost from morning till late in the evening. As said earlier, these songs (*sokre-sene*) are taboo after the first two days. No work is done in the fields during the first eleven days of the festival. At least work on the first four days is a complete taboo, even the Christians do not go to their fields (as observed in Kidima). The eleventh day is *mekra*, i.e., a community taboo on cutting of meat and going to the fields.

The Sekrenyi ritual is geared towards cleansing of both physical and metaphysical aspects of the body. The cleansing and purifying principles of water and fire combine in this ritual which has for its object the prevention of illness during the coming year.

Performed communally, it aims not only at bodily health but also aims to ensure healthy functioning of the society. As stated earlier, the rituals are carried out only by men who in the traditional Angami system performed the roles of warriors and hunters. The rituals performed have parallels with the rituals that are performed after head-taking and after a lasting illness. The body of the performer is washed and presumably any ill-luck clinging to it is washed away.

It is worth noting that the fire made at the time of Sekrenyi is used for rekindling the family hearth. Thus a clean fire, produced after keeping chaste for duration of the ritual and after cleansing oneself at the village spring, which was kept clean by not allowing the women to pollute it, is used for rekindling the hearth. This hearth fire is meant to last for another year. Thus we see that Sekrenyi also marks the beginning of a new year.

Thus the Angamis assign positive qualities to water and both positive and negative qualities to fire. Water is perceived as having cleansing properties. So in case of prolonged illnesses a special water hole is dug and this water, supposedly clean from all kinds of pollutants is thought to remove the illness-causing agent. A similar idea seems to surround the act of men washing themselves at the village spring during Sekrenyi and after the taking of head. Whether such rituals are performed by the women is not known. Fire, on the other hand, though not capable of cleansing is regarded as an agent of good and bad fortunes. Thus we see that at the time of building a new house fire is brought from the house of a socially recognized person. That is, a person whom good fortune has favoured. Conversely, the same fire which was brought from such a source is relit at the beginning of each year. The fact that extinguishing the hearth of somebody's house is considered a serious offence also confirms the idea that with the extinguishing of fire the good fortune brought by it also dies.

Notes

1. Angamis have a complex system of water distribution. Water from springs is tapped through water channels to irrigate the rice fields.
2. It was narrated to me by three Khonoma villagers, two of them had taken part in the celebrations when they were very young and had not converted of Christianity. The sequences listed below are by no means complete. I was told that it is rather difficult to recall the names of all the rituals that take place unless the details and meanings are asked when the festival is in progress.

References

Durkheim, E. and Mauss, 1963. ***Primitive Classification.*** (trans. R. Needham), London, Free Press.

Edsman, C.M., 1987. 'Fire', ***The Encyclopaedia of Religion,*** vol. 5, ed. by M. Eliade. pp. 340-46. New York, Macmillan Publishing Company.

Hutton, J.H., 1969. ***The Angami Nagas,*** Bombay, Oxford University Press. (first published in 1921 by Macmillan & Co. London).

Rudhardt, J., 1987. 'Water', ***The Encyclopaedia of Religion,*** vol. 15, ed. by M. Eliade, pp. 350-61. New York, Macmillan Publishing Company.

15

Bhutas in Oral Ayurvedic Tradition

V. Verma

The general belief among those influenced by western education is that Ayurveda mainly constitutes innumerable medicinal formulations and information about the natural products to cure ailments and diseases. The more important aspect of Ayurveda is its system of totality and the cosmic view of looking at the human body and its functions. Ayurveda's preventive and curative methods are based upon establishing 'inner' and 'outer' harmony. The importance of medicines described in Ayurveda is secondary as they are subject to change depending on place and time, and their pharmaceutical properties are dependent upon the prevalent environmental conditions. The most important contribution of Ayurveda is its fundamental theory of equilibrium based on the three humours. This tradition continues in many Indian homes even today.

The *bhutas* or the five fundamental elements (ether, air, fire, water and earth) constitute the material reality of the universe including the physical self. They are organized in a variety of forms, shapes and proportions which account for the diversity of our phenomenal world. The cause of life and consciousness, however, is *jiva* (soul), which is without any substance. It is essence or energy. It is a part of the universal soul which is the animating principle of the cosmic substance. The physical body undergoes changes with time and decays, while the *jiva* does not undergo any change and is indestructible. At the time of death, the *jiva* leaves the material body and the five elements constituting the physical form return to their main pool.

All physical and mental functions of the body are governed by three humours – *vata*, *pitta* and *kapha*. These humours are derived from the five elements of which the body and the rest of the universe are constituted. For cosmic balance and harmony, it is essential that the five elements are in equilibrium as their imbalance causes catastrophes. Similarly, for physical and mental health it is essential that the humours are in equilibrium. Their imbalance and derangement (termed vitiation) leads to various disorders. The function of each humour is related to the fundamental element(s) from which it originates. *Vata* is derived from ether and air, and, like these elements, is all pervasive, light, dry, abundant, cold, mobile and rough. It is responsible for the entire body movements and mind activities, blood circulation, respiration, excretion, speech, sensation, touch, hearing, feelings like fear, anxiety, grief, enthusiasm etc., natural urges, formation of foetus, sexual act and retention. *Pitta* is derived from the fire and is hot. It is also characteristic in being sharp, sour, pungent and has a fleshy smell. *Pitta* is responsible for vision, digestion, hunger, thirst, heat regulation, softness, luster, cheerfulness, intellect and sexual vigour. *Kapha* is from water and earth and like these elements, is soft, solid, dull, sweet, heavy, cold, slimy, unctuous and immobile. It constitutes all the solid structure of the body and is responsible for unctuousness, binding, firmness, heaviness, sexual potency, strength, forbearance and restraint.

Since everything in this manifest world is derived from the five basic elements, all have humoral qualities. Nutrition, environment, weather, social and psychological behaviour – all these alter our bodily humours constantly. Varying degrees and intensity of humours determine the basic human constitution.

Longevity and quality of life depends upon two principle factors – *daiva* and *puruskara*. *Daiva* is the result of the deeds or *karma* of the previous lives and *puruskara* is what we achieve in this life. The basic constitution of each person at birth are due to *daiva*. Through one's deeds in the present life, that is *puruskara*, one is capable of improving one's bad health and ruining one's good health. The basic principle of health is to create an equilibrium of the three humours with personal effort and knowledge. It is done by acting according to one's constitution and by living in harmony with weather, climate, nutrition, personal behaviour, social environment, etc. This harmony is created by an appropriate knowledge of one's constitution as well as with the knowledge of one's surroundings. It will be soon clear how all this is related to the five elements.

Warm and dry climate will give rise to *pitta* as these are the characteristics of fire. Cold and humid climate gives rise to *kapha,* and so does living in dark humid rooms with lack of light and sunshine. Hot dry winds will enhance *vata* as these are the characteristics of air. Deserts are *vata-pitta* dominating, whereas mountains are *vata-kapha* dominating. Anger enhances *pitta* whereas fear enhances *vata*. Excess of sleep vitiates *kapha*, lack of sleep increases *vata*. These will make a never-ending list. It can be generally stated that these fundamental facts are reflected in our daily lives, not just in India, but all over the world. This ancient wisdom is also reflected in the languages. The words 'brilliant', 'bright', 'shining', etc., are used to appreciate one's intellectual capacities and power of assimilation. Sexual vigour is universally symbolized with fire. Similarly, the words 'radiant', 'lustrous', 'glowing', 'beaming', etc., are used to describe one's complexion. With subdued *pitta*, even an intelligent person will lack power of assimilation and intellect. A beautiful person in the conventional sense may look unattractive without the luster of *pitta*.

Many of the expressions in English can be traced to the cosmic laws of the *bhutas* and the humours, 'to get cold with fear', 'to get stiff or shiver with fear', 'to get a dry throat or to tremble with certain emotions', 'to be overwhelmed and be unable to speak', etc. All these are *vata*-related emotions and *vata*-related functions.

No phrases can be found for *kapha* as this humour is not related to activities but to binding, firmness, heaviness and inactivity. However, the *kapha*-related effects are well-known. In Western Europe, 'autumn depression' is very frequent. Autumn is cold and humid with often covered sky and lack of sunshine. One is forced to stay indoors. These are *kapha*-promoting factors. *Kapha* is derived from water and earth and vitiation of this humour causes inertness, lassitude and depression. If appropriate measures are not taken, the humour vitiates and one suffers from its negative effects on the body and the mind.

The relationship of *bhutas* and the medicinal practices in India can be traced back from the Vedic period. Prayers were addressed to the god of wind and healing *mantras* were chanted by the *pandit*-cum-*vaidya* at child birth. As mentioned earlier, the formation of the foetus is the function of *vata*. "The way wind and mind move fast, the way birds move around in the sky without any hindrance, similarly, oh ten months old baby, you come out from the uterus and let the placenta also fall out." In this citation, we have the mention of both wind and sky, the movements of the mind, the other movements in nature and the physiological process of child birth. These physical and mental functions are *vata*-related and there is a mention of the two formative elements of *vata*.

Vata (the wanderer) also called *vayu* (the purifier), is the breath of life (*prana*). It is *marut* (without whom one dies); it is *anila* (one lives with it); it is *pavana* (the cleanser). In the living Hindu tradition, Hanuman, the god born from wind, is worshipped. Prayers are specially addressed to him for courage, fearlessness and strength. All these qualities are the attributes of *vata*. In certain parts of India, Tuesday is the day for Hanuman's worship and some people observe a semi-fast on this day. During this fast, salt is prohibited, grain food is taken only once a day and milk and fruits are taken. This diet also helps to keep *vata* in equilibrium. Similarly, the fast of Friday is attributed to the goddess of satisfaction. On this day one is supposed to take a light meal and strictly avoid sour foods. Sour enhances *pitta*, which is from fire and devouring in nature. It is responsible for the digestion and assimilation of food in the body. This fast is on Friday because *sukra*, the bright one, is symbolic of the element fire. The shining quality is the quality of *agni* and worshipping it, one gains brilliance, intelligence and beauty. The worship of these objects is also done to gain fame. All these ceremonies and rituals are an integral part of tradition and it is not possible to analyze them separately and neither are they meant for such an analysis. As has been already stated, everything is undergoing a constant change and is interrelated and interconnected. It is not possible to separate the Ayurvedic tradition from religious, social, ritualistic and ceremonial aspects of life. Although, the term holistic has been often used in the context of health and medicine in the recent years, in the true sense holistic health is not possible without a holistic way of life.

Kapha is responsible for the solid structure of the body and derives from water and earth. These two elements are worshipped and are important in various ceremonies and rituals. In traditional health care practices, these elements form a large part of healing practices. Worship of certain trees and medicinal plants, planting of certain trees (specially *peepal*, holy fig), wearing gems, seeds, etc., visiting holy places specially the confluence of rivers, worshipping mountains, are some of the frequent practices. Worship of earth, related to the fertility and sexual potency, is one of the attributes of *kapha*.

Ayurvedic tradition of nutrition is alive in most Indian homes. Intuitively and spontaneously people add a bit of coriander in their potato-based dishes, garlic and ginger in cauliflower dishes, cumin and pepper in yogurt, tamarind to digest lentils and beans, *ajwain* in fried foods. This is basically done to nourish with a diet which is balanced not only in its quantity and variety but also by universal laws of harmony to keep the body and mind in tune with the cosmic rhythm.

Similarly, an Indian kitchen is a little apothecary and usually an elder of the family has the knowledge of using various grains, spices, herbs and minerals for curing minor ailments. In their own way, people have the knowledge of the pharmaceutical properties of the substances they are using. Indeed their knowledge is limited to the practice of these products only and is not as refined as described in the scriptures; but the fundamentals of it lie in the concept of five elements.

Classification of pharmaceutical properties of the substances is done according to six major *rasas* which are derived from the five elements. *Rasa* is the complete sensuous experience belonging to one particular category. For example, if you eat something sour, you know that it is sour because of a particular taste on your tongue. Tongue only qualifies the taste. It, however, does not mean that the effect of the sour is limited to your tongue. Tongue is only an identifier of the sour, but its effect is felt in the whole body. It has an immediate effect on *pitta*. It is like fuel. It increases *agni* in the body. *Pitta* further effects so many physiological and psychological functions of the body. Thus, pharmaceutical properties of the substances are related to the humours. Both *rasas* and humours are from the five elements.

(i) Sweet is derived from earth and water and because of the cold character of these elements, sweet substances are cold in nature and decrease *pitta*. Because of the heavy character of these elements, the sweet substances also decrease *vata*. As earth and water are the formative elements of *kapha*, they will obviously increase *kapha* and vitiate it if taken in excessive quantity.

(ii) Sour is derived from elements water and fire. Because of the fire element, they increase *pitta*. Because of water, the sour substances also increase *kapha* but decrease *vata*.

(iii) Saline and salty substances are derived from earth and fire; they increase *pitta* and *kapha* but decrease *vata*.

(iv) Pungent or *katu rasa* is derived from the elements air and fire (e.g., pepper, ginger, garlic, cardamom, bay leaves, etc.). This *rasa* increases *vata* and *pitta*, and decreases *kapha*.

(v) Bitter *rasa* is derived from elements air and ether (e.g., *curcuma*, *neem*, *katuka*, etc.). Since *vata* is derived from these two elements, this *rasa* increases *vata* and decreases the other two humours.

(vi) Astringent *rasa* is derived from elements air and earth (e.g., spinach, *jamun*, dates, etc.). The astringent decreases *pitta* and *kapha* because of the very dry nature of the air but it increases *vata*.

The five *bhutas*, three humours and six *rasas* have similar action and are interconnected. It is very easy to understand their logic. However, in day-to-day existence, where this mode of thinking and acting is a part of life, their logic is not sought. The sun god is offered water every morning to keep a cosmic equilibrium in a symbolic manner. Somebody suffering from excessive *pitta*, whether it is from staying too much in the sun or eating too many sour, salty or pungent food or chemical drugs or from anger, is cured simply by drinking few glasses of cold water, a cold bath or by the intake of substances with bitter, sweet or astringent *rasas*. If we put sand on the fire, the fire diminishes. Similarly, an excess of *kapha* which is from water and earth, diminishes the bodily fire, causes lack of hunger and other symptoms of vitiated *pitta*. This equilibrium is reestablished again by hot, pungent and salty food.

In the oral Ayurvedic tradition, the terminology of the three humours may not be exact and may vary from one region to another, but their basic functions are understood very exactly and their principles are followed effectively.

It is very interesting to note that the familial wisdom of Ayurveda, which is as ancient as the Vedas, and whose rationale is so explicitly been given by our great physicians and sages like Caraka, Susruta and others of those times, is often distrusted by those influenced by western education. Ayurveda is being taken out of its cosmic context and extracts and chemicals from Ayurvedic drugs are tested in laboratory on animals for proving their validity. Besides, people suffering from inborn disorders get a sense of satisfaction when their ailments are proven with machines with exactly-set standards and highly-sophisticated foreign terms. Let us take an example of irregular blood pressure, which may sometimes be caused due to dry and cold weather or stressful circumstances. At the initial stages, it is easy to cure sometimes only with an appropriate quantity of water and avoiding certain food stuffs and life-styles. A wise person or astrologer may also tell the ailing person to wear a special gem or seeds, pray to god Hanuman and observe a fast in his reverence. As already explained, this fast recommends all what brings equilibrium of *vata*. Besides, this also gives the patient the complete therapy recommended by Ayurveda, which works at the rational, psychological and spiritual levels. But the moment the patient begins to live in the belief that he/she is a patient of blood pressure, the ailment becomes grave. The healing capacity is diminished with fear, and fear further enhances *vata*, and excess of *vata* enhances the blood-related disorder. As *vata* is derived from ether and air, which are mobile and all-pervasive, all functions of the body which are mobile and are everywhere in the body are the domain of *vata*. Taking the above example, with increased *vata*, the so-called 'patient of blood pressure' may also become a prey to insomnia, as sleep is also an attribute of *vata*. A holistic oral tradition enables one to break away from a vicious cycle of inborn ailments which can be cured simply by keeping oneself in harmony with the cosmic rhythm. Inner imbalance increases one's vulnerability to external disorders and enhances several degenerative processes in the body.

The oral tradition of health care intrinsically takes into consideration the social, psychological and economical aspects. In the familial tradition, health care becomes the responsibility of each family member and they take care of each other. This provides psychological therapy, healing and comfort. The old people take care of the younger ones with their wisdom and provide them comfort and care; whereas the younger people help the old with their resources and energy. Oral tradition of Ayurveda, based on the concept of balance and harmony of the *bhutas*, are preventive in their approach and help reduce the costs of health care considerably.

Just as *vata*, *pitta*, *kapha* are the bodily humours, *rajas*, *sattva*, *tamas* denote the qualities and activities of the mind. Thinking, planning, taking decisions, etc., are the *rajas* activities of mind. During sleep, the mental activity is termed *tamas* as the mind is closed to new knowledge. Emotions like greed, jealousy, laziness, paining and killing, telling lies, stealing, etc., are also the *tamas* qualities of mind. *Sattva* activities of the mind are those which lead us towards equilibrium, truth and self-realization.

These are the qualities of self-discipline, self-restraint, control over the senses, concentration practices and *pranayama*. *Rajas* is related to *vata* and hence to the elements ether and air. *Sattva* is related to *pitta* and hence to the element fire. *Tamas* is related to *kapha* and hence to the elements water and earth.

In everyday life, *tamas* balances *rajas* in certain life situations like over-activity with laziness. Our daily activities cannot be dissociated from *tamas* even as a very 'good' and 'moral human being'. For example, eating meat involves killing and tormenting. There are times when we have to tell lies to handle a situation. *Sattva* is also a part of living as nearly all people in the world try to find peace within themselves through various means like religion, nature worship or other devotional ways.

In the oral tradition of India, a balance between these three qualities is very important and is an integral part of the familial education. In traditional homes, a child grows up learning breathing and concentration exercises, along with training in worldly activities and keeping away from emotions like greed, anger, excessive attachment, etc. A particular state of mind or domination of one of the three qualities is not only limited to the activities of mind but to the whole way of life. A person with predominance or *rajas* will not only have a hectic mental activity but also a hectic way of living and excess of *vata*. Similarly, *tamas* qualities give rise to excess of *kapha* and related disorders. A person leading a worldly existence, if only preoccupied with means of salvation rejecting his activities and essential duties, will suffer from physical and mental disorders arisen from this imbalance.

In the living tradition of Ayurveda, these qualities have a great importance as they not only apply to the activities of the mind but practically to all other aspects of life. Food, life-style, colours, and, above all, the personality and nature of a person, are described in terms of these qualities.

It is very difficult to separate oral from textual tradition, as oral is only a simpler, practical and interesting version of the textual. For example, when a woman gets pregnant, after a few weeks, a ceremony is performed and special dishes are prepared on that day. This ceremony is done to bring in her the consciousness of being temporarily physiologically different, to teach her to have *sattvic* state of mind and to prescribe her a special diet which includes certain herbs to give her strength and food supplements. All these instructions are not different from what is written in *Caraka Samhita*. When all this is taught to her in an atmosphere of festivity and done as a ritual, it becomes more fascinating, interesting and easier to follow. It becomes a familial responsibility rather than medical.

The oral tradition of medicine is interwoven in the lives of the masses and is the results of thousands of years' effort of the sages. Every effort should be made to preserve this and save ourselves from the impact of western mechanistic view of life which is apparently illogical, and, in medicine, it ignores health and treats only the disease. We cannot fit Ayurveda in the concepts of modern medicine and should do all to keep our tradition of worshipping the sun and fire, rivers, mountains and trees and the great, powerful and all-pervasive wind and sky, let these cosmic forces maintain an equilibrium of this cosmic energy in us.

In medicine and health, textual tradition is extremely important, as without it we could not have had such an enriched tradition as we have today. But for this enrichment, oral tradition played a tremendous part. We have enriched our knowledge of medicine in the past with methods from the middle-east and Persia. In fact, much of this knowledge is lost in their home countries. We could preserve this because we have both oral and textual tradition of Ayurveda which is not only concerned with the preservation of human life but includes the whole cosmos of which the human beings are a tiny part.

16

Peasant Perception of Bhutas

Uttara Kannada

M.D. Subash Chandran

Sanskrit textual tradition holds that man has a fivefold constitution, called *bhuta* or *tattva* (element). The *pancabhutas* (five elements) are *bhumi* (earth), *jala* (water), *agni* (fire) *vayu* (air) and *akasa* (sky). For generations, this textual tradition has been monopolized by the Brahmin community who formed bulk of the scholars, teachers and priests. At the same time in India live thousands of other communities are expected to have their own oral traditions regarding the *bhutas*. We could indeed hope for a wealth of information and concepts emerging from this probe into the oral tradition of these diverse human groups who live in a bewildering diversity of ecological conditions prevalent in this country. However, it should be noted that, for more than 2000 years, most of them have been interacting with the influential Brahmin community, more so in the plains and plateaus of India, and is expected to have imbibed from them the textual tradition, displacing or modifying the oral tradition. In the last century, with the universalization of education, the flood-gates of knowledge have opened for all. Nevertheless, we can attempt to reconstruct the oral tradition from the rather isolated human groups, like those living in the hilly areas and are expected to have a more secure oral tradition.

Uttara Kannada or North Canara is a district of Karnataka situated towards the middle of the western coast of South India. The hills of the Western Ghats cover major part of Uttara Kannada except a narrow coastal strip, the continuity of which is broken by wide river mouths and backwaters. Bountiful rainfall promotes the growth of luxuriant forests which, though subjected to heavy commercial pressures, specially in the last 150 years, cover about 60 per cent of the district's 10,000 square kilometres of the land surface. The cultivation is mainly of rice, coconut, areca nut, spices like cardamom and pepper, other crops like banana, sugarcane, groundnut, cocoa, nutmeg and vegetables, as well as fruit trees like mango, jack, garcinia, cashew, etc. These are grown on about 13 per cent of the land surface.

Though the first man did appear along the west coast and Western Ghats in the pre-historic period, these regions were colonized by agricultural communities only after the introduction of iron in India around 1000 BC (Bhat, 1979). Historical evidecne shows that the influence of Buddhism in the district could be as old as the third century BC (Sundara, 1979). Agriculturists and pastoralists who colonized this region between 1000 BC and AD 300 (Bhat, 1979), in the special ecological situation of the west coast, evolved a combination of rice cultivation in the estuaries and valleys with growing of millets in the slash-and-burn style along the hill slopes. This was supplemented by hunting, fishing and gathering of forest produce and, to limited extent, pastoralism. The natural resources were largely controlled by the village communities with several regulations to ensure sustainable utilization (Gadgil and Iyer, 1989).

The oral tradition of the early peasantry, related to the perceptions of *bhutas*, in a region with high amount of heterogeniety in nature, is expected to have undergone a tumultuous effect with the arrival of the Brahmins in the region. They were probably introduced by the Kadamba king of the fourth century. The Havik Brahmins, who claim to have descended from these early Brahmins, have even today considerable influence on the peasant population. Though originally they were all engaged in priesthood, in due course a major section of them became experts in raising the well-known spice-gardens of the region. Exponents of Sanskrit textual tradition the Haviks became keen observers of natural phenomena and formed important links between textual and oral traditions. In course of time the illustrious Haviks became consultants to the local peasants in many matters pertaining to culture and religion, climate and soil and even astronomical and astrological phenomena. Nevertheless, compared to most other regions in India, in the hilly and wooded Uttara Kannada, with several physiographic barriers, there persisted a wealth of oral tradition.

Though there are equivalent words for the five *bhutas* among all the peasants, most of the non-Brahmin peasantry are not aware of the *pancabhutas* of textual tradition. The names of the *bhutas* are *bhumi* (earth, also *mannu* which is more a term for soil than earth), *neeru* (water), *benki* (fire), *gali* (air) and *vaana* or *akasa* (sky).

Earth

The peasant perceives the *bhumi* as mother or Bhumitati. She is also a divinity Bhumdevi. The agricultural operations begin with *bhumipooja* (worship of the earth). It may be for the peasant *gaddepooja* (worship of the field). The peasants often identify themselves as *mannina makkalu* (children of the soil). Traditionally, the peasants have a terriotorial distribution based on soil or other earth-related characters. For instance, the Gamvokkals or Patgars are found in the coast and are specialized in cultivating the estuarine salt-resistant rice and protect their crops from inundation of salt-water by building earthen dams called *gajanikettu*—their fields being known as *gajanis*. The

Halakkivokkals cultivate rice and vegetables in the coastal plains and valleys. The Karivokkals grow rice in hill-top villages. The Namadharis combine rice-cultivation with toddy-tapping of the wild palm *Caryota urens* in the interior hilly villages (Kandivar group) or practice rice cultivation in the coastal villages and tap toddy from coconut tree (Tengidivars). In this fashion the different communities of peasants divided the resources of the earth, without unhealthy competition, between them and on sustainable basis. These peasants are knowledgeable about various qualities of different soils as related to the crops each type could support. These qualities include particle size, fertility, water-holding capacity and drainage characteristics.

The peasants have a strong tradition of using different local strains or varieties of crops, each suited to the type of soil. For instance, in Kumta taluk, only about one-fifteenth of the total area of the district, has about fifty local varieities of rice, suited to different soil conditions. This fact reflects that the peasants know their soils well and through generations have developed by selection and introduction the different varieities suited to the habitat heterogeneity. Further, they also understand that the river floods, bringing materials from the forest-clad hills, enriched the soil and gave bountiful crops. The peasants who cultivate the hill soil understand their proneness to severe erosion and quick depletion of feritlity. To overcome this, they have developed *hakkal* (shifting cultivation) involving a rotation of fields. During the fallow period the growth of vegetation in the field built up the soil and restored its fertility. This vegetation is chopped and burnt into ashes which return the depleted elements back to the soil. Further, traditional cattle-keeping in the district is mainly for manure. The peasants also understand that organic matter like leaves from plants contain the necessary components helpful in restoring soil-fertility and structure.

The estuarine farmers realize that the ideal time to grow rice is when the salinity of the soil declines during the rainy season. The tradition of planting mangrove trees along the earthen protective bunds not only prevents their erosion but attracts flocks of birds, the castings of which enriches the rice fields with phosphates and nitrogen.

The Havil Brahmin farmer is one of the best experts in soil management. Buchanan, who travelled through Uttara Kannada in 1801, reports about three grades of areca garden soils – cagadala, *gujiny,* and *betta.* The farmer uses various soil and water-management practices in these different soils and has different manuring practice (Buchanan, 1870).

Water

In most parts of the country water sources and water bodies are considered sacred. In Uttara Kannada many of the water bodies like *hole* (river), *halla* (stream), *kere* (pond), *bhavi* (well) are supposed to be guarded by spirits. Choudi or Choudamma is the most common water-guarding spirit. Spirits like Kere Bhutappa or Bhuta guarding the *kere* are also worshipped (*appa* is suffix for father, therefore Bhuta is considered a fatherly spirit). In the densely wooded lime-rocks of Yana, an interior village of Kumta taluk, are numerous springs, which are sacred to the people. During floods pesants offer prayers to the rivers and even throw eatables into the flood waters.

Rain (*male*) is the most important cosmic phenomenon influencing the life of the peasant. The *panchanga* (almanac) prepared by the Havik Brahmin is popular among the Hindus and widely used to decipher the timing of different rainy spells so as to co-ordinate with the agricultural operations. The *panchanga* divides the time span of a year into 27 periods, each presided over by a *nakshatra* (star). The rainy season of Uttara Kannada commences under the Rohini *nakshatra* in early June. The early agricultural operations continue up to the commencement of *ardra*, the peak of rains in July. In the coast of Uttara Kannada the harvesting of rice is completed during Swati *nakshatra* in October.

The peasants have their own oral tradition pertaining to the rains. They can read the imminence of rainy season from several environmental phenomena. One indication is the blowing of wild west wind (*birugali*) for seven to fifteen days. The first rains are preceded by *minchu* (lightning) and *gudugu* (thunder). The peasants correlate the high temperature and high humidity of summer months as indicating the formation of *moda* (clouds) and possible thunder-showers towards the evening. The *karimoda* (black clouds) are considered a sign of the rains, unlike the *bilimoda* (white clouds).

The profuse fruiting and simultaneous ripening of *neerilu* (*Syzygium cumini*) is a signal of the approach of rainy season and commencement of the agricultural operations. Profuse flowering of *nandi* tree (*Lagerstroemia microcarpa*) is yet another sign. More fruiting of the *kanigala* tree (*Dillenia pentagyna*) towards the base, middle or top foretell poor, normal and excess rains respectively during the season. A Havik Brahmin priest-cum-farmer told me that the climatic phenomena which promote heavy fruiting of *neerilu* also promote high production of rice. Mass movements of ants related to shifting of their colonies also point that the rains are around the corner. A species of spider weaving its web in the grass is taken as indicating the end of the rainy season.

The peasant community, in general, holds the view that the forests have a favourable effect in rainfall. The Havik priest-cum-farmer is of the opinion that deforestation need not be followed by a local decline in the rains; if there is better vegetation elsewhere, even that contributes towards attracting the rains. The peasants believe that water is more in the forest areas. That evergreen sacred groves (*kans*) were important sources of water was known by both the British administrators as well as the forest-dwelling peasants. Several of these sacred groves are associated with water-bodies even today.

Most peasant settlements are, for obvious reasons, located in places where water is easily available. The Havik Brahmin priest-cum-farmer explained how an ideal location is chosen for digging a well. An important sign indicating water at a shallow depth is the type of tree-growth present around it. If trees llike *alu* (*Ficus bengalensis*), *atti* (*Ficus glomerata*), *neerilu* have bright green foliage throughout the year as well as symmetrical branching, then ground water is available nearer to the surface. *Huthu* (anthill) also indicates water at short depths – say within 20 to 25 feet. The reasoning here is that the white ants bring wet soil from not-so-deep in the ground. Anthills are sacred in Uttara Kannada also because of their association with the cobra.

The early peasants who experienced the phenomenon of quick loss of soil and soil fertility, especially in the hills, attributed this to the torrential rains of the region. To combat this, they evolved *hakkal*, terracing of hill slopes and building of stone wallls around the fields. Moreover the clearances were small with belts of forests left in between. For the regularly-cultivated fields, the peasants added large quantities of leaf-manure to improve the fertility and protect the soil structure. The Havik spice-gardener usually makes an elaborate system of channels for drainage during rains and irrigation during the dry period. He has also developed the practice of covering the entire soil-surface of the garden with leaf-litter and dry grass to prevent erosion, moisture loss during dry season and to increase soil fertility. In fact, for the purpose, every gardener maintains special leaf-manure forests (*betta*) near his garden.

Fire

Fire has a prominent place in every household. The *hoge* (smoke) emanating from the hearth of the household is considered an auspicious sign – of life and warmth. The peasants light the lamps before the household gods, within the sacred groves and below the sacred trees. More lamps are lit on special occasions and sacred fires lit with plant exudates like frankinscence, camphor, a balsamic exudate from wild trees of the region like *Vateria indica, Canarium strictum, Ailanthus malabarica*, etc. Oil lamps are lit on all important occasions like birth, marriage, death, etc. In certain temples and sacred groves dedicated to Masti and Gramadevaru, annual fire-walking programmes are organized and the devotees, to fulfil their vows, walk over the *kenda* (burning ember).

Fire is widely used for *hakkal*. The farmers are knowledgeable about the power of fire to convert plant biomass into elemental nutrients necessary for the crops. The ash from the household is carefully conserved and used as a fertilizer. The rubble of the field and dry leaves gathered from the forest are set on fire to enrich the fields with nutrients. Fire is used to destroy weeds and insect pests. The peasants inhabiting the forest tracts know the value of fire to keep away wild animals detrimental to life and property. Fire-based systems of traditional vegetational control, as practised by the peasantry of Uttara Kannada, resulted in the region becoming a mosaic of plant communities in different stages of vegetational succession in harmony with climax patches of natural forests. The rich habitat heterogeneity made the district a haven for wildlife. The peasantry carried out subsistence hunting unimpeded, up to the advent of the British period in the nineteenth century (Subash Chandran and Gadgil, 1991).

Air or Wind

The changing patterns of wind also bring changes in the routine of the peasants. When *birugali* (strong winds) blow from the west, beginning towards the end of May, the peasants expect the rains to follow in one or two weeks and start preparing the fields for this great cosmic phenomenon. The moisture-laden monsoon winds from the south-west (*neerugali*) last up to the Deepavali festival in early November. Then the *mudagali* (east wind) begins. This is a drying wind, signalling the end of the rainy season (*malaikala*) and beginning of winter (*chelikala*). Special prayers are made to the spirits of the sacred groves and sacred trees. A season of leaf-fall and drying up of *karada* grass starts. Most of the peasants plant broad beans (*Dolichos lablab*), groundnut (*Arachis hypogea*) and other legumes favoured by *mudagali.* Winter vegetables like raddish, knol-kohl, onion, cabbage and different varieties of brinjal, gourds, amaranthus are grown by the peasants. The tropical sun and the drying winds kill the weeds and insect pests of the ploughed fields. The peasants rise in the pre-dawn hours, as soon as Belli (Venus) is sighted in the eastern sky, and start their work. Many go to the nearby woods to gather dry leaves for manure and dead twigs for fuel. The *karada* grass is cut from the *bena* (pasture) and stored.

Suggi celebrations of the Halakkivokkals, during March, coincides with the Holi festival, the *mudagali* slows down and *besigekala* (summer) starts. The *samudragali* (west wind) from the Arabian Sea starts. It is a humid wind and is associated with the sprouting and flowering of several cultivated and wild trees. This is the seasaon for collection of fruits, like mango, jack, garcinia, *neerilu, karvanda* (*Carissa carandans*), *sampige hannu* (*Flacourtia montana*), etc.

Sky

The Havik Brahmin farmer's knowledge of *vaana* or *akasa* (sky) is more rooted in the textual tradition. For him *akasa is space. It is the home for countless nakshatras* (stars) and other celestial bodies like *surya* (sun), *chandra* (moon) and *grahas* (planets). The *brahmanda* (universe) is endless. Many *nakshatras* are visible and many are not. Among the stars knwon to him may be mentioned Arundhati, Dhruva or pole star, Saptarishi or Seven Sages, etc. Out of the multitude of *nakshatras* the most influential on man and his environment are 27 in number. Their influence is felt during different times of the year. The influence of some of the stars on the monsoon rains has been already mentioned. The Haviks are experts in preparing the *panchanga*. Most peasants refer to the *panchanga* to know in advance about the proper timings under different ruling stars for any agricultural operation as well as find auspicious timings, free from any evil influence, for the commencement of any important activity. It is a common practice for them to consult the Havik Brahmins when they are not literate enough to go through the *panchanga*. The period under each *nakshatra* is subdivided between the *navagrahas* (nine planets) which are Surya, Chandra, Budha (Mercury), Shukra (Venus), Mangala (Mars), Brihaspati (Jupiter), Shani (Saturn), Rahu and Ketu. Of these Shani, Rahu and Ketu have bad influence on people.

Surya has the most important influence on man and the living world. The Havik Brahmin farmer's multi-storeyed spice-gardens, for which Uttara Kannada is famous, are marvellous instances of traditional tropical agriculture attaching great importance to the controlled use of sunlight. The ideal garden is one located in a narrow valley with a perennial water-source and a rising hill to the west to shelter the garden from the western sun, supposed to have a scorching effect on it. Withing the garden, under the unbroken canopy of tall betel trees are shade and dampness loving crops like cardamom, pepper, betel vine, nutmeg and cocoa. Buchanan (1870) found blocks of evergreen forests specially maintained by the peasants in which wild pepper was grown.

The peasants recognize the impact of sun for growth of several plants. Whereas most plants bloom during the day, some like *ratkirani*, (*Cestrum nocturnum*), *Nyctanthes arbor-tristis*, jasmine, etc., bloom towards the dusk or in night hours.

Though the non-Brahmin peasantry do not have the textual tradition pertaining to the *akasa*, celestial bodies do have an influence on them. The warmth of summer and chill of winter are associated with the phases of the sun. The sunshine produces *ubha* (steam) from water and the steam becomes *moda* (cloud) which creates *male* (rain) and *ibhini* (fog). The coastal peasants associate waxing and waning phases of the moon with the tides of the sea.

The peasant communities have names for certain stars, constellations and planets which are helpful to them during nocturnal activities like hunting, toddy-tapping, etc. The *nakshatras* are to the peasants *sarkalu*, *arkalu* or *chikki*. The Halakkivokkals name a cluster of six stars *arlu sarkalu*, a second one of three is called *gotikuli* (marble pits); a third constellation of five stars are called *gotisarkalu* (playing 'marble stars'). The evening star is known as *deepa bachuva sarkalu* (lamp-lighting star).

The rise of Belli in the pre-dawn hours stirs up activities in the peasant household. The Havik Brahmin considers the rise of Belli as the start of good time, a time free from evil spirits. It is safe to start a journey at this time. Their children wake up soon after the rise of Belli for studies. It is generally believed that the people who get up before the sunrise are healthier.

The Karivokkaligas call a group of four stars as *halkinakudige* (assembly of four) and another cluster as *vokkaligarakudige* (assembly of peasants).

Kandivars, a section of Namadharis, mostly inhabiting the evergreen forest areas, traditionally carry out tapping of toddy from *Caryota urens*, a wild palm. The tapper goes to the forest after dusk when a cluster of three stars *murukashina chikki* is visible. In the early hours, the tapper goes to the forest soon after the rise of Belli, or even before that, when the brighter Dodda-arkalu (big star), i.e., Jupiter, rises. The tappers who also did some traditional hunting for subsistence are able to read time in the sky by locating the positions of *manchadakalu* (legs of the cot), evidently referring to the four corner stars of the Orion or Hunter. Some other constellations are *hakkimatti* (flock of birds) and *dhanakayuva hudugaru* (shepherd boys).

The *grahana* (eclipse), of the sun and the moon, is generally considered as an evil happening. But the observances associated with *grahana* like fasting and abstaining from any serious physical work and other rituals apparently arose out of the Brahmanic influence in the region. An elderly Gamvokkal peasant expressed that *grahana* is a difficult time for *surya* and *chandra* which are divine bodies benefitting mankind and there is no harm in our viewing it and praying for an early end to it.

Amavasi (new moon day) is not considered a good day. The Haviks hold the view that *amavasi* has a disturbing effect on the psyche. It is a time of aggravation for the mentally ill. All the peasantry abstain from difficult physical work on *amavasi* day, neither do they strain their working cattle. Tree-climbing is almost a taboo on this day.

The Cosmocentric Vision

The different peasant communities, each forming a coherent group, notwithstanding the differences between them, which are more due to the diversity of environments in a humid tropical hilly region, are unified in their perceptions of *bhutas*. These perceptions are reflected more in their practical life and approach to nature than in their views. The peasants live in a cosmocentric universe having accepted them as part of their ecosystems, subjecting themselves to the elemental powers, in spite of their inherent capacities to dominate these powers as members of the human race. The early peasants, who inhabited the difficult Western Ghats region with its torrential rains, dense forests and ocean to the west, in the twilight period of the evolution of

Hinduism, were able to preserve their views and life-styles for centuries in spite of the arrival of Brahminism about sixteen-hundred years ago. Along with Brahminism came elaborate ritualism and new textual traditions of religion and culture. Yet, by and large, the peasants lived in close communion with *bhutas* (elements of nature) without the barriers of elaborate rituals, *mantras* or priesthood. Many of their practices, carried forth to this day or to recent historical times, form the basis of our study.

The oral tradition and practices of the peasants of Uttara Kannada, in many ways, reflect the cosmocentric vision of man. Major incursions into their lives began with the arrival of Brahmins. Yet the tumultuous impact was with European colonialism – the Portuguese becoming the masters of Goa in the sixteenth century and the British domination in the nineteenth century. Before these incursions, the peasants, including the Havik Brahmin, lived in harmony with their ecosystems, modifying nature in several ways to secure niches of existence for them and, at the same time, making efforts to maintian the balance with its elements. The district is rich in the wreckage of the lofty oral traditions, which, in many ways, are in agreement with modern ecological principles, reflecting the cosmocentric vision of the peasants. We also find many peasant groups, even today, inhabiting some of the interior villages, clinging on to the ruins of their age-old traditions. According to the philosophical tradition, it is generally held that the reality of the subtler planes is responsible for the grosser planes, and, that, at a higher level of understanding, the distinction between the gross and the subtle gets obliterated.

The peasant who lives in the microcosm of his ecosystem is linked to several other ecosystems with material circulation and energy flow between them and all of them together form the biosphere. Indeed, according to the modern landscape approach, the peasant is not merely part of an ecosystem but of several ecosystems forming a landscape. Landscape is defined as 'a wide area where a cluster of interacting stands or ecosystems is represented in similar forms'. No ecosystem within a landscape is an island (Janzen, 1984). All ecosystems are 'open' and exchange energy, mineral nutrients and organisms (Noss, 1983).

In the traditional land use system of Uttara Kannada, the peasants, while clearing natural forests for cultivation, conserved substantial patches of them as inviolable reserves called *kans*. These *kans* often merge with ordinary forests (*adavi* or *kadu*), shifting cultivation (*hakkal*) fallows in different stages of vegetational succession, grazing lands (*bena*), cultivation sites (*gadde* or *bailu*), garden (*totta*), water bodies like *kere*, *halla*, *hole* etc. Such a mosaic landscape accounted for the high diversity of plant and animal life for which Uttara Kannada is famouns. Daniels (1989), in agreement with the principles of modern landscape ecology (Forman and Godron, 1986), recommends for the conservation of the birds of Uttara Kannada a landscape approach which 'ensures that the most valuable birds and also the gamma diversity of birds is maintained in the district'. Thus we find in the traditional landscape management, linkages between ecosystems ideal for conservation of maximum diversity.

The modern alternative agricultural systems, recommended for the Third World farmers, based on ecological principles of sustainability and stability (Altieri and Anderson, 1986) are surprisingly similar to the traditional landscape management system of the peasants of Uttara Kannada.

SPIRITUALIZED NATURE AND UNITY OF THE BASIC ELEMENTS

To the peasant, nature is itself spiritualized. In his world, woods, trees, soil, water, cliffs and caves are animated with spirits. Yet he has to clear forests, work with soil and tame water-bodies as well as hunt animals. The peasant communities, while clearing forests for cultivation or for pastures take care to leave substantial portions of the primeval forests untouched as sacred groves-cum-safety forests. Often known as *kans* or *bana*, these forests conserve biodiversity, protect the watershed, increase the heterogeniety of the landscape and supply many non-wood produce to the community which can be safely taken without affecting the forests in a major way.

We studied several of the sacred groves in an area with the least influence of Brahminism. Many of these groves have vacant spots as worshipping places, where the devotees make offerings to deities and stick tridents to fulfil their vows or make sacrifices of fowl or goat to propitiate them. The deities may be sometimes represented by anthills or crude stones. Of late icons with human forms are replacing the older ones, as the wild spirits are getting linked with the gods of the Hindu pantheon. The spirits permeating the sacred groves may be male or female. The common male spirits are Bhutappa and Jatakappa. The common female spirit is Choudi or Choudamma. There may be other male spirits like Betedevaru (hunter's god), Birappa (hero), Masti, Rachamma, etc. There is hardly any difference in the concept of the people between these several male spirits as well as female spirits. In a sense the male and female spirits are comparable to the *Purusha* and *Prakriti* of the ancient texts of India. In their original forms, retained even today, in many of the *kans* or *bana* the male and female spirits, especially Bhutappa or Jatakappa and Choudamma have no icons, though elsewhere, and more so outside Uttara Kannada, these deities have been identified with gods and goddesses of the Hindu pantheon. These deities permeate the entire sacred groves. The appellations *appa* and *amma* applied to the male and female spirits signify that to the peasants these spirits are guardians of fields, cattle, water resources, forests and people. It seeems that these spirits of the village communities have been unfairly treated as evil spirits or *shudradevatas* in the texts on

Indian religion, mainly because they are to be propitiated by animal sacrifices and are notorious for spreading diseases. However, for the peasants of many villages of Uttara Kannada, the sacred groves are temples. They worship the spirits who favour them if they go in the right path shown by the ancestors or do harm if they deviate. It should be noted that the deviations meriting such divine wrath include cutting of trees especially within the groves, untimely hunting, killing of wrong species of animals which may be totemic or sacred ones, as most of these wrong-doings have adverse environmental consequences.

The village landscape is dotted with several sacred trees with or without deities underneath them. For instance, the ficus tree, wherever it occurs, is sacred to the people. Many times the tree itself is permeated with the holy spirit. Recently, biologists have recognized the value of ficus sps. as a keystone plant resources of the tropical forests, fruiting at crucial times when most other trees do not bear fruits and thereby supporting many birds and animals (Terebogh, 1986).

INEVITABILITY OF DESTRUCTION

Forests are to be cut down for agriculture, animals hunted for food or domesticated and killed for the same purpose. These activities are inevitable for subsistence. Cycling of elements through living organisms and environment and energy flow from sun passing through green plants to the animal consumers of first (herbivore), second (primary carnivore) or third (secondary carnivore) orders are important attributes of eco-systems of which man (a born omnivore) is merely a part. The peasant understood the inevitability of this destruction. He atoned for this destruction through protection of sacred groves and sacred trees, worship of cows, bull and monkey. Even deadly animals like cobra and tiger were worshipped in sacred groves dedicated to them: Hulidevaru *kan* for tiger and Nagara *bana* for cobra.

The peasants consider Sunday as the birthday of the coconut palm and abstain from climbing it or hurting it in any way on that day. Most peasants do not plough on Monday, the birthday of the bull. That people do not easily cut down trees or forests is evident from Buchanan's observation made in 1801, near Karwar:

> The forests are the property of the gods of the villages in which they are situated, and the trees ought not to be cut without having leave from the Gauda or headman of the village, whose office is hereditary, and who here also is priest (*pujari*) to the temple of the village god.
>
> *Buchaman, 1870*

The peasants hunted most of the time, communally, during specific seasons of the year only, and that too with the 'permission' or 'knowledge' of the guardian spirits of the village. They consumed flesh of domestic animals mostly after sacrificing to their deities. The peasants traditionally lived in earthen houses thatched with grass and palm leaves in spite of the abundant and the finest timbers of the world like teak and rosewood. The peasants did not destroy forests for timber and timber was not an important commodity for sale in the pre-British days. Their houses became one with the elements of nature once they were abandoned or when whole villages were vacated.

HAKKAL CULTIVATION AND MATERIAL CYCLING

Hakkal (shifting cultivation), as practised by the small number of peasants during the pre-colonial period of the west coast of India, was perhaps the best mode of cultivation suitable for the hilly terrain. There are instances of land and civilization perishing due to over-exposure of tropical soils. Such may have been the case with the early Mayan civilization. Millet cultivation in the Yellow river basin of China, carried out as early as 4000 BC by unregulated clearing of forests resulted in enormous soil erosion of the uplands (Treshow, 1976). By the system of shifting cultivation, the abandoning of cultivation after a time to allow for the resprouting and reseeding of wild woody growth the soil is replenished by nutrients carried to the surface by deep-rooted trees and shrubs to spread over the ground as litter (Sauer, 1955).

HABITAT CONTINUITY AND ISLAND BIO-GEOGRAPHY

The sacred groves, many of them as they exist today in Uttara Kannada, after over 150 years of forest-management by the state, have reduced to small vegetational islands. According to Mac Arthur and Wilson (1963) small or remote islands and islands with uniform topography have fewer species than large or complex islands or islands nearer the source of colonization. The new arrivals are virtually balanced by the extinction of older species within the islands. There is strong evidence to state that the Uttara Kannada peasants, with their cosmocentric outlook and spiritualization of nature, were able to modify the landscape in such a fashion so as to overcome the isolation effect of islands. The sacred groves were often continous with ordinary forests, shifting cultivation fallows in different stages of vegetational succession, grazing lands and several other natural and man-made habitats which provided continuity for complex cycling of matter and flow of energy. The sacred groves of Uttara Kannada, their attenuated form of the present-day notwithstanding, continue to be the best centres of bio-diversity, sheltering rare species and even helping in the restoration of natural vegetation in the surroundings.

In their view of the ecosystem, all social activities impinge directly or indirectly on ecological processes and are themselves affected by those same processes. Fauna, including man, vegetation, soil structure and micro-climate are intricately linked and mutually interdependent (Ellen, 1932). The traditional peasants of Uttara Kannada basically held such an outlook in his interaction with nature and was conscious in keeping the balance of the eco-system.

Need for Rethinking and Reorientation

Hindu cultural heritage, according to Sharma (1975), identifies and believes the oneness that identity in all lives and the same energy pervade in each and everything. The *Bhagavad Gita* states in Dhyana Yoga st. 30:

> He who sees Me everywhere and sees all in Me, he never becomes lost to Me, nor do I become lost to him.

This approach is reflected in the life of the Uttara Kannada peasants and in his perception of the living and non-living environment. Such perceptions have declined in most of India with the ritualization of Hindu *samskaras* or sacraments, the pursuit of which according to Pandey (1949), was meant for, 'sanctifying the body, mind and intellect of an individual, so that he may become a full-fledged member of the community'. What caused this failure was that the keepers of these *samskaras* thought they could not create anything new and their only business was to collect and preserve. They regarded a slight variation as sin. Pandey continues, "To make the matter worse, the language of the procedure and *mantras* became unintelligible in course of time. This was the stage when the true spirit of the *samskaras* depart and their sculptures were left behind to be wroshipped by their blind followers."

Such a stage in the cultural and religious life of the Indian elite had adverse consequences on the peasantry as well. His attitude towards elements changed gradually as is reflected in his treatment of nature and the quality of his cosmic life which got eroded as well. His life which became more individualistic and discrete, estranging him more from the environment. The spirits pervading his universe vanished, subdued as *rakshasas* or evil bodies by the gods of the Hindu pantheon which evolved side by side. The more benevolent spirits or deities inhabiting the sacred groves or hill tops related to the major gods of the Hindu religion idolized in temples which replaced the sacred groves.

Dr. Radhakirshnan (1949), in his discourse on the conflict of religions, refers to the epics which relate the acceptance of new tribes and their gods into the old family circle. "The clash of cults and the contact of cultures do not, as a rule, result in a complete domination of one by the other. In all true contact there is an interchange of elements, though the foreign elements are given a new significance by those who accept them. The emotional attitudes attached to the old forms are transferred to the new which is fitted into the background of the old. Many tribes and races had mystic animals, and when the tribes entered the Hindu society the animals which followed them were made vehicles and companions of gods. The enlistment of Hanuman in the service of Rama signifies the meeting-point of early nature worship and later theism. The dancing of Krishna on Kaliya's head represents the subordination, if not the displacement, of serpent worship. Rama's breaking of the bow of Siva signifies the conflict between the Vedic ideal and the cult of Siva, who soon became the god of the south."

Kumar (1974) affirms this by pointing out to the cult of Shakti in India, which "has been an offshoot of primitive and universal worship of the cosmic energy visualized as the Divine Mother. This concept of Shakti, as we find in the Puranas, and other literature, is related more to the creative faculty, whereas in the Tantras and primitive beliefs, her descriptive aspect, is elaborately described." It may be observed that the concept of Choudamma in Uttara Kannada, as it exists in many interior villages unaffected by Brahminism, is more related to this creative faculty.

Bhattacharya (1975) is more specific in this matter. He considers aboriginal, tribal, non-Aryan genesis of the Mother-power who lives in the mountains, valleys, dales and caves. "In the Sakti temples of the South India preponderance and importance of tribes as chief participants is cleverly kept under cover by Brahminical interests. This cover is easily supplied by legendary tales about the Great Mother assuming many forms." In the more populated areas of Uttara Kannada, temples were erected to house this newly-evolved mother goddess. In the whole of Kerala, Bhagavati temples appeared presumably replacing the groves, a process which is infilterating into the remotest villages of Uttara Kannada. This is the repetition of the process started during the epic period and it has had a significant influence on man's approach to the elements.

Similar transformations have taken place for the male spirit also. Williams (1883) points to the classical male deity, Ayenar, of South India. He is a very popular village god, who guards the fields, crops and herds of the peasantry and drives away their enemies the devils and fiends. Ayenar was always associated with groves of trees. He was also known as Sasta. Thus we find that Ayenar's concept role are similar to the roles of the *Bhutas* of Uttara Kannada. Just like Ayenar is addressed as Ayenar-*appan* (father), the *Bhutas* are known as Bhutappa to the peasantry. The popular deity of Kerala, Aiyappa, is also known as Sasta. Most of the Aiyappa temples are situated in groves or dense forests, e.g., the famous Aiyappa of Sabarimala forests. It is significant that this Aiyappa has been accepted in the Hindu pantheon as one of the sons of Shiva.

With the evolution of the Hindu gods and the arrival of the "popular Hinduism" in a big way, the masses became more estranged from the elements, as represented by nature itself. The sacredness of the plant kingdom itself got reduced to a few symbols like the *peepal* tree and *tulsi* plant and of animal kingdom to the holy cow or monkey. The elaborate ritualism prescribed by the scriptures and blindly practised by the priests symbolized the Hindu culture and outlook, and narrowed down the cosmocentric vision.

The peasants of Uttara Kannada, isolated as they were through several centuries in densely-forested hilly terrain of torrential rains and ferocious wild animals, have suddenly woken up to the 'development of' the rest of India. As modern ecology grapples to trace its links with the elements and marvels at the discovery of the amazing resource management systems of the traditional people (Gadgil and Berkes, 1991), the simple life-style of the peasants of Uttara Kannada, is rapidly transforming into an anthropocentric one and losing its millenia-old links with the primary elements.

References

Altieri, M.A. and Anderson, K., 1986. An ecological basis for the development of alternative agricultural system for small farmers in Third World. In *American Journal for Alternative Agriculture.* Vol. 1, No. 1, Institute for Alternative Agriculture.

Bhat, P.G., 1979. Pre-history of Coastal Karnataka. In *The Quarterly Journal of the Mythic Society.* Vol. 70, January-June, 1979, Nos. 1-2; 86-96.

Bhowmick, S., 1984. Brahmanisation in border Bengal : A case study in Western Midnapur. In *Man in India,* Vol. 64, No. 1.

Buchanan, F.D., 1870. *A Journey from Madras through the countries of Mysore, Canara and Malabar.* Vol. 2. Higginbothams and Co., Madras.

Daniels, R.J.R., 1989. *A Conservation Strategy for the Birds of Uttara Kannada District,* Ph.D. thesis, C.E.S., Indian Institute of Science, Bangalore.

Elden, R., 1982. *Environment, Subsistence and System: The Ecology of Small Scale Social Formations.* Cambridge University Press.

Forman, R.T.T. and Godron, M., 1986. *Landscape Ecology,* John Wiley and Sons, New York.

Gadgil, M. and Berkes, F., 1991. Traditional resource management systems. In *Resource Management and Optimization* 18 (3-4), 127-41.

Gadgil, M. and Iyer, P., 1989. On the diversification of common property resource use by the Indian society. In: F. Berkes (Ed.) *Common Property Resources: Ecology and Community Based Sustainable Development.* Belhaven Press, London.

Gadgil, M. and Subash Chandran, M.D., 1989. On the history of Uttara Kannada forests. In *Changing Tropical Forests,* Dargavel, J., Dixon, K. and Semple, N. (eds.) Australian National University, Canberra 47-58.

Janzen, D.H., 1983. No park is an island : increase in interference from outside as parksize decreases. In *Oikos,* 41: 402-10.

Mac Arthur, R. and Wilson, E.O., 1963. An equilibrium theory of insular zoogeography. In *Evolution,* 17: 373-87.

Morab, S.G., 1980. Chamundesvari temple as pilgrim centre. In *Man in India,* 60; nos. 1-2; 98-101.

Noss, R.F., 1983. A regional landscape approach to maintain diversity. In *Bioscience* 33, 700-06.

Pandey, R.B., 1949. *Hindu Samskaras: A Socio-religious study of the Hindu Sacraments.* Vikrama Publications, Banaras.

Radhakrishnan, S., 1949. *The Hindu View of Life* (8th impression). George Allen & Unwin Ltd. New York.

Sandra, B. and Lugo, E., 1990. Tropical secondary forests. In *Biological Abstracts,* 89; no. 10 Ref. 103832.

Saraswati, B.N., 1986. Thinking about Tradition. In *Man in India,* 66; no. 3 : 199-219.

Sauer, C.O., 1955. The agency of man on the earth. In Williams (ed.) *Man's Role in Changing the face of the Earth,* 49-69.

Seuffert, O., 1991. Ecomorphodynamics and soil erosion. In *Applied Geography and Development,* 38: 7-21.

Sharma, O.P., 1975. *Dynamic Indianism,* O.P. Sharma, Chandigarh.

Subash Chandran, M.D. and Gadgil, M., 1991 (a) Kans-safety forests of Uttara Kannada IUFRO : Forest History Group meeting on "Peasant Forestry" 2-5 September 1991, Freiburg, Germany.

Subash Chandran, M.D. and Gadgil, M., 1991 (b). State forestry and decline of food resources in tropical forests of Uttara Kannada in Southern India. Symposium on "Food and Nutrition in the Tropical Forest" 10-13 September, 1991. UNESCO-CNRS Paris.

Terebogh, J., 1986. Keystone plant resources in the tropical forest. In: M.E. Soule (ed.) *Conservation Biology: The Science of Scarcity and Diversity.*

17

Danda Ritual

Five Elements

Ileana Citaristi

The two seasons during which two new *rasas* flow on earth are spring (March-April) and the autumn (September-October). Both these periods mark the transition between different and opposite activities at the social and agricultural level. During the monsoons all kinds of collective works are interrupted and substituted by indoor and introverted ones; it is only after the rains that the military and trade expeditions as well as the harvesting operations will start. Similarly, after the winter months spent in social and collective gatherings, spring paves the way to a new awakening of nature and to all the fears and expectations linked to a new agricultural year.

Among the rural communities of the coastal and central Orissa, both these periods are marked by rituals related to the Shiva-Shakti cult, in which the deities are worshipped in their benevolent and terrific aspects.

Differently from the orthodox Hindu section of the population, among these communities, Durga or Devi is never represented by an iconographical image but by various symbols such as a pole, a pitcher, a sword, a dagger, and so on.

In the performances of these rituals, traces of ancient cults belonging to the Tantric Buddhist, Tantric Saiva and Shakti traditions as well as tribal and indigenous features can be observed, making it a fascinating example of a cultural synthesis achieved along the centuries.

Both the Sola Puja (sixteen-days-puja) culminating in Vijaya dasami performed in the month of Aswina and the Danda yatra (called also Jhamu Nata, Patua Yatra, Uda Parva) performed in the month of Chaitra, have in common, among other things, the embodiment of the power of Devi in the form of a pitcher of clay filled with water.

The *kalasha* worship is usually associated with a psychological state where the fulfilment of a vow or desire is involved; it can be interpreted as a womb containing generative lymph (symbol of fertility) or as a symbol of the human structure where the pot is the trunk of the body, the coconut placed on the top is the head, the five mango leaves are the five senses, the water contained in it is a symbol of the mind, the turmeric spread on it is the soul and the germinated paddy placed in front of it is the main nourishment.[1]

While in the last four days of the Sola Puja the *kalasha* is worshipped with sacrifices of animals (especially goats which are associated with *kama* or desire as one of the six *ripu* or enemies), during the *danda* rituals it is the human body which undergoes a series of punitive tests, once again in relation to a vow undertaken or a desire to be fulfilled.

According to the dictionary, the word *danda,* besides signifying staff, club, stick, rod, has also the meaning of corporeal punishment, chastisement, subjection, control, restrain. Self-control is exercised by the *danduas* (devotees) not only by the way of fasting for a number of days which varies between 18 and 21 (starting from the full moon of the month of Chaitra up to the beginning of the solar month of Baisakh), but also by performing physical exertions of different kind.

Although all sections of population can take part in the rituals, we find that in most villages where *danda* is performed, the majority of the *danduas* are from the *paik* or martial communities[2] and the *pata dandua* himself is the leader of the *paik akhada* of the same village.

It is certainly difficult to trace the historical reasons for this connection, but elements of self-discipline, physical fitness and vigorous dance involved in the performance of *danda* together with the fact that both forms of physical expressions placed in the background of the Shiva-Shakti cult can be brought to explain at least in part the cultural link.

Another reason can be due to the fact that geographically the Danda rituals, besides being performed in some coastal areas of Orissa, are specially found in the *garjats* or fortified ex-feudatory states of central Orissa, like Talcher, Angul, Denkanal, Hindol, Daspalla and Nayagarh, where the population is mainly composed by the military caste. The fact that the *paiks,* besides being warriors, were all along also involved in agricultural works in times of peace is another important aspect to be considered in this regard.

An interesting variant to the Danda rituals of central Orissa can be found in the Bhokta cult of Baripada, the capital of the northern district of Mayurbhanj.

Here the main Bhoktas who undertook fasting and performing of some of the physical penances during the same part of the year, still hold their titles in a hereditary way and they were allotted special gifts and privileges by the royal dynasty of the state to undergo penances for the welfare not only of the family members of the Maharaja but for the whole community as well.

Among the *danda* (self-punishments) performed are, *bhumi* or *dhuli danda*, group pantomimes enacted on the ground (literally, in the dust), *pani danda*, acrobatics in the water, *agni danda* (which includes, *jhuna khela*, play with resin, *nia pata*, walking on burning coals, *ugra pata*, swinging upside down on burning ashes) and *swanga* (folk plays) which are enacted in different places every night for 13 days culminating in Pana Sankranti or the first day of the month of Baisakha.

Although there are variations in the performance of the various phases between one area and the other, and although now-a-days some part of the rituals may not be performed regularly everyday, the physical interaction of the devotees with dust, water, fire and air is a common feature whenever *danda* is performed.

Under the hot sun of April, in the middle of the day when the earth is most burning, the *danduas* gather around the *kamana ghara* in the village and under instruction by the *pata dandua* perform *dhuli danda* or short sequences which represent the art of ploughing, cultivating and harvesting. Goddess Kamana herself, represented by the permanent *kalasha* kept in the *kamana ghara*, gives them orders through the words of the *pata dandua*. In the enactment of the different agricultural operations, the *dhuli* is used in the most imaginative ways – at times it represents the black grams which are sown in the ground, at times the paddy which is ventilated after thrashing and at times the weeds to be extirpated.

The bodies of the *dandua* become at times the plough, at times the boundary between the fields and again the cart over which the harvest is carried or the bullocks which trample over the new paddy during the thrashing operations.

According to a principle which seems to be universally applicable, wherever we find that the faith in the magical chain of events still predominates over the cause-effect relation of the scientific outlook, the enactment of certain action in a ritualistic set-up is bound to influence the course of similar events at the time of their accomplishment.

In the same way the physical enactment of all these agricultural operations performed as ritualistic acts of offering and penance is believed to assure the success of these operations when they will take place during the new agricultural year. After the last act which simulates the smearing of oil and *haldi* over the body is time now to proceed towards the nearest tank for the ritual bath and *pani danda*.

The procession moves along with the *pata dandua* carrying the Gauri *beto*, which is composed by two cane sticks covered with red bangles, black strips of cloth and a *sari* and the bundle of straw containing the sacred fire.

The first immersion is done along with the Gouri *beto*; all the *danduas* stand around her and after a full immersion they pour water over her again and again and wash her with leaves of mango tree while chanting invocations to the goddess.

They then wash themselves in the same way and perform acrobatic feats in the water.

Now-a-days, in many places this feature is omitted, but *dandua* belonging to the village of Manikagoda in the Khurda sub-division of Puri district, confirmed to me that it used to be performed up to one generation ago. The aerial somersaults which are part of the *pani danda* are the same which are part of the *paik* training even today. According to the *paik* terminology they are called *suna* and include backward somersaults from different heights as well as pyramidal formations of various kinds.

After the bath and *pani danda* follows a very important ritual – the *danda jia* (re-lighting of the sacred fire).

It is interesting to note that here the word *danda* assumes yet another meaning – it relates to the handles which support the torches which are re-lit everyday at this time and are carried in procession along the village together with the Gauri *beto*.

As a phallic symbol, the handle like the stick can be regarded as symbol of Shiva, to whom *agni* or *teja* as creative power has always been mythologically connected.

The Danda are four in number and every year two new ones are made while the old ones are stored in the *kamana ghara* at the side of the permanent *kalasha*. They are constituted of two parts – the handle made of clay supports a cup made of straw; when the *jhuna*, (hard oily substance derived from the *sal* tree) is thrown into it, it creates a coat by melting which prevents the straw from burning fully.

The fire which had been carried from the *kamana ghara* stored in a bundle of straw is revived by rubbing it vigorously against the ground.

The four *danda* placed on the ground in a cross-shaped way with the four cups facing each other are first lit with the bundle of straw and repeatedly made to blaze by pouring resin. With each blaze, invocations to Agni, Durga, Kali and various terrific aspects of Shiva Bhairava rise to the sky.

A procession around the village is taken at a very fast pace; each *sahi* and corner is passed through and outside each house *bhogo* is offered to the deity. One of the *dandua* blesses each offering along the way and collect a portion of it. Each shrine is circumambulated and outside certain houses designs made of coloured powders are drawn on the ground and *bhogo* of different types are placed on it.

These are the outer spaces where the *nata* will take place at night; the ordinary space, sacralized and circumscribed on the four sides by the ritualistic power of the square and circular designs is a medium of transaction between the secular and the sacred. The evening performance is not just for entertainment but a continuation of the process of expiation in which the whole community participates through the physical enactment by the *dandua*.[3]

The procession finally return to the *kamana ghara* when the evening sets in; the deity is deposited inside, the fire switched off and the *dandua* takes the only meal of the day – a liquid preparation, called *pana*, made out of milk, fruits, black pepper, green gram and fried rice.

The fire is re-lit in the night and some more physical exercises called *danda bhanga* take place. These are performed by one of the *danduas* who, while holding the lit *danda* in his hands, perform some ground acrobatics.

The *pata dandua* goes around the *kamana ghara* in a special *chali* called *jhaleri*, while the blazing flames activated by the *jhuna* rise to the sky, breaking into the darkness of the night.

The scene is now set for the apparition of *parva*, the terrific aspect of Goddess Kali. This character always opens the night performances and it is taken out only during the period of the *danda nata*.

The *dandua* which interpretes this role is dressed with a red and black *sari*, wears female ornaments and has an arch-like structure of bamboo strips covered with cloths tied at the back. The latter is the *parva* (radiance) and it is kept all through the year inside the *kamana ghara* together with *kamana* and the *danda* or handles for the fire.

The themes of the *nata* performed in front of different houses for thirteen consecutive nights are drawn from ordinary events and relations of the tribal people. The steps of the dances are quite vigorous and performed at a fast tempo. They are accompanied by dialogues with the main player, songs directed to the audience and interludes of pure dances. A lot of stamina is required on the part of the dancers who have to talk, sing and dance without pausing.

The items can be performed in a shorter version accompanied only by the *dhol* or in a longer one called *swanga* (in Sanskrit, meaning graceful acting) accompanied by an ensemble of instruments, such as *pakhawaj*, *dholak*, *jodinagara*, (played with sticks), *jhumka* (metallic balls with pieces of iron inside), harmonium, *gini* (cymbals), *mahuri* and *kahali* (wind instruments).

Among the most popular characters are *chadeya* (bird hunter), *babaji* (sanyasi), *hata khata* (mendicants), *kandha kandhuni* (tribal couple), *pattara saura* (nomads), *sabara* (tribals), *vinakar* (who holds the *vina*).

In certain villages *nachwa* (the dancers) are different from the *dandua* who perform the rituals, but in this case the *nachua* are equally under a vow, don't observe full fasting like the *dandua* but are strictly vegetarian throughout the period of the *danda nata*.

The houses in front of which the *nata* are performed usually belong to well-to-do families who, themselves under a vow, choose to fulfil it and manifest their devotion towards Shiva by inviting the party and sponsoring one of their performances.

The invitation is done by cleaning up the frontage of their houses with cow dung and water, drawing decorative floor designs with coloured powders and placing over it offerings of food and a jugful of water.

The money collected after each performance is used for the *puja* and the deity; the entire community acts under a vow and for a common goal and thus all participate, in their own way towards the successful fulfilment of their expectations.

The rituals reach a climax in the last two days when the *dandua* subject themselves to the trial of *ugra* and *nia pata.*

At midday of the Meru day, under the hot sun, in front of the *kamana ghara*, each of the *dandua* swings, for a few seconds, in an upside down position over burning coals and the day after, on Sankranti, they walk on a bed of burning charcoal spread to about 25 feet.

The last act, performed at 2 a.m. in the night after Sankranti, is the emptying of the *kalasha* into the tank from which water had been taken and consecrated at the beginning of the rituals.

The circle is thus complete and the entire process is ready to start once again; macro and microcosm have attuned to each other's wave-length through the medium of the physical performance by the *dandua.*

Notes

1. This anthropomorphic interpretation of the symbol of the *kalasha* has been given to me by a tantric *pujari* whose forefathers had performed rituals for the Royal dynasty of Seraikhella in Bihar.
2. From the Sanskrit word *padatik*; they were the infantry soldiers of the rulers of the feudatory States in Orissa. In exchange for the military service rendered, they received free *jagir* (land), which they cultivated in times of peace.
3. This link between the ritualistic penances enacted by the devotees in the daytime and the evening performance by the dancers is not so evident in the Bhokta cult of Baripada in Mayurbhanj. Although the sacralization of the performance-space is carried out by the Chhau dancers before the dances begin on the first night by spreading, on the arena, some earth brought in procession from the *akhada*, it is only when the dance performance is quite advanced that the Bhokta visits the arena with the sacred pitcher of water on the head. The whole procedure gives the impression more of a juxtaposition of events than of an originally integrated process.

18

Kerala Fisherfolk
Ritualistic and Cosmic Elements

P.R.G. Mathur

Numerous spirits have influenced the behaviour of the Hindu and Mappila (Muslim) fishermen of Kerala. Listed out here are some of the beliefs of the Hindu fisherfolk connected with certain important spirits, demons and deities.

Pretham (Ghost): The Element of Air

The *pretham* (soul) of a person who commits suicide hovers around the place where he took his life or by the side of his house. The marine Hindu fisherfolk believes that when a *pretham* enters the body of a person he begins to act like a lunatic. When such symptoms appear, the Kaniyan (village astrologer), is immediately consulted, to identify the *pretham* and locate his abode. The astrologer, after identifying the spirits, directs the next of kin to contact a particular Mantravadi (sorcerer) for conducting a Homam (propitiatory rite) in order to get rid of the *pretham*. Accordingly, the Mantravadi is invited to perform the Homam. The Mantravadi draws a *kalam* (cabbalistic figure) in the courtyard with coloured powders. The figures of the supposed *Pretham*, Gandharvan and his wife Yakshi are drawn in the *kalam*. The Homam is performed after this. The belief is that once the propitiatory rites are conducted the *pretham* is consigned to flames. Sometimes an amulet is prepared for wearing around the waist of the possessed.

Akasa Gandharvan: Personification of the Sky

The supernatural power of Akasa Gandharvan, an ethereal goblin of the Mappila fisherfolk of Tanur, is described in my monograph, *The Mappela Fisherfolk of Kerala*. The Hindu fishermen believe that the Akasa Gandharvan is responsible for causing dissention between Lord Krishna and Arjuna. Krishna Kunhu, my Araya informant, said that Akasa Gandharvan possessed supernatural powers. Once when Krishna was offering prayers taking water in his right hand, the Gandharvan appeared in the sky in his chariot and disturbed the Lord's mind. The Lord's prayer stopped as froth from the Gandharvan's horse's mouth fell on his palm, thus polluting the water. Krishna became infuriated and vowed to teach the Gandharvan a lesson for his misbehaviour, and kill him before the sunset. Hearing this the Gandharvan was distressed. In order to save his life, he approached Brahma, Vishnu and Siva, but they did not oblige. Meanwhile, Narada appeared on the scene and advised the Gandharvan to seek the help of Arjuna who was spending his life *incognito* in the mountains along with his brothers. Narada then informed Krishna that the Gandharvan had gone to Arjuna's abode and decided to bring about a solution. He appeared in disguise before Arjuna and told him to go to sleep when Krishna killed the Gandharvan. He promised that he would restore the life of the Gandharvan. Krishna killed the Gandharvan before sunset as promised, but his life was restored by Brahma at once. Thus, the Hindu fishermen believe that the Gandharvan is still at large.

Kadutha: Ethereal Element

The Aryans of Cochin believe in a large number of spirits like Kuttichathan, Karumkutty, Pookutty and Kalladimuthan. The spirits of the dead wizards belonging to different castes like the Nairs, Irvas and Cherumans or Pulayans are also capable of making mischief, it is believed. For instance, the Aryans of Elangkunnapuzha propitiated on all important occasions Kadutha the spirit of a dead Nair sorcerer of the village. The spirit is housed in a shrine. This Nair sorcerer is believed to be a great devotee of Lord Ayyappan, whose shrine is at Sabarimala Kerala. Thus, Kadutha is worshipped by the Aryans for getting bumper catches and warding off diseases. Special propitiatory rites are performed in Kadutha's honour. The oracle of Kadutha dances before the shrine and predicts whether or not there will be good catches and about the recovery of the sick.

Marutha: Ethereal Spirit

The Aryans of Elangkunnapuzha believe that Marutha, the spirit of a Pulaya woman sorcerer, has supernatural powers in curing incurable diseases and preventing capsizing of boats at sea and getting bumper catches. Sometimes the Aryans worship her by making special offerings of liquor and meat ostensibly for getting ownership in fishing units. During the Mandalam (fast days from first of Vrichikam to the tenth of Dhanu), Marutha is offered beaten rice, puffed rice, molasses, plantains and camphor. It is interesting to note that although Marutha is the spirit of the Pulaya woman (scheduled caste), she is housed in a special shrine by the Aryans and propitiated on all important occasions, besides offering special worship.

Kotha: Ethereal Element

The Aryans of Elangkunnapuzha say that the spirit Kotha possesses miraculous powers in curing illnesses and saving the fishermen from hazards of the sea. Kotha is the spirit of a departed woman sorcerer who belonged to the Pulaya caste (agrestic serf). She is believed to be the sister of Marutha. The spirit is frequently worshipped by the Aryans by offering liquor and meat. A shrine has been built in her honour in the village for offering worship to her. During the Mandalam period only vegetarian dishes are offered to gods and goblins.

CHEMBAN MUTHAPPAN, UNNIKKA MUTHAPPAN, SURANAT KAIMAL

The spirits of the ancestors are propitiated by Hindu fishermen on all important festive occasions. The Aryans of the Elangkunnapuzha village have installed three unhewn stones in a shrine representing three ancestors, namely, Chemban Muthappan, Unnikka Muthappan, and Suranat Kaimal. Chemban Muthappan and Unnikka Muthappan belonged to the Arya caste whereas Suranat Kaimal was a Nair. These three spirits are propitiated for 41 days during the Mandalam days by making an offer of vegetarian dishes.

THOTTAM KAZHIKKAL

The Thottam Kazhikkal ceremony is performed on the last three days of the Mandalam. Pullavans and Velans are commissioned in the performance of the Thottam Kazhikkal ceremony. They draw cabbalistic figures using coloured powders, five in number. They also draw human figures of deities like Vigneswara and Yessaswari. Pulluvans and Velans beat their drums and sing songs in praise of the deceased sorcerer. The she-oracles possessed of the spirits of Chemban Muthappan, Unnikka Muthappan and Suranat Kaimal dance before the Kalam (the figures drawn on the floor) and circumambulate the shrines. The ceremony lasts for about six to eight hours. The oracles predict the future welfare of the fishermen. The Pulluvans and Velans are paid from ten to fifteen rupees for their services.

MUNNODI APPAN

Munnodi Appan, the spirit of the dead ancestor of a family belonging to the village of Tarayakadappuram in the Alleppey district, is propitiated by the Aryan fishermen. The spirit is housed in a shrine and it is worshipped as a *devan* (male deity). The local tradition is that long ago the fishermen offered their prayers to different Gods for getting bumper catches to meet their livelihood. Munnodi Appan, and Aryan, employed his magical powers and got bumper catches for the entire villagers. Thus, he saved the villagers from starvation. A shrine was built in his honour by the villagers when he died. Whenever the Aryans of Quilon, Alleppey and Trivandrum do not get good catches, they take a vow to offer special *pujas* in honour of Munnodi Appan either at home or in the shrine. They make votive offerings consisting of meat, liquor, fried fish, etc. when their prayers are heard. Now, vegetarian dishes only are offered in the shrine of Munnodi Appan. When Munnodi Appan is propitiated at home, the species which the fishermen want to haul, are offered to him. Avoli and Ayala (Mackerel) were relished by Munnodi Appan. Apart from fish and meat, liquor and *pappad* are offered to this spirit.

Hindu fishermen of the erstwhile Travancore state particularly those of the Alleppey district make periodical offerings and perform special rituals in the honour of Munnodi Appan at his shrine, if they get bumper catches or if serious illness is cured within a given time. Once their wishes are fulfilled, they conduct the special ritual at his shrine spending as much as Rs. 500. The mode of worship at the Munnodi Appan's shrine is very interesting. The office of the priest is hereditary in the family of Munnodi Appan. The women folk are forbidden from entering the shrines and have to keep a distance of a furlong during the propitiation of Munnodi Appan. The priest is not allowed to wear any cotton clothes when he performs the worship. His dress is made of banana leaves (*ada*). He has to observe vegetarianism and celibacy. Neither liquor, nor meat is offered to Munnodi Appan now-a-days. The Aryans of Travancore generally set apart three-and-a-half per cent of their day's catch for Munnodi Appan's worship. When the amount increases to Rs. 500 the special ritual at Munnodi Appan's shrine is conducted. Sometimes, when they are enable to save Rs. 500 for his worship in the year, they borrow funds from moneylenders to propitiate Munnodi Appan.

PARASSINIKADAVU MUTHAPPAN

Hindu and Muslim fishermen of Malabar send their votive offerings to the Parassinikadavu Muthappan. His shrine is at Parassinikadavu, a village in the district of Cannanore, and belongs to a Thiyya family. The local tradition says that once Siva, under the spell of Shani (Saturn), went to the forest of Parassini for penance. He attained *moksha* during his penance. A structure was raised by a Thiyya family in his honour at Parassinikadavu, then in a forest, and later on it came to be known as Parassinikadavu Muthappan's shrine. This Muthappan is a non-Sanskritic deity. Meat, fish and liquor are offered to him. It is noteworthy that the members of almost all castes in this region propitiate the Muthappan. His devotees are generally given free boarding and lodging. Even Nambudiri Brahmins and Nairs are sent offerings to the Muthappan in fulfilment of their wishes and vows. The Hindu fisherfolk of Malabar, Mukkuvans and Mogayar (Mukkuvans) propitiate the Muthappan at home as well as in the shrine for getting bumper catches, relief from illness, protection from the hazards of the sea and for becoming owners of fishing units. His favourite dishes are a mixture of fried millets, *pappad* (wafers) and *katala* (bengal gram). Hindu fishermen frequently vow to set apart five per cent of their daily haul before launching if they are blessed with good catches. They exhort the Muthappan thus: "Oh Muthappan: Let our net be filled with bumper catches; we shall send our offerings to you." Sometimes a fishing unit has workers from both the Hindu and Mappila communities. In that case the expenses in connection with the propitiation of the Muthappan are borne by the entire crew.

The Muthappan is worshipped daily but special offerings are made once a week, once a month and once a year when his festival is celebrated. He is frequently propitiated at home by the fishermen for getting bumper catches and for getting relief from sickness. The propitiation of the Muthappan is called *pazhamkuttivekkal*. Another important offering to the Muthappan is called *vellattam* or *tiruveppu*. Two or three *mannans* (washermen) impersonate the Muthappan for *vellattam* and perform the dance in front of his shrine. This performance of dance is conducted as the main *vazhivadu* (votive offering) for getting bumper catches and rid of incurable diseases. It costs Rs. 13 for conducting this ceremony. On the other hand, only one Mannan is required for *tiruveppu* who assumes the guise of the deity and dances before his shrine. The Mannan's fee for performance of this rite is Rs. 1.25. *Vellattam* is performed at night.

Gulikan: Ethereal Element

Gulikan or Mandi is propitiated by the Hindu fishermen all over Kerala. The Gulikan is connected with diseases and death. Horoscopes are cast by every Hindu of Kerala in which the position of the Gulikan is clearly indicated. The Gulikan's position indicates when the person will die. When death occurs in a fisherman's house, it is customary to plant a stone outside the house representing the Gulikan. An informant informed me that stone representing the Gulikan will never be installed in the room reserved for ancestors or in any of the house. However, the fishermen believe that once the Gulikan is propitiated by installing a stone on the earthen platform, it will prevent death. The Gulikan is generally worshipped to get big fishes like *etta* and *avoli*. They vow to conduct a special *puja* in honour of the Gulikan by offering *etta* and *avoli*. They fulfil their vow by making votive offerings when they get these species of fish. The Gulikan is periodically propitiated by the offer of *kuruthi* (water mixed with turmeric and lime), today, bananas and flowers. A wick lamp is lighted for the worship. A red fowl and a ram are sacrificed in the Gulikan's honour on important festive occasions like Omam and Vishu. Sometimes, the oracle of the Gulikan, in trance, directs the fishermen to handle times of crisis. The oracle reveals the causes of illness and discloses the remedy.

The Mukkuvans of Malabar believe that there are four kinds of Gulikans: Brahma Gulikan, Vishnu Gulikan, Abhimanyu Gulikan, Asura Gulikan. They further believe that if the Asura Gulikan is displeased tensions in the family are bound to arise, besides infights among the members of the crew. In such cases the Mukkuvans consult the *kaniyan* (village astrologer) and seek their advice to ward off the wrath of the enraged Asura Gulikan. The *kaniyan* prescribes the remedy in the form of a magical rite called Puramneekkal which is similar to Uzhinhu Vangal. A magician is invited to conduct this rite. The articles required for the purpose prescribed by the magician and the astrologer are: a cooked fried fish (*etta*, *aikkora*, and *narimeen*), coconut oil, potato, lady-finger, bengal gram, beaten rice, puffed rice, etc. A thigh of the cock is roasted in the fire and given to the Asura Gulikan. The total expenditure for conducting the rite comes to Rs. 100.

Brahma Gulikan: Ethereal Element

The Brahma Gulikan is worshipped for getting bumper catches and also for warding off the misfortunes and illness caused by him. Sometimes the Mukkuvans call the Brahma Gulikan as Brahma Yakshasu, the spirit of a dead Brahman. The Mukkuvans believe that the Brahma Gulikan is capable of causing separation of a husband and wife. An amulet is prepared by the magician and given to the patient to wear or a Puramneekkal ceremony is conducted to appease him. Sometimes the *mantram* 'Oh Gulika, Brahma Gulika, Vishnu Gulika, Asmara Gulika and Abhimanyu Gulika' is chanted for 21 times over a string for putting on the waist of the patient. The same *mantram* is written 21 times on a copper plate and an amulet is prepared for wearing. Sometimes rice powder mixed with molasses is given to the Brahma Gulikan to appease his wrath. The Mukkuvans say that the Vishnu Gulikan and Abhimanyu Gulikan are not wicked. The Abhimanyu Gulikan is the spirit of Abhimanyu, son of Arjuna, who died in the Kurukshetra war.

Pottanmar: Ethereal Element

The Mukkuvans of Malabar believe that Pottanmar are the bodyguards of the Goddess Bhadrakali. They are propitiated on festive occasions like Mandalam, Karkitaka Sankranti and Sivarathri. Pottanmar are offered vegetarian dishes consisting of balls of rice, jaggery and coconut. The ordained oracle of the Pottanmar speaks a *mukabhasha* (gesture language) in their frenzy and declare what offerings would please the Goddess. They predict future events that affect the fishermen and divine the causes of illness in their families.

KANDAKARANAN

The Mukkuvans of Malabar hold that Kandakaranan is the defence minister of

Bhadrakali. They say the deity does not like meat and liquor. It seems he has been elevated as a Sanskrit deity. The main offerings of Kandakaranan consist of boiled rice, jaggery and coconut. He is worshipped for getting bumper catches, getting rid of illness, particularly, smallpox, and for protection from the hazards of the sea. The Izhvas of Palghat propitiate this deity by sacrificing a fowl.

Kadalamma: Water-element

The Aryans of the Kanjirachera village, Alleppey district, perform an annual festival called Ponkala in honour of Kadalamma (mother or Goddess of sea). It is reported that this ceremony is also conducted by the fishermen of Trivandrum Quilon and southern parts of Ernakulam. *Ponkala* the cooking of rice or pudding in the open air by women is an offering to Kadalamma, who is worshipped daily. A *mandapam* (open shed) is erected for this. The offerings consist of flattened rice, puffed rice, jaggery and *navadhanyam* (nine pulses), *ghee*, camphor, benzoin, sugarcane and coconuts. The *mandapam* is decorated with tender coconuts and mango leaves before the actual ceremony. Fisherwomen who have reached their menopause assemble on the morning of the forty-first day at the sea coast with *ponkala* pots containing the necessary rice, jaggery, coconut and firewood. The ladies cooking the *ponkala* should abstain from sexual intercourse and observe vegetarianism for the day. Two kinds of *ponkala* are prepared, one with rice, jaggery, coconut shavings and plantains, and the other without jaggery. Forty-one women participated in the festival of 1971 at the Kanjiranchera village in Alleppey. Each lady cooked the *ponkala* in a new earthen pot and propitiated the Kadalamma jointly. Formerly, the *ponkala payasam* (pudding) was thrown into the sea in sealed pots. This practice has been discontinued in recent times. However, it is reported that this custom is still in vogue in the Azhikkal village, Alleppey district. Charms and sacred formulas are uttered while throwing the pudding into the sea. Krishnan Kunhu, my informant, told me that in olden days, the *ponkala* pots thrown into the sea used to return the following day to the ovens on which the pudding was prepared. Many of his ancestors, he claimed, had seen such miraculous deeds of Kadalamma. A few coins and a little rice pudding are the only items thrown into the sea today instead of *ponkala* pots. A night long *nadaswara cutchery* (a music concert played with Nadaswaram – a snake pipe with 12 holes and other accompaniments) is held on the occasion.

The Akasa Gandharvan, Gulikan, Kadutha Kotha, Munnodiappan, etc., represent the cosmic element of sky, ether, air, etc. Kadalamma is the proeification of the cosmic element of water. The rituals connected with the propitiation of various gods and goddesses represent the element of fire and water.

References

Iyer, L.K.A., 1912. *Tribes and Castes of Cohin.* vols. I and II.

Mathur, K.S., 1964. *Caste and Ritual in a Malva Village.*

Mathur, P.R.G., 1978. *The Mappila Fisherfolk of Kerala.*

Mathur P.R.G., (forthcoming) *The Hindu Fisherfolk of Kerala.*

Menon, K.P.P., 1934. *History of Kerala.*

Pereira, J.J., 1989. *Narayana Guru: A Social Educator.*

Saraswati, B.N., 1977. *The Brahmaic Ritual Tradition.*

Swami Sarvananda, 1973. *Taittriopanishad.*

List of Contributors

Ashim Kumar Adhikary	Palli Charcha Kendra Vishva Bharati Sriniketan - 731 236
Jan Brouwer	"KALAUKAS" 222, Gangotri Layout Mysore - 570 009
M. D. Subash Chandran	Dr. Baliga College Kumta - 581 343 (Karnataka)
Tan Chung	Indira Gandhi National Centre for the Arts New Delhi - 110 001
Ileana Citaristi	C/o Shri Sailen Roy Bakhrabad Cuttack - 753 002 (Orissa)
M. M. Dhasmana	Institute of Indology and Himalayan Studies 286, Mahesh Nagar Ambala Cantt. - 133 001
Vibha Joshi	Indira Gandhi National Centre for the Arts New Delhi - 110 001
L. K. Khubchandani	270/212, Sind Society Ganesh Khind Road Aundh Pune - 411 007

P. R. G. Mathur	Srinivas Nilayam P.O. Agrharam Palghat - 678 571
Sujata Miri	Deptt. of Philosophy NEHU Mayurbhanja Complex Nongthymmai Shillong -793 014
Kanak Mital	Indira Gandhi National Centre for the Arts New Delhi - 110 001
Pradeep Mohanty	Deptt. of Archaeology Deccan College Research Institute Pune
R. S. Negi	29/A, Circular Road Dehradun - 248 001 (U.P.)
Richa Negi	Indira Gandhi National Centre for the Arts New Delhi - 110 001
N. Patnaik	Social Science and Development Institute Plot No. 1243, Nageswartangi Lewis Road Bhubaneswar - 751 002
Poornanand	Deptt. of English University of Garhwal Srinagar - 246 174 (U.P.)
Onkar Prasad	Ratanpalli Santiniketan - 731 235
D. R. Purohit	Deptt. of English University of Garhwal Srinagar - 246 174 (U.P.)

B. N. Saraswati — Indira Gandhi National Centre for the Arts
New Delhi - 110 001

Kapila Vatsyayan — Indira Gandhi National Centre for the Arts
New Delhi - 110 001

V. Verma — A-130, Sector 26
Noida - 201 301 (U.P.)

Index